LOWE'S®
Home Improvement Warehouse

COMPLETE
Landscaping

Editor: Michael MacCaskey
Photo and Contributing Editor: Lynn Ocone

Project Director: René Klein

Art Director: Bill Harvey
Page Makeup: Eugenie Delaney, Michele Fairchild, Sylvie Vidrine

Writers: Steven Cory, Scott Gibson, Doug & Karen Jimerson, Diane
Slavik, A. Cort Sinnes, Lance Walheim, Ann Whitman
Senior editor: Tere Drenth
Consulting editor: Margaret McKinnon
Technical review: Denny Schrock
Indexer: Kathy Barber

Principal Illustrators: Rik Olson and Mark Pechenik
Additional Illustrations: Anthony Davis, Debra Lambert, Lois Lovejoy,
Jane McCreary, Mimi Osborne, Erin O'Toole, Lucy Sargeant, Wendy
Smith-Griswold, Catherine M. Watters

Photographers: See page 432

Cover design: Vasken Guiragossian
Cover photos: Top left, Susan A. Roth; Top right, Marion Brenner;
Middle, Karen Bussolini; Bottom left, courtesy of Southern Living;
Bottom right: Greg Ryan and Sally Beyer. Spine: Mark Rutherford.

Production: Lory Day

Special thanks to Danielle Javier, Marianne Lipanovich

LOWE'S COMPANIES, INC.
Bob Tillman, Chairman/CEO/President
Karena Bailey, Merchandise Manager
Melissa S. Birdsong, Director, Trend Forecasting and Design
Robin Gelly, Merchandiser
Bob Gfeller, Senior VP, Marketing
Jean Melton, VP, Merchandising
Mike Menser, Senior VP, General Merchandise Manager
Gregg Plott, Director, Marketing
Dale Pond, Executive VP, Merchandising
Mary Taylor, Marketing Manager
Amanda Dillard, Merchandising Assistant

Be sure to visit our web site at www.lowes.com

10 9 8 7
First Printing January 2002
Copyright © 2002 Sunset Publishing Corporation, Menlo Park, CA
94025. First edition. All rights reserved, including the right of
reproduction in whole or in part in any form. Library of Congress
Control Number: 2001099253. ISBN 0-376-00913-6.
Printed in the United States.

Preface

America's Home Improvement Warehouse, where you'll find everything you need for your landscaping projects, including the best selection of plants for your region, is pleased to bring you a practical guide to making your garden dreams a reality. *Lowe's Complete Landscaping Book* was written by landscaping experts around the country. It covers the subject from top to bottom. Whether you want to beautify an underused side yard, build a deck or privacy fence, raise award-winning roses sheltered from the kids' play areas, or wind an inviting path to a secluded corner of the garden, this book will give you the tools, tips, tricks, and techniques you need.

With full-color photos and landscape plans, you can take an inspiring walk through some of America's most beautiful home gardens, borrowing a patio design from one, a soothing fish pond from another, and a pergola from a third. All of the gardens in this

book are lushly planted with a variety of annuals, perennials, bulbs, shrubs, vines, trees, grasses, ground covers, vegetables, herbs, and wildflowers, and all offer ideas for your own garden.

Every plant in this book is identified by both its common and botanical names, so it should be no problem to spot them at your local Lowe's nursery department. When you see a plant you think may be well suited for that hard-to-grow shady spot by the front door or that sun-blasted wall next to the barbecue, stop by and get further advice from our gardening experts.

Our professionals are ready to help you, whether you're planting your first annual or designing and building an entire patio surrounded by plants. Lowe's is known across the country for the very best selection of landscaping products—from lumber for arbors, decks, and fences to the tools and materials for irrigation systems, outdoor lighting, and do-it-yourself garden ponds.

You'll also find a wide variety of pavers, concrete blocks, grilling equipment, even outdoor furniture. And if you want to dress up an existing fence, trellis, or arbor, only your imagination can limit the paint colors we can create for you.

But even if you only stop by for a box of galvanized nails, take advantage of one of our learn-by-doing classes. If you don't have time for a class, check out the Lowe's web site at www.lowes.com and click on the How-To Library tab. Under the Outdoor Projects category, you'll find an extensive list of step-by-step instructions on everything from building a deck to installing a mailbox and maintaining your outdoor furniture. You'll also find a category called Lawn & Garden that may add a few tips to all that you find in this book.

Lowe's is proud to assist you in every way possible to make your property as beautiful, unique, and livable as it can be. Enjoy!

Contents

CHAPTER 1   6
What Makes a Great Landscape?
All great gardens share certain traits. Include them in your plan and success is guaranteed.

CHAPTER 2   22
Landscape Styles for Today
Searching for an overall look for your garden? Here are some favorites.

CHAPTER 3   68
Places to Sit, Walk, and Play
What could be more essential? Here are some ideas to consider.

CHAPTER 4   114
Creating Privacy
You've got to have some, even in the outdoors. Will yours come from a screening fence, a hedge, or some combination of both?

CHAPTER 5   144
Making Your Plan
We demystify the process and guide you step-by-step.

CHAPTER 6   176
Landscape Plans
Actual landscape plans from great gardens around the country, including detailed plant lists.

CHAPTER 7   204
Laying the Foundation
These are the jobs that come first—grading, drainage, and sprinklers.

CHAPTER 8   220
Building Patios, Decks, and Paths
Every garden needs such structures.
Here's what you need to know to get started.

CHAPTER 9   252
Landscaping Projects
These are some of our favorites projects for weekend builders.

CHAPTER 10   272
Artful Touches
It's those details—a brightly colored wall, attractive furniture—that make a garden livable and personal.

CHAPTER 11   296
Choosing Plants
Need plant ideas? We got 'em, more than 500 in fact, our favorites in all catgories.

CHAPTER 12   386
Gardening Basics
What you need to know about watering and mulches, fertilizers, pruning, lawns, and pests.

INDEX   424

CHAPTER 1

What Makes a Great Landscape?

A great landscape can take many forms: grand or modest, formal or casual. It is whatever works for you and your family. In all cases, it's a place where you can relax, entertain friends, and reconnect with nature.

But how do you get there? This chapter shows some successful landscapes and boils down each to its essence, explaining what works about each of them. We present these gardens hoping that one or more of the ideas you find in them will provide the inspiration you need to create your own.

IN THIS CHAPTER
PRIVACY • COMFORT
STYLE • NATURE • SEASONS
PRACTICALITY • BEAUTY

Keep It Private but Open

PLAN FOR PRIVACY, BUT NOT FOR TOO MUCH

In whole or in part, well-planned landscapes contain the right combination of private and open space.

Visually and literally, a fence, wall, hedge, or a planting of shrubs and trees transforms a space into a quiet, restful retreat. They also do practical jobs like keeping your children and pets in and unwanted intrusions out.

Depending on its height, location, and screening properties, an enclosure can also provide privacy—an increasingly valuable commodity. The right amount of privacy allows you to live and work in the garden just as you wish—from singing to yourself as you sow seeds or stretching out on a chaise longue in the sun.

Does enclosing a garden always mean you're keeping the rest of world away? Yes and no. Even if your landscape includes the most gloriously unlimited natural vista—whether a forest, mountain range, canyon, coastline, or desert—you'll need to enclose a portion of it.

Maiden grass partially screens and softens the edges of a meandering path, drawing visitors to a private garden bench. Tall plants behind the bench and upright columns along the path frame this retreat.

Conversely, if it's on a Manhattan rooftop, you'll want to leave a view of the city or a glimpse of neon.

Walk around your property, identifying areas that require covers or screens. Also try to evaluate how plantings and additional structures will affect your neighbors, the patterns of sun and shade in your garden, and any views you want to preserve.

TOP LEFT: An arbor, covered with climbing roses, provides just enough privacy while not completely blocking the neighboring view.
TOP RIGHT: The most beautiful screen of all—an artful combination of flowering trees and plants—allows some privacy for front-porch loungers.
BOTTOM LEFT: Classic picket fence and covered gate at the front of this house create a charming division between public and private spaces.
BOTTOM RIGHT: Gate set within a tall hedge marks a threshold between garden areas, adding an air of mystery and an invitation to explore.

Set off in a secluded corner of the garden, this small patio features a vine-covered arbor. When in bloom, the long panicles of Japanese wisteria create a fragrant bower, perfect for shady alfresco dining.

Be Comfortable

MAKE YOUR LANDSCAPE AN EASY PLACE TO RELAX

Landscape designers think about outdoor space just how architects and interior designers think about indoor space: The needs, desires, and comfort of their clients come first. In an outdoor setting, this means providing just enough shade in summer and sun in winter and convenient places for sitting and lounging.

Because walls, ceilings, and floors are such an essential part of any home, architects and interior designers

don't need to discuss the importance of these structural elements with their clients. But people may have difficulty thinking about elements they associate with indoor spaces as essential to an outdoor space. Yet every well-designed landscape, large or small, has "walls," "ceilings," and "floors" that must be considered from the very beginning of the design.

Beyond structural elements, landscape designers

have concerns that are typical for indoor spaces—furniture, lighting, traffic patterns, and cooking equipment—in addition to the kind of style the homeowner desires.

When you think of landscaping, don't think only of plants. Instead, think first about how you and your family and friends want to live outdoors. Put your own needs ahead of the plants you want to grow. Once you've taken care of those needs, go ahead and plant.

TOP LEFT: A lantern illuminates a romantic dining nook, creating a private space in an evening garden. A leafy trellis defines the ceiling.
TOP RIGHT: A fireplace creates an inviting focal point in this stone-paved outdoor dining room. Sturdy pillars support the lath ceiling.
BOTTOM LEFT: Striking red Adirondack chairs have a high visual impact on a grassy lawn. Under the trees, a hammock invites a shady nap.
BOTTOM RIGHT: Commanding the best view, this combination of arbor and old-fashioned swing makes a comfortable place to relax.

Develop Your Style
AFTER ALL, IT'S YOUR LANDSCAPE

Keep in mind that your landscape belongs to you and that the best outdoor landscapes reflect the personalities, tastes, and interests of their owners. Wouldn't it be boring if people used only one standard to judge a successful landscape? Luckily, many people feel freer to express themselves in their outdoor surroundings than they do in their interior spaces, perhaps because the outdoor canvas is larger and has looser boundaries. And even if you're a little timid about expressing your own taste in the front yard, in the relative privacy of your backyard, your only rule may be that anything goes.

You're allowed to say, "It's my garden, and you don't have to like it." A treehouse with a rope ladder? Brightly painted garden walls? Patio trees festooned year-round with little twinkling lights? A Victorian fretwork design on the deck railing? A pathway enlivened with a mosaic of bits of broken crockery? Why not?

Visitors pass a collection of unusual potted dwarf conifers at the entry arbor before seeing the plants beyond the gate. The potted plants demonstrate a restrained color palette and variegated foliage.

TOP LEFT: Annual flowers and colorful foliage plants surround an old-fashioned red metal chair, flanked by matching gazing balls.

TOP RIGHT: Spring flowers and ivy spill from whimsically planted garden boots. Stuff crumpled newspaper into the bottom of the boots and then fill with potting soil.

BOTTOM: A school of fish carved from weathered wood appears to swim over waves of foliage below a wall of cedar shakes.

Embrace Nature

INVITE IT IN, BUT STRIVE FOR BALANCE

Great landscapes embrace nature. They borrow certain practicalities from their indoor counterparts, but they effortlessly make the most of all that nature offers.

Do what you can to bring in the natural world—the sky, clouds, birds, butterflies, a breeze, shadows, stars, and views of the surrounding hills or of water.

The trick is finding the right balance. Practically speaking, this may mean reducing the size of a patio and screening it, or making an overhead structure more open, to bring creature comforts into balance with the natural setting. Does this mean that you may

This stucco wall encloses a private garden but allows views of the hillsides beyond it. A shallow birdbath, along with yellow coreopsis and purple Spanish lavender flowers, attracts butterflies. The vine-covered arbor shades a cozy bench swing.

still experience times of the day that are too hot to sit outside or too windy for an outdoor meal? Yes, but you may feel that's a small price to pay for all the other joys of outdoor living.

Finding the right balance goes for wildlife, too. Encourage birds and butterflies by providing food, shelter, and water and by growing the plants they prefer. But also provide the right kind of barriers or deterrents to mosquitoes and deer, for example.

TOP LEFT: A rich tapestry of shapes and colors—from chartreuse lady's mantle to burgundy Japanese maple—nearly envelops this natural-looking miniature pond.

TOP RIGHT: Where natural woodland is in short supply, wrens, bluebirds, and chickadees are among birds that may decide to nest in well-placed birdhouses.

BOTTOM LEFT: This simple arbor, soon to be cloaked by flowering vines, provides a quiet refuge to watch hummingbirds drawn to the hanging feeder.

BOTTOM RIGHT: In a backyard pond, a northern leopard frog surfaces among the water plants. It helps keep insect pests in check.

Celebrate the Seasons
REMEMBER IT'S A GARDEN FIRST, NOT A LIVING ROOM

One thing is certain: A landscape shows off the seasons in ways interior rooms cannot. To get the most enjoyment, design for year-round interest. Trumpet spring with a display of flowering bulbs and annuals if you like, but don't neglect the beauty of a crab apple in fall. Place a dogwood prominently for its spring flowers, but also to highlight its bare branches in winter.

Changing the look of your interior rooms to match the seasons is doable and even fun, but really only sensible for a few of us. But outdoor spaces are another matter. Nature is in charge, and the landscape will change whether you're ready or not. So make the most of it, from the profound seasonal changes of the Northeast and Midwest to the more subtle but equally commanding variations of the South and Far West.

Imagine how your use of the landscape will vary from season to season. In spring, you'll want to be outdoors as much as possible. Summer is for entertaining and perhaps quiet times in the shade. And during winter, more often than not you'll be inside looking out.

Pink cosmos, purple coneflowers, and towering phlox practically shout, "Summer!" This blend of annuals and perennials promises a long season of butterfly-attracting blossoms, while seeds of coneflowers and cosmos draw finches.

TOP LEFT: A mix of trees and shrubs of varying densities and heights gives this snow-covered garden plenty of shape and visual interest.

TOP RIGHT: Red, golden, white, and pink zinnias bloom in autumn against a backdrop of orange pumpkins ready for Halloween carving.

BOTTOM: Fiery autumn foliage of liquidambar and maple trees glows behind the bent-stick loveseat. Beside it, golden grasses cascade over the patio stones.

A shed designed in harmony with the garden can serve several functions. This one shelters a seating nook and provides enough room for tool storage, counter spaces, and trash or compost bins—or even firewood.

Be Practical

ACCOMMODATE YOUR FAMILY'S NEEDS

The best landscapes address the practical needs of their owners. Just as indoors, people need room for their clutter, tools, equipment, and supplies. Every homeowner has to deal with trash cans and yard waste bins and find a place to store them. And then there are the nuts-and-bolts aspects of accessories, like pool equipment, irrigation timers, air conditioning units, and outdoor lighting systems.

Side yards offer one of the most logical spots to locate these practical necessities, especially if they can be grouped in one area. Bear in mind that pool and air-conditioning equipment can be annoying when running so try not to locate them under a bedroom window, or where they could ruin an outdoor dinner party.

Plan for safety and ease of movement. Gates, fences, and railings safeguard people against dangers posed by swimming pools, driveways, busy streets, and elevated decks. Ramps and graded paths with smooth, firm surfaces will ease passage for the disabled and elderly. Night lighting permits safe movement and discourages intruders.

How much time are you willing to invest in maintenance? Lawns, swimming pools, hedges, and rose and vegetable gardens all need frequent upkeep. To ease watering chores, an automatic irrigation system can cut many hours of hand-watering from your schedule.

While practical concerns may seem relatively minor in the overall scheme of things, you'll be glad you addressed them early in the planning stage instead of trying to figure out how to deal with them after the landscape is completely installed.

TOP LEFT: This gracefully curved stone path is wide and smooth enough for two people to walk side by side on its firm surface.

TOP RIGHT: In regions where lawn irrigation is a regular task, invest in an underground sprinkler system to save time and energy.

BOTTOM LEFT: A fenced service area hides trash cans from view of this well-planned deck. Shrubs screen the service area and provide a pleasant backdrop for the deck seating.

BOTTOM RIGHT: Built-in storage on this arbor is cleverly concealed behind a lattice-covered door. When the door is closed, the compartment is completely invisible.

Water tumbles from a terra-cotta jug in this leafy oasis. Shade-loving ferns, mosses, and pink impatiens illuminate the small pool.

Let Beauty Reign
FINDING WAYS TO ADD THAT EXTRA SOMETHING

Beauty in the garden takes many forms. Most often, it is conceived as colorful flowers, and rightly so. The diversity of flowers guarantees the possibility of endless fascination.

Leaves are also a rich source of garden color, usually lasting longer than flowers. Besides a host of remarkably diverse greens, you can find plants with shades of yellow, red, purple, blue, or gray.

Perhaps you assume that beauty is derived mostly from artfully chosen and combined plants. That may be so, but not necessarily: A single plant displayed in a special container can be stunning.

To be beautiful, plants don't need to be exotic or rare. Sometimes the most ordinary plants become

extraordinary when grown or presented well. A common but vigorous ivy is more beautiful than a rare plant that struggles to live.

Some landscapes are beautiful by virtue of their details, such as an artfully finished deck railing, a carefully laid pathway, or a well-placed sculpture. Brightly painted walls and fences can elevate a simple landscape to a memorable one.

Great landscapes can take many forms and styles, but in the end, all are an unabashed celebration of beauty. Wherever it occurs, beauty is the reason you want to relax on the deck in the morning and linger outdoors as long as possible in the evening.

TOP LEFT: Foliage of evergreen shrubs, Japanese maples, and grasses provides both color and texture in this Asian-influenced garden.
TOP RIGHT: A few dramatic plants, such as New Zealand flax and bold blue-green agave against airy lavender, add beauty to a Mediterranean-style poolside garden.

BOTTOM LEFT: Flamboyant 'Pink Impression', 'Holland Glory', and 'Orange Emperor' tulips echo the colors of this brick-walled garden.
BOTTOM RIGHT: 'Pink Crystals' ruby grass with pink-and-silver flower heads glows against a backdrop of ornamental grasses and wildflowers.

CHAPTER 2

Landscape Styles for Today

Different approaches to outdoor living and gardening—from a variety of regions and situations—help you refine your own needs and desires. You may find that you like a patio or deck from one approach, a natural-looking pond from another, and an outdoor kitchen from a third. And that's exactly how to create a landscape that is uniquely yours.

IN THIS CHAPTER

CURB APPEAL • ROSES • FORMALITY
ASIAN STYLE • EASY-CARE
FAMILY-CENTERED • WATER
OUTDOOR ROOMS • COURTYARDS
SMALL SPACES • COTTAGE STYLE
PLANT LOVERS • A COOK'S GARDEN
CONTAINERS • AN ARTIST'S GARDEN
WILDFLOWERS • SHADE GARDENS
BACKYARD HABITATS • ROCK GARDENS
TROPICAL FLAIR • WATERWISE
FIRE SAFETY

Creating Curb Appeal

IF IT LOOKS GOOD, IT IS GOOD

Landscaping that enhances your house's curb appeal is one of the best investments you can make. Yet for most homeowners, the front yard is far from ideal. It may be a virtual blank slate, with neither personality nor character, or be outdated, with a narrow walkway, a ring of shrubs around the foundation, and a concrete slab at the door. Conversely, your front yard may be so overgrown with foliage that the house is hidden.

To transform your front yard, focus first on the entry walkway. Make it so clear and obvious that guests are never confused about the best route to the front door. Also make the path wide enough for two adults to comfortably walk side by side (see the diagrams on page 95). In addition, use materials for the path and driveway that complement and enhance your house's façade.

All landscapes should be a mixture of permanent and short-lived plants, but in the front yard, this mix is doubly important. Permanent plants, such as conifers, look lush and green from season to season. They create structure and provide a stage for showier annuals and perennials. Be sure to select low-growing or dwarf conifers and broadleaf evergreens that are in scale with your home and won't soon block paths or windows.

Define the front entryway with accents of bold, colorful annuals, in containers or in a small planting bed; replant seasonally. Containers also make the most of tight quarters, on the steps of a front porch, for example.

Create a show-stopping entrance to your front yard with an arbor of climbing 'Phyllis Bide' roses, as in this garden. Blooming all season long, the apricot blooms greet visitors and passersby.

TOP: A robust planting of favorite perennials forms a mosaic of flowers and foliage in this sunny driveway border and entrance garden.
BOTTOM LEFT: In place of a street-side lawn, a profusion of perennials greets passersby and creates a favorable first impression.
BOTTOM RIGHT: This crisp, clean entry is defined by a brick path and tidy Japanese hollies. Bricks are laid in a herringbone pattern.

In a formal rose garden, align structures and ornaments along well-defined sight lines. Plant roses together in their own beds, so it's easy to give them the extra care they require.

A Passion for Roses
THEY OFFER BEAUTY, VARIETY, AND LUSCIOUS SCENTS

With the recent introduction of the so-called landscape roses—low-maintenance, disease- and pest-free varieties that bloom more or less continuously throughout the growing season and demand little pruning—roses can now be considered easy-care plants.

If, however, you favor the familiar long-stemmed hybrid tea or other types such as grandifloras, floribundas, and English roses, you'll pay a price for all that beauty and fragrance.

To do what they do so well—namely, produce quantities of beautiful, often fragrant flowers—these roses need special attention. Although hybrid teas can be planted among other plants, it's far easier to lavish them with the attention they require if they grow in a small bed of their own. Ten to twelve hybrid teas make a magnificent dis-

play, provide plenty of flowers for cutting, and require a bed only 8 by 12 feet or so. Any shape of bed will do, but generations of gardeners have favored the formal look of square, round, or rectangular beds edged with stone, brick, or clipped boxwood. Often, a birdbath or sundial is placed in the center for added interest.

Nearly all roses demand a location that receives at least 6 hours of sun each day. Ideally, the bed will provide good air circulation and receive morning sun to help dry the plants' leaves early in the day (damp leaves invite disease).

Before planting, pay special attention to improving the soil with organic matter. The extra effort you put into improving the soil now will pay off in superior growth for years to come.

TIPS

- Choose varieties suited to your climate and landscape needs.
- Amend soil before planting.
- Provide 6 to 8 hours of sunshine daily and good air circulation.
- For more information about roses, see page 354.

TOP LEFT: Double your rose-gardening pleasure by planting sprawling landscape roses at the feet of tall, single-trunked standard roses.

TOP RIGHT: Arching over a split-rail fence, the 6- to 10-foot canes of 'Zéphirine Drouhin' rose explode with fragrant cerise pink blooms.

BOTTOM LEFT: Just 3 feet tall, 'The Fairy' landscape rose shows off pale pink flower clusters and glossy leaves from spring through fall.

BOTTOM RIGHT: Old-fashioned shrub roses dominate the borders along this gravel walkway, creating a delightfully fragrant garden scene.

A Formal Look

IT'S UNDERSTATED AND ELEGANT

Formal gardens may be large or small; rural, suburban, or urban; filled with plants or featuring practically none. What defines a formal garden is a predominance of straight lines, geometric shapes, and classical symmetry; that is, what appears on one side of the garden is mirrored, sometimes with near perfection, by what appears on the other. The outermost dimensions are frequently rectangular, and this shape is repeated elsewhere in pools, patios, flowerbeds, and borders. Often a single object, such as a statue, sundial, or large urn, serves as the center of interest. It's placed for optimum effect, usually toward the rear of the garden and directly in the line of sight from a favored viewing spot.

If formal landscapes seem to be governed by rules, they are. The precedents of today's formal gardens stretch back to ancient Greece and Rome. Interestingly, while other garden styles come and go, formal gardens have remained popular.

Formal gardens are well suited to Georgian-, Mediterranean-, French-, and Victorian-style houses, though they can also suit the geometric style of some modern houses.

TIPS

- Rely on symmetry and geometric shapes for the overall design.
- Keep the design simple, clean, and spare.
- Choose plantings that enhance the geometry of the design.

Perfect symmetry marks this tidy planting. The carefully clipped creeping fig vine against a gray wall fools the eye, enlarging the cozy garden. The low boxwood hedge encloses the classical-style fountain.

TOP LEFT: Close-clipped boxwood hedges and strict symmetry, hallmarks of the formal style, give this entryway timeless appeal.

TOP RIGHT: A birdbath provides a focal point for the garden bench in this formal arrangement. Note the geometric shapes of the beds and paths.

BOTTOM: Designed to be viewed from above, formally clipped evergreens offer year-round appeal, while the flowering border changes with the seasons. A sundial marks the garden's center.

A sheltered bell and weathered fence give this garden a Japanese look. Creeping plants and moss-covered boulders surround large paving stones that form a meandering path between rhododendrons, Japanese maples, and evergreens.

Asian Style

TAP INTO CENTURIES OF GARDEN-MAKING KNOW-HOW

Inhabitants of Asian countries have one of the world's most ancient gardening traditions. What has taken thousands of years to refine and perfect would be impossible to capture in just a few words. It's enough to say that one of the most important underlying tenets of Asian-style gardens is a reverence for nature.

Today's most successful and authentic Asian gardens embody the same spirit that led early Chinese garden makers to study and contemplate the beauty and mystery of wild landscapes. Returning to civilization, these early landscape designers attempted to re-create that beauty and mystery, essentially by miniaturizing it. Along the way, design ideas developed that included a system of profound symbolism: a rock of a certain shape depicts male energy, a placid pool represents female attributes, a crooked path deters the passage of evil, and a turtle-shaped rock represents nothing less than ten thousand eons.

Given this reverence for the natural world, it's not surprising that Asian cultures revered gardens. An important part of any Asian-style garden, grand or small, is a place to sit and contemplate and appreciate beauty. If you intend to create a garden in this style, don't forget this important component. And remember to keep the design simple. Like any formal landscape, much of the allure and beauty of Asian-style gardens relies on simplicity and purity of vision. Avoid the temptation to overdo it; instead, ask yourself at each turn, "Will this add to or take away from the scene I'm trying to create?"

• Take cues from nature; don't be afraid to imitate.
• Learn about the symbolism contained in Asian gardens.
• Simplify at every step in the design process.

TOP LEFT: Water is an important feature in Asian gardens. Red azaleas accent this overflowing stone basin fed by a traditional bamboo spout.
TOP RIGHT: Simple lines and angles of this wooden deck give it an Asian flair. Stones line the edge of a pool that flows under the walkway.
BOTTOM LEFT: A rustic fence with a pagoda-style roof is complemented by the weeping Atlas cedar growing next to it. Note how the elements of the house and garden present a unified vision.
BOTTOM RIGHT: Small details are important. Here, a diminutive bamboo gate echoes the living bamboo lining the pathway.

Easy-Care Landscapes
FOCUS ON MINIMIZING UPKEEP

An unkempt landscape makes both gardener and guests uncomfortable. The patio furniture may look romantic when littered with a few fallen leaves, but if the plants appear uncared for, the atmosphere is depressing.

One way to keep up with maintenance is to install a garden that essentially takes care of itself, with automatic irrigation, large areas of paving, and tough evergreen shrubs. However, if you love to use a hose and to see the garden change dramatically with the seasons, this low-maintenance solution won't appeal. One alternative is to develop a garden that reduces the tasks you hate—pruning vigorous vines, perhaps—and includes tasks you enjoy, such as raking oak leaves off a gravel path or deadheading roses with much-loved old pruners.

Excellent soil combined with plants that are well suited to your climate and conditions will get the garden off to an good start. Mulching will reduce the need for weeding, and an automatic irrigation system will reduce the need for hand-watering. If you dislike sweeping and raking, avoid planting trees and shrubs that drop messy fruits, flowers, and leaves. Unless you enjoy pruning, choose plants that won't outgrow their space. Group plants that have similar needs so they are much easier to maintain.

In place of a lawn, a tranquil "streambed" of gravel meanders around the garden, punctuated by a few well-chosen, low-maintenance flowering annuals and perennials. Prominent plants include annual pink cosmos and purple Russian sage, a perennial.

TIPS

- Amend and prepare weed-free soil before planting.
- Choose well-adapted plants that fit your space.
- Suppress weeds and save water with mulch.
- Install an automatic irrigation system (details on page 212).

TOP LEFT: Paved patio and path surfaces reduce yard maintenance; low-growing evergreen ground covers eliminate the need for mowing.

TOP RIGHT: Easy care 'Autumn Joy' sedum offers masses of deep rose flower clusters that turn coppery as autumn advances.

BOTTOM LEFT: A brick mowing strip not only makes trimming lawn edges easier but also provides strong definition and a sense of order.

BOTTOM RIGHT: Bold and simple plantings, including river birches, grasslike liriope, and sedums, make for easy upkeep of this garden.

Family-Centered Backyards

MAKE SPACES FOR PLAYING, GROWING, AND LOUNGING

Landscapes designed with the needs of a busy family in mind take into consideration the full range of activities that occur outdoors, with the accent on fun. Anything and everything—from swimming pools, built-in kitchens, tree houses, sport courts, gazebos, children's play areas, dining areas, saunas, swings, and spas—can and should be considered as a part of a landscape that's designed for active outdoor living.

The popularity of such landscapes began in suburban neighborhoods in the 1950s and was centered around the barbecue. Sun and wind control, as well as areas for dining, entertaining, playing, relaxing, and working, became primary considerations. Along the way, a new definition of landscaping emerged, one that included all these elements for outdoor living.

Fun and function mix company in this backyard flower and vegetable garden. The whimsical scarecrow and casual child-sized chair set the tone, inviting young gardeners into a space designed for their needs.

TIPS

- Locate areas designated for outdoor cooking and dining close to the house.
- A well-maintained lawn is one of the most versatile surfaces for outdoor living and playing.
- Ask your children what they'd like in the garden. Listen to their answers.
- For a sample landscape plan created with families in mind, see page 186.

TOP LEFT: Broad benches in this arbor create a poolside space that's perfect for sharing a board game, a cool drink, or a conversation.
TOP RIGHT: A vine-covered arch divides garden spaces. Potato vine scrambles up a pair of gateposts and across sturdy timbers.
BOTTOM LEFT: Surrounded by a carpet of wood chips, a carved and cushioned stump makes a comfortable chair for reading or reflecting.
BOTTOM RIGHT: Eye-catching lattice paneling and wooden shingles make this doghouse a charming and functional addition to any yard.

Nestled in a private garden, this cobble and concrete pool offers a tranquil place for reflection. Small rocks, flagstone, and boulders add textural interest and blend with the muted tones of surrounding plants.

Just Add Water
EVEN A LITTLE GOES A LONG WAY

Water gardening is booming because homeowners have discovered the big impact that even a small pond can make—and also how easy it is to include one. Because of this popularity, options are increasing. Fountains and ponds are the most common choices, but even something as simple as a birdbath adds a little of water's reflective charm to the garden, while at the same time doing something nice for the birds.

If you decide on a fountain or pool, the choice is largely a matter of personal preference and the layout of your garden. Many terra-cotta and cast-concrete wall fountains come with recirculating pumps. Vinyl pond liners and fiberglass shells are available in many shapes, sizes, and depths, and they make installing a pool almost as easy as digging a hole (see pages 262 through 265). And you always have the option of adding a custom-

designed pool, which is formed from reinforced poured concrete. Keep in mind that geometrically shaped pools look best in formal gardens, while free-form pools and waterfalls are best suited to informal landscapes.

Goldfish and koi add an exotic shimmer of life to the water. Both live for decades. Even in cold-winter climates, they can dwell year-round in the pool as long as it is outfitted with a pool heater.

TIPS

- Place a water feature where it can be easily viewed and enjoyed.
- Remember that waterlilies require at least 6 hours of sunlight to bloom.
- Protect goldfish and koi from predators.

TOP LEFT: Placed among colorful flowers and foliage, a mossy stone basin invites birds to drink and bathe.

TOP RIGHT: Splashing water from a reproduction antique fountain enlivens this garden retreat and masks intrusive noises.

BOTTOM: Water bubbling from a fountainhead inside a boulder cascades down its sides, sending soothing sounds across the patio.

Outdoor Rooms

CREATE INTIMATE NOOKS FROM BIG, OPEN SPACES

When a fence, hedge, or masonry wall encloses an outdoor space, the space becomes, essentially, an outdoor room. The question, then, for homeowners and landscape designers is whether they want one big multipurpose room or a series of rooms designed for specific needs. For example, you may want separate areas for outdoor cooking (and eating) and a vegetable garden. Or you may want a divider between a patio area and a utilitarian cutting garden or dog run.

You can separate one area from another in a variety of ways. Fences, hedges, low walls, rows of shrubs, and lattice screens serve well. Being able to catch a glimpse of the adjoining room through an opening in a hedge or fence adds to the mystery and appeal, and beckons visitors from one room to the next.

Although you might not think of garden areas as outdoor rooms, many landscapes already employ the concept to shield a utility area for trash cans and garden equipment from view. They can also hide a vegetable garden behind a vine-covered lattice. How far you take the idea is up to you, but it can add usefulness and livability to any size of garden.

Dividing this cramped, steep yard into outdoor rooms made creative use of a difficult site. A sunny dining terrace offers low walls for comfortable seating and overlooks a colorful, cozy flower garden below.

- To unify a garden of rooms, repeat materials throughout the landscape.
- On a flat site, even minor grade changes add drama.
- A series of well-designed garden rooms makes even a small garden seem large.

TOP LEFT: This arbor-covered gate creates the impression of entering an outdoor room. On the gate, note the weighted chain that makes it self-closing.

TOP RIGHT: Steps and angled hedges suggest distinct spaces in this small garden. Its well-arranged design offers smaller nooks for relaxing and entertaining.

BOTTOM: Four simple plaster columns create the impression of an outdoor room with little intrusion. Trees provide an airy enclosure.

Showing the character of years, this Mediterranean-style courtyard blends terra-cotta tile squares with diagonally set blue-glazed accents; it also features a vibrantly tiled fountain. A small flowering tree provides dappled shade.

Courtyard Sanctuaries

WHERE IT'S HOT AND DRY, THEY COOL AND REFRESH

From their origins in arid climates, courtyard gardens contain the tradition of blocking out harsh surroundings while enclosing a bit of a cool, welcoming paradise. These oases are wonderful gardens to live with and in, functioning much like outdoor rooms.

Because they are enclosed, courtyard gardens are like distilled versions of larger landscapes. All of the elements are there—the floors, ceilings, and walls; the flowers, trees, and shrubs. But because the space is confined, each element is brought out in high relief, combining to make an impact out of proportion to its size.

The peace and calm afforded by these special landscapes invites people to linger, but without plenty of comfortable seating as a part of the plan, that invitation is no better than a tease.

If you're considering a courtyard garden, don't fall prey to the "bigger is better" notion. For courtyards, small is beautiful—and comforting. You won't need to go overboard with plantings. A couple of well-chosen small trees (possibly even in containers), a few vines for the wall, perhaps a small boxwood hedge surrounding a fountain (don't forget the fountain!), and a pot or two of flowering annuals are all you need.

- Small courtyards are intimate—don't make yours too large.
- Don't try to crowd in too many plants.
- Include comfortable seating.
- For a desert courtyard design, see page 192.

LEFT: Arched entry frames view of private courtyard and issues invitation to come inside and visit. Dappled shade and cooling brick create comfortable summer retreat.

TOP RIGHT: This narrow, L-shaped side yard has all the charm of a more traditional, square courtyard. Note the space-saving wall fountain and comfortable seating.

BOTTOM RIGHT: Complete with koi pond and ample seating, this courtyard garden was created in a narrow space. It includes a rill set in the middle of the stairs.

Small Spaces
THEY CAN STILL PACK A LANDSCAPE PUNCH

The average size of home landscapes is shrinking. Instead of expansive open spaces, most gardens are pocket-sized—perhaps just a balcony or rooftop—in which to create a private paradise.

Size is relative. What matters most is not the physical dimensions of the space, but a commitment to create a good design and to invest ingenuity in the effort.

Small gardens have certain advantages. Condensed spaces are naturally cozy and inviting. They bring each plant into sharper focus, making even a common red geranium in a terra-cotta pot seem special. Although weeds, dead leaves, and other garden debris stand out in a small space, the effort to keep a small garden tidy is minimal, leaving more time simply to enjoy it. And because there is less to buy, you can create a great small landscape on a modest budget.

Scale is perhaps the most important element to consider in small spaces. Choose plants that are naturally compact and fine-textured and furniture that is small but comfortable. Likewise, choose features, such as a fountain or pool, that are small in scale without sacrificing their function. The fact is that you can shoehorn all the elements of a larger landscape into the smallest of spaces if you pay careful attention to the size of every element.

The painted trompe l'oeil gate at the end of this small courtyard fools the eye into believing that a larger garden lies ahead. The curved path and repeating flower colors also move the eye and create interest.

TOP LEFT: This pocket-sized patio seems large, with inviting old brick pavers, mature vines, plenty of comfortable seating, and beautiful views.

TOP RIGHT: The angled patio and gently curving pathway make this small garden look larger than it is. A koi pond adds a swirl of motion.

BOTTOM LEFT: A place to get away from it all, this small corner garden provides seclusion and relaxation. The wall planting of geraniums and ivy takes advantage of vertical growing space.

BOTTOM CENTER: A clever design divides the garden in diagonals, disguising the narrowness of the space while creating intrigue.

BOTTOM RIGHT: An inviting path leads to a small stone patio—just the place to stop and smell the roses. No space is wasted here, where plants fill every nook and cranny.

The charm of this cottage garden starts with the strong structural elements of a white picket fence and an arbor that gives glimpses of the flowering perennial gardens beyond. 'New Dawn' roses cover the arbor.

The Cottage Garden Ideal

IT'S A STYLE THAT'S LIGHT AND LOOSE

A landscape with the personality of an English cottage garden has great charm. Plants are grown and added at the taste and whim of the gardener, and the only guiding principle is to include the gardener's favorite plants.

The effect is likely to be kaleidoscopic, with an old climbing rose, a clump of daylilies, a mat of nasturtiums, and a towering stand of hollyhocks surrounded by spots of color from cottage pinks, basket-of-gold, veronica, poppies, and other plants. The true cottage garden has a wild and woolly look, but it is also an engaging spot in which to lose oneself.

While this loose design approach may appeal to you, the more random and chaotic the plantings, the more important it becomes to have a strong skeleton underlying everything and contributing a subtle, but discernable, sense of order to the scene. As with any other landscape, start the design by defining utilitarian areas—pathways, patios, decks, and so on. Bear in mind that because cottage gardens are naturally unruly, paths need to be extra-wide to accommodate plants' exuberant growth. Leave enough room for outdoor activities, such as cooking, dining, and lounging, and then decide the shapes and sizes of the flower beds and borders.

The profuse, bountiful look associated with cottage gardens depends on plants that are not merely growing but *thriving*, and in order to thrive, they need the best possible soil. Improve it before planting. You'll probably never get a second chance to do it right, so be sure to add generous amounts of organic matter to the soil, till it in deeply, and add whatever amendments may be necessary.

TIPS

- Design beds with bold lines and curves.
- Use roses as landscape plants, filling in around them with billowy companion plants.
- Arrange plants to create drifts of flower colors.

TOP LEFT: There are no strict rules for planting a cottage garden. Include as many plants with as much variety as you like. The more variety of blooms and colors, the better.
BOTTOM LEFT: Morning glories frame the windows at the end of the this exuberantly planted path. Roses punctuate the planting beds.
RIGHT: Pink blossoms cover 'Ballerina' rose. Across the path, dianthus, catmint, and scabiosa mingle beside yellow 'Sun Goddess' rose.

When Plant Lovers Garden

IF PLANTS ARE THE FOCUS, THE RESULTS ARE ALWAYS INTERESTING

If you're a plant lover—if you buy plants at nurseries, garden centers, plant sales, garage sales, and grocery stores without having the faintest idea of where you intend to plant them—you need a special kind of landscape.

You might assume this approach would result in a chaotic landscape, but usually the opposite is true. Plant lovers constantly pinch, tweak, rearrange, and reorder their gardens. It's that constant fussing that, in the end, creates a beautiful garden.

The examples on these pages show that you can be a plant lover and still leave some room in the garden for human inhabitants.

TIPS

- Well-defined beds and edged paths keep an overflowering garden from looking unkempt.
- Choose plants that interest you and label them so you can keep track.
- Rearrange and reorder plants frequently; there's no such thing as too much trial and error.

Borders are bigger and lawns smaller when plant lovers garden. This border combines perennials, such as phlox, heliopsis, coreopsis, salvia, sedum, and speedwell, with oakleaf hydrangea.

TOP: Stepping-stones lead to a bentwood chair from which to contemplate the eclectic mix of flowering plants and grasses in this casual garden.
BOTTOM LEFT: Plant lovers can always find room for one more, even if it has to be wedged into a terra-cotta container. Here, a variegated agave accents the planting.

BOTTOM RIGHT: Without apparent rhyme or reason, self-sown pink foxgloves pierce the air in a beautiful spring display. Neatly clipped yew hedges contain them.

Both kids and vegetables thrive in this packed kitchen garden overseen by a scarecrow. Just step out the back door for baskets of summer vegetables. Fragrant herbs and bouquets add to the mix.

A Cook's Garden
WAYS TO KEEP HERBS AND VEGETABLES CLOSE BY

Nothing is quite so satisfying to cooks as being able to walk out the back door to grab a sun-ripened tomato for a salad or snip a sprig of parsley or basil for a pot of simmering soup. While a sprawling vegetable garden may work for some, those with smaller spaces can enjoy the convenience of home-grown vegetables and herbs, too.

Even if you're a novice gardener, creating a garden that's both edible and attractive is well within your reach. You can mix edibles with flowering perennials and annuals, essentially using vegetables as ornamentals. This allows you to enjoy small amounts of home-grown produce without a big commitment of time and space.

Use herbs, with their distinctive fragrances and interesting colors, to line pathways and use long-lived vegetables, such as cabbage, to fill decorative containers. The colors and textures of leafy greens, such as Swiss chard, brighten late-season borders, while the shapes of dramatic plants, such as artichoke or rhubarb, lend an sculptural touch to a border.

- Choose a location close to the kitchen that receives at least 6 hours of sunlight a day.
- Make sure there is a supply of water near the garden.
- Include flowers for color.
- For an edible garden plan, see page 184.

TOP LEFT: Easy-to-build raised planters provide perfect conditions for golden sage, basil, rosemary, and other fragrant and culinary herbs.
TOP RIGHT: The shapes, colors, and textures of leafy lettuces and 'Purple Vienna' kohlrabi brighten both the garden and the salad bowl.
BOTTOM LEFT: Free-blooming gold signet marigolds wind among blue-green, red, and curly-leafed cabbages and smoky-colored kale.
BOTTOM RIGHT: In compact landscapes, use vegetables as edible ornamentals. Plant them among flowers in borders and containers.

Container Gardens

Plants in containers, long a staple in city gardens, lend versatility to any garden. Containers can go almost anywhere—into sun or shade—to provide a bright splash of color or fill out a bare spot. They can become a focal point in their own right if the container has sufficient presence. Moreover, during a long winter, you can move them to a protected spot and perhaps prolong bloom.

Container gardening allows you to display plants where the soil is poor or even nonexistent. Place them along paths, on stairs, in sitting areas, and even on the tops and sides of walls and fences.

Among shade plants suitable for containers, some of the most striking effects come from those with unusual leaf markings and colorful foliage. Purple, red, and yellow foliage, such as that found on coleus, caladium, and Persian shield (*Strobilanthes dyerianus*), makes a stunning foil for bright flowers and lush green leaves.

Bold leaf shapes, such as those of hostas, can contrast handsomely with fine-textured foliage, such as that of fringed bleeding heart (*Dicentra eximia*). Strap-leaved plants, such as agapanthus, can add drama and soften the harsher lines of other plants.

Choices for sunny locations are practically unlimited. Try flowering annuals, such as rosy pink petunias, with erect blue mealycup sage (*Salvia farinacea* 'Victoria') and white African daisies. Or match the pink floribunda rose 'Nearly Wild' with red-and-pink maiden pink (*Dianthus deltoides*). For large mixed plantings, select the central plant first, then choose plants with flowers that complement its growth habit and color. Annuals are perfect for containers, thanks to their shallow roots and vigorous growth, but most plants perform well as long as the container is large enough to accommodate the plant's roots.

Containers hold cushions of flowering plants, rambling vines, bamboo, and small trees in this small concrete and brick-paved courtyard. Water spilling from a lion mask on the wall cools the air.

TIPS

- Make sure containers allow for good water drainage.
- In containers, use a lightweight soil mix, not garden soil.
- Water and fertilize container plants on a regular basis.
- For a collection of container gardening ideas, see the garden plan on page 194.

TOP LEFT: Native prairie grasses rub shoulders with blanket flower, gloriosa daisy, and purple coneflowers in this stone bowl composition.
BOTTOM LEFT: Bottomless culvert pipes lend an architectural element and give billowing annual flowers a place to take root on this sunny deck.
RIGHT: Annuals and sculptural desert plants fill pots on both sides of this courtyard fountain, softening the brick and stucco surfaces.

An Artist's Garden

QUIRKY PERHAPS, BUT ALWAYS FUN AND ALWAYS INTERESTING

Whether their owners are actually artists or not, the landscapes pictured on these pages are certainly works of self-expression. Their creators let loose in their own backyards.

Strong forms and bold colors alternate with soft textures and quiet corners. No surface is sacred. The door of a garden shed might be Day-Glo green, a patio may be made from an intricate mosaic of broken bits of crockery, or an old wheelbarrow might recall a Currier & Ives painting. Whimsy abounds, and simply delighting in the results is reason enough to enjoy these gardens.

It's interesting to note that artists' gardens are usually the expression of a single personality. Rare is the couple who can agree on what ornament goes where in the garden or whether fluorescent purple is a good color to paint a lawn chair.

TIPS

- Be willing to experiment—and fail.
- Trust your own eye and experience.
- Look at familiar materials in new ways.

The trompe l'oeil gate, painted on an otherwise blank wall, welcomes visitors to an imaginary land beyond the wall. The painted scene visually enlarges the landscape, while planting up to the wall adds to the illusion.

TOP LEFT: A colorful mosaic of square blue, purple, orange, pink, and red tiles marks the points of the compass in this flagstone path.
MIDDLE LEFT: Dramatically painted stucco walls provide a foil for plants with bold foliage and sculptural form, such as red-leafed kalanchoe.

BOTTOM LEFT: Dymondia carpets the ground between paving stones, surrounding an artistic sofa made from fieldstone and cement.
RIGHT: With its yellow door and contrasting eaves, this artist's garden is bright with color even when no flowers are in bloom.

A vibrant planting of springtime wildflowers under a palo verde tree includes reddish spikes of Parry's penstemon and gold Mexican poppies, a simple yet powerful combination.

Wildflowers Unleashed

BEAUTIFULLY FREE SWEEPS OF STUNNING COLOR

When many people think of wildflowers, they see them as suitable only for large plantings—ones measured in acres instead of square feet. Wildflower mixes, however, are delightful, low-maintenance additions to landscapes of any size, whether planted in traditional borders, in a rough area out back, or as a replacement for a lawn.

For the greatest success with wildflowers, pay attention to regional recommendations. Wildflowers that grow well in some regions are utter failures in another. For example, California poppies return year after year in the desert Southwest but are quickly overwhelmed by weeds and tall grasses in the rainy Southeast.

Also, take time to prepare the soil properly before planting. Remove all weeds from the planting bed by hand, by tilling, or by using an herbicide.

TIPS

- Select a seed mixture specifically formulated for your region.
- Start with a weed-free planting area.
- In all regions, planting in the early fall is best; early spring is second best.

TOP LEFT: Red poppies glow in a casual meadow planting, reflecting the brilliant setting sun. Comfortable chairs invite visitors at day's end.

TOP RIGHT: For drama, choose wildflowers with complementary colors, such as orange California poppies and blue love-in-a-mist.

BOTTOM LEFT: A peeled board fence is the background for fescue and wildflowers, including red poppies, purple penstemon, and yellow sundrops.

BOTTOM RIGHT: A cheery welcome begins at the curb where orange California poppies predominate in this casual entryway planting. The poppies provide a surprisingly long season of bloom.

Diminutive irises rise early in spring and are attractive planted in clusters around the base of pine tree and among mossy rocks.

Shade Gardens

GOT SHADE? HERE ARE WAYS TO USE IT

As forests age, a whole new microclimate is created, along with a unique set of plants that flourish in the protection provided by the canopy overhead. An amazing variety of ferns, the nodding bluebells of early spring, the lyrical beauty of a dogwood tree in bloom, and azaleas. Rhododendrons and camellias add their resplendent blossoms to the spring green, and these are just a few of the extraordinary plants associated with woodland landscapes.

If you're interested in creating a woodland garden (and are lucky enough to have the natural conditions that would foster one), your best bet is to mimic nature's own designs. If possible, at different times of year take as many walks as you can through natural woodland areas in your region. Take along a notebook and a camera to record what you see. If plants catch your eye but are unknown to you, take photographs of them to a nursery where staff should be able to help you identify them. Don't be tempted to dig up plants from the wild—not only is it bad form, but it's illegal in many areas.

Add a patio or deck where the view is particularly pleasant. You'll undoubtedly want to spend as much time as possible enjoying your plants at close range.

TIPS

- Choose plants adapted to shade conditions under trees.
- Never collect woodland plants from the wild.
- For more ideas, see the plan on page 196.

TOP LEFT: Drifts of bleeding heart, accented with primroses and bluebells, make a naturalistic spring display in this shaded garden.
TOP RIGHT: Bold, white-edged hosta, purple hebe, and chartreuse lady's mantle light up the shade under Douglas fir and myrtle trees.
BOTTOM LEFT: Snowdrops emerge in late winter as snow recedes from under leafless trees. These flowers signal the beginning of spring.
BOTTOM RIGHT: Mature trees shade a carpet of wildflowers and ferns. This woodland slope makes a smooth transition from lawn to house.

Backyard Habitat
WELCOMING VISITING CREATURES

While some people dream of planting a rose garden or vegetable patch, wildlife gardeners have visions of butterfly gardens and bird sanctuaries. Often, this type of landscape has no lawn, or it's only a small one. Gone, too, are neatly trimmed shrub borders. In their place are informal plantings of annuals and perennials and meandering

LEFT: This naturalistic Southwestern garden features red-flowering autumn sage and bunny ears cactus, plus a visiting bunny.
TOP RIGHT: When snow covers the ground, cardinals enjoy red hawthorn berries and other persistent fruits, such as crab apples.
BOTTOM RIGHT: Trumpet honeysuckle, a favorite of hummingbirds, clambers over a birdhouse intended for other feathered friends.

walks covered with pine needles or bark. Most contain at least one birdbath, fountain, or small pool for the fresh water that's essential to all forms of life.

All landscapes require regular upkeep, but informal plantings that attract wildlife are far less demanding than more traditional ones. Allow plants to find their natural forms instead of trimming them into tidy shapes. A weed here or there isn't such an eyesore when it's growing amid a profusion of billowing plants. And birds and butterflies won't notice whether it's a weed or a cultivated plant.

Even though wildlife landscapes are informal, be sure to define places to sit, relax, and take in the sights and sounds of your private sanctuary. A wooden bench under a spreading tree, a couple of chaise longues on a patio overlooking a small pond, or a clearing in a grove of trees for a picnic table and benches will provide human comfort and a vantage point.

TOP LEFT: Adult monarch butterflies are attracted to a variety of sun-loving flowers, including these purple coneflowers.
BOTTOM LEFT: A rustic homemade bird feeder is right at home in this wildlife-friendly garden planted with an appealing assortment of annuals and perennials.
RIGHT: When you create a wildlife habitat, be sure to leave room for the garden's human inhabitants, too. That way, you'll have a ringside seat.

TIPS

- Choose plants that provide food and shelter for the wildlife you want to attract.
- Don't keep the landscape too tidy.
- Provide a source of fresh water.
- For an example of a landscape planned with wildlife in mind, see page 182.

Perched on the slope, this garden blends dwarf conifers and low-growing perennials, such as red penstemon, blue catmint, apricot poppies, and yellow alyssum, that echo the wildflower fields of the Rocky Mountains.

Rock Gardens

IF YOU'VE GOT 'EM, USE 'EM

Rock gardens are landscapes in miniature, simulations of boulder-strewn mountain slopes, rocky outcrops of coastal bluffs, or windswept high plains—all created with diminutive flowering and evergreen plants. Your property may be suitable for a rock garden if it contains natural outcrops of rock or slopes with thin, gravelly soil that makes landscaping difficult.

Traditional rock gardens rely on plants from high altitudes. Called alpine plants, they grow beneath a winter blanket of snow on high mountain slopes. Low and ground-hugging, they send roots deep into rocky crevices and put forth brilliantly colored—and often surprisingly large—flowers. Modern rock gardens use any type of plant, as long as it is relatively delicate in scale.

Strict practitioners of alpine gardening insist upon using plants and rocks that are native to alpine regions. Casual rock gardeners insist only that a plant look right in its rocky surroundings, caring little for the origin of the plant and even less about where the rocks might have come from.

The best rock gardens attempt to re-create a natural rocky landscape, whether from the mountains or by the shore. Most plants adapted to rocky sites are naturally dwarf and low-growing. Most rock gardeners avoid annuals, such as petunias, dahlias, and zinnias; preferred are low-growing junipers, dwarf conifers, compact ground covers, and various mosses.

TIPS

- Make your garden about 40 percent rock and 60 percent plants. Plant around stone steps or along the tops of retaining walls.
- For a realistic look, copy nature. High mountain meadows usually have one type of stone and only two or three kinds of wildflowers.
- To make a rock outcropping on a flat site, mound soil into a berm and place jagged rocks onto the face of it so they look as if they've been forced upward out of bedrock.

TOP: Colorful conifers and flowering perennials, such as lady's mantle with chartreuse blooms, offer a perfect contrast to the muted boulders.
BOTTOM LEFT: Crevices in lichen-covered rocks are home for hen-and-chickens, which thrives on neglect in poor, rocky soil.
BOTTOM RIGHT: Variegated sedum dominates this rockery planted with succulents, each tumbling over the next for a natural-looking display.

Tropical Flair

WHEN THE CLIMATE'S RIGHT, BRING THE TROPICS HOME

More than any other landscape style, tropical landscapes are about plants. Swaying palms, neon-flowered bougainvillea spilling over the top of a roof, cannas rising rocket-like beside a garden pool, and aptly named elephant's ears putting forth leaves the size of a table-cloths are just a few of the treasures.

A mainstay of gardens in the Lower and Tropical South, as well as the mild-winter West, tropical plants are hot items for gardeners just about everywhere. Tropical and semitropical plants revel in long hot summers. In addition, many of these plants bloom nearly nonstop through warm weather with flowers that are nothing short of spectacular.

Combining the different shapes and sizes of leaves of these plants is as rewarding as combining different colors of flowers. Try juxtaposing large-leaved plants with ones that have small, delicate foliage or combine plants with different-colored leaves.

Don't let the prospect of cold winters keep you from trying tropicals in your garden. In marginal climates, gardeners can often preserve tropicals just by mulching them heavily in the autumn. Where this isn't enough, grow them in containers, bring them indoors before the first fall frost, then back outdoors the following spring.

This miniature tropical paradise was created from an assortment of palms, tree ferns, and an angel's trumpet, with its large, wonderfully fragrant hanging blossoms. The small pond makes room for exotic water lilies and adds the soothing, cooling sound of water.

- Mix and match textures, colors, and sizes of tropical plants.
- In cold-winter regions, grow tropicals in containers.
- Check out the plan for a tropical oasis on page 202.

TOP LEFT: A tall canna 'Grande' and variegated ficus tree preside over this lush planting of colorful caladiums and sweet potato vine, bringing a little bit of the tropics to the city.

TOP RIGHT: The finely cut fronds of the Mediterranean fan palm provide intricate tropical texture in this entryway garden.

BOTTOM LEFT: Slate tiles set off a grove of sculptural palms, a planting of tall horsetails, and furniture draped in tropical colors.

BOTTOM RIGHT: Nothing succeeds like excess. Green-and-white variegated caladiums makes a bold, exotic statement.

Drought tolerant sedums and grasses in this California border provide textural contrast throughout. Blue-green agave adds drama to the top of the wall; golden poppies add splashes of color. All take heat in stride.

Waterwise Landscapes

HERE'S PROOF THAT DRY DOESN'T MEAN BORING

Where rain is scarce or reservoirs easily overtaxed— whether from a temporary weather condition or the prevailing climate—more and more gardeners are becoming conscious of their water usage.

Many homeowners are forgoing large lawns and sprawling beds of annuals that demand more in water than they return in pleasure. Good alternatives are water-conserving plants that are well adapted to the region's natural conditions. These gardeners group plants wisely, placing drought-resistant plants together, and putting only the plants that need regular watering on a separate irrigation system and schedule.

The good news is that Lowe's stocks plants that are well adapted to your particular region—plants more or less content to survive on the area's natural rainfall (or occasional lack of it). To make the most out of what water you have, choose less-thirsty plants.

Make sure your watering practices and devices deliver water as efficiently as possible (see page 212) and routinely incorporate organic matter to improve your soil's ability to resist evaporation and retain moisture. Don't forget the value of mulch. A layer of organic material over soil and around plants reduces moisture loss, reduces weeds, and slows erosion.

- Select plants that are native to your region or to a region with a similar climate.
- Water only when plants need it, not by the clock.
- Keep the landscape free of weeds; mulch liberally.
- For good examples of waterwise landscapes, see pages 188 and 190.

TOP LEFT: Thyme happily creeps between the crevices of this flagstone patio, demanding little care or water. Scarlet penstemon brightens the foreground.

TOP RIGHT: Early spring, when intense blue pride of Madeira and golden California poppies are in bloom, is the showiest period for this Mediterranean garden.

BOTTOM LEFT: Spiky yucca (far left) and purple Dutch irises rise over flowering perennials in a Colorado garden. These drought-tolerant plants withstand harsh winters.

BOTTOM RIGHT: Weeks of drought won't faze yellow fernleaf yarrow or red-and-yellow blanket flower, but too much water can kill them.

Fire Safety

HOW LANDSCAPING MIGHT SAVE YOUR HOUSE

Wildfires are a fact of life in the West and are becoming so in other regions of the country. One of the most important steps you can take to prevent losing your house to fire is to landscape it properly. Fire officials believe that clearing the brush within 30 to 400 feet of the house can halve the odds of losing your house to fire. That's a big range, but the exact distance is determined by slope, wind, neighborhood density, and your house's architecture and materials.

For years, common wisdom was to landscape with fire-retardant plants. Fire specialists now say this practice is misleading. The 1991 fire in the hills of Oakland, California, showed that fire-retardant plantings gave a false sense of security, especially when those plants were affected by drought, poorly maintained, or adjacent to a house with a wooden roof. In a high-intensity fire, everything burns. But some landscapes are safer than others. The following guidelines offer the best information to date.

Above a fire-prone canyon, this garden has been landscaped with fire safety in mind. The lawn acts as a buffer between the house and any fire that may travel up the canyon. As added protection, low-growing fire-resistant plants surround the lawn.

- Eliminate fire ladders—plants of different heights that form a continuous fuel supply from the ground up to the tree canopy.
- Create a transition zone, if your lot size allows, 30 to 50 feet out from the house. In this area, leave only enough shrubs and low-growing plants to stabilize a slope.
- Regularly clean up leaves and other plant litter and remove overgrown brush.
- Clear all vegetation and debris from your roof and gutters several times during the year.
- Keep plants well watered (assuming water supplies permit), especially those within 30 feet of the house. Keep grasses watered and green year-round.

TOP LEFT: Sprinkler system keeps lawns and landscape trees from drying out and becoming fire hazards. Water as needed, not by the clock.
BOTTOM LEFT: A defensible landscape helped these firefighters save a rural home from wildfire in San Diego County, California.
RIGHT: A professional pruner, secured by ropes and harnesses, thins the deadwood from crown of this tree to make it more fire resistant.

- Thin crowns of clustered trees, trim limbs to 20 feet or more off the ground, and cut back any branches to 15 to 20 feet from the house. Prune out all dead branches.
- Clear out overhanging tree branches along the driveway and prune back bushy shrubs to ensure that fire trucks have easy access.

CHAPTER 3

Places to Sit, Walk, and Play

Extend your living areas into the great outdoors! By transforming your backyard into outdoor rooms, you can double the square footage of your home's living area for little cost. Outdoor space may consist of a patio or deck, one path or several, or special places for fun and adventure. You can turn an underused area into the perfect spot for an outdoor playroom, a dining area under the stars, or a private flower-and-foliage-filled retreat for yourself.

IN THIS CHAPTER
PATIO OR DECK? • OUTDOOR LIVING
DECK BASICS • LUMBER CHOICES
HARDWARE AND FINISHES
PATIO PRIMER • KITCHENS
PAVING • EDGING • PATHS
STEPS • PLAY AREAS

Patio or Deck?

WHICH WORKS FOR YOU?

First things first: Do you prefer patios or decks? Sometimes, this decision is simply a matter of style or is dependent on your site.

Decks have a number of advantages. Deck lumber is durable and resilient underfoot, and it won't store heat the way stone, brick, or concrete does. Hardwoods add a furniture-like elegance, and choices of man-made and recycled products are also on the rise. Decks can also tame sloping, bumpy, or poorly draining sites.

Patios, on the other hand, lend an unmatched sense of permanence and tradition to a formal garden or house design. You might choose traditional brick or tile or elegant stone. Concrete pavers are rising stars, and they're easy to install yourself. And don't rule out concrete—you may be amazed at the jazzy techniques for coloring, retexturing, and softening the concrete slab. Loose materials, such as pea gravel, bark, or wood chips, are still other options.

Or why not combine both patio and deck in one design? A blend of masonry and wood allows great flexibility in space, texture, and finished height.

Bricks placed diagonally fill a path leading to a color-matched garden seating area paved in traditional fieldstone. The path jazzes up the fieldstone and echoes the brick wall of the house and entry steps.

LANDSCAPING PRINCIPLES

Whatever type of outdoor surface you choose, let basic landscaping principles guide your thinking. These principles are abstract concepts, such as unity, variety, proportion, and balance. Return to these principles repeatedly as your plan develops. For more examples of how these concepts affect landscape design, see Chapter 5, beginning on page 144.

Here are examples of how some of these ideas apply to the design of your patio.

Unity Unity means that everything looks as if it belongs together. Paving, overhead structures, and screens complement each other; furniture suits the patio's architectural style; and the patio's plants relate to each other and to other plants in the landscape.

Unity between the patio and house is an important consideration, too. If, for example, your patio is built off a casual-style kitchen, the patio should have the same feeling.

Variety Variety keeps unity from becoming monotonous. A good design offers an element of surprise: a path that leads from a large main terrace to a more intimate one, a plant display that brings the garden

TOP LEFT: An outdoor hearth with sofa and chair drawn up to it makes an idyllic sanctuary in all seasons, both day and night.
TOP RIGHT: Different paving materials and flower-filled planting pockets create a private area adjacent to an active swimming pool.
BOTTOM: Colorful squash and potted plants add an autumn touch to this patio, tiled in earthy tones to match the house.

into the patio, a subtle wall fountain that gives dimension to a small space, or trees that provide varying degrees of light at different times of day.

You can make use of variety on vertical planes, too. Patios that step up or step down, low walls, raised beds, privacy screens, and container plants of varying heights help draw the eye away from a vertical expanse.

Proportion Proportion demands that the patio's structure be in scale with your house and garden. Keep in mind that as outdoor rooms, patios are built on a different scale than indoor rooms. Although many patios are scaled to the size of the living room, don't be afraid to design something larger. Outdoor furniture usually takes up more room than indoor pieces, and you may want room for containers of plants, too. (Choose plants with their mature sizes in mind.)

There are sensible limits, however. If your lot is so big that you need a large patio to keep everything in scale, try to create a few smaller areas within the larger whole. For example, squares of plants inset in paving

LEFT: Overhead timbers, supported on massive posts, harmonize with the natural surroundings, softening and shading the patio's hard surfaces.
TOP RIGHT: Formal brick patio mirrors the traditional lines of this stucco house. Even the handrails match the house trim.
BOTTOM RIGHT: Mossy stone patio blends almost seamlessly with its shady surroundings. The plantings mimic Mother Nature, too.

break up a monotonous surface. Use plantings or fences to divide one large area into one or more functional spaces.

To maintain proportion in a small patio, keep the design simple and uncluttered—clean lines make elements seem larger. Stepped planting beds lead the eye up and out of a confined area. Tall vertical screens used to enclose a small area actually make it appear larger, as does such a solid paving material like brick, with its small-scale repetitive pattern.

Balance Balance is achieved when elements are artfully combined to produce the same visual weight on both sides of a center of interest. For example, if a mature tree shades one side of your patio, balance the tree's weight with perimeter benches on the other side.

ORIENTATION TO THE SUN

Another consideration as you plan your patio is weather. Exposure to the sun is one of the most important factors in your enjoyment of outdoor space. Knowing the sun's path may prompt you to adjust the site of the patio, extend its dimensions, or change its design in order to add a few weeks or months of sun or shade to your outdoor room. Often, the addition of a patio roof can moderate the sun's effects.

Reflecting the façade of the house, this patio of brick set in sand has an informal look. Despite the patio's expansiveness—which means no grass to mow—the herringbone pattern lends a sense of containment.

Theoretically, a north-facing patio is cold because it rarely receives the sun. A south-facing patio is usually warm because, from sunrise to sunset, the sun never leaves it. A patio on the east side is cool, receiving only morning sun. And a west-facing patio is often unbearably hot because it receives the full force of the sun's midafternoon rays. In addition, late-afternoon sun often creates a harsh glare.

Generally, the patio temperature will follow this north-south-east-west rule. Exceptions occur in climates where extreme summer or winter temperatures are predictable. For example, mid-July temperatures in Phoenix regularly climb above 100°F, and a north-facing patio there could hardly be considered cold. In San Francisco, on the other hand, a patio with a southern or western exposure could hardly be considered hot because chilly fogs and stiff ocean breezes are common during the summer months.

For more about planning your landscape and its orientation to the sun, see page 152.

This wood-fired outdoor oven sees plenty of pizza baking and chicken roasting. The carefully crafted granite structure houses a prefabricated oven insert, a chimney, a wood bin, and even a digital timer.

Dining Outdoors

An outdoor dining area is often the centerpiece of an attractive patio or deck and can double as a sewing spot or as a perfect place to play board games and enjoy other leisurely activities.

A functional and inviting outdoor dining area incorporates a careful balance of many of the site con-

siderations and structural and design elements described in this book. For example, ensuring privacy, sufficient shade, and shelter from the elements—with shade trees, overhead structures, screening, and fences—will add significantly to your enjoyment of the space. Defining the area with colorful plantings also adds appeal. In general,

TOP: The wide, even surface of this flagstone path eases walking through the landscape. Lighting allows for nighttime strolls.
BOTTOM RIGHT: The path itself is the focal point here. Its mix of shapes, textures, and materials draws the eye through the garden.

Use solid paths Use brick, concrete, pavers, or stone for routes that you're likely to travel barefoot (the path from hot tub to house, for example), so your wet feet won't pick up dirt. Use bark or gravel in places that call for a more natural look.

Make it wide enough Main paths should be wide enough for two people to walk side by side: 4 to 5 feet is about right. Small subsidiary paths should be wide enough for a wheelbarrow (handles have a 24- to 30-inch spread): 2 feet is a generous minimum, as long as plants don't crowd the edges. Organize a network of paths like a river system, with smaller paths branching off larger ones.

Add plants wherever possible Allow some space between pavers, stones, or bricks in which to plant thyme or other low creepers. Amend the soil well so that plants can establish roots; it should be on the sandy side, so it won't become packed down with foot traffic and kill the plant's roots. Don't tuck plants in paths used for main walkways or where snow removal will be necessary.

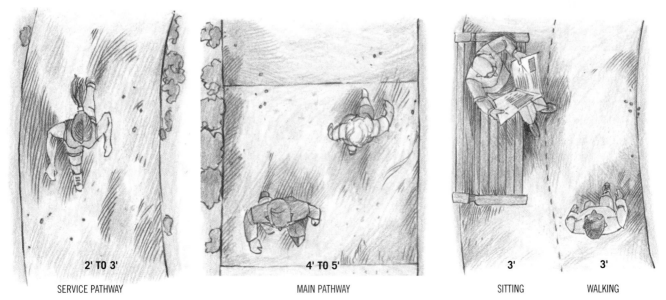

PATHWAY CLEARANCE

BENCH CLEARANCE

2' TO 3'

4' TO 5'

3'   3'

SERVICE PATHWAY

MAIN PATHWAY

SITTING   WALKING

Bricks are extremely versatile. They can be mortared or laid on sand and arranged in a wide variety of patterns and colors. This garden path was made with used brick pavers laid in a basket-weave design.

Brick Paths and Walkways

Brick is probably the most adaptable and frequently used patio surfacing material available. Set in sand or mortar, brick provides a handsome surface that blends with nearly any architectural style and looks at ease in almost any setting.

Bricks are available in a range of colors, sizes, and finishes and can be laid in a number of patterns, from basic to complex. You can combine patterns in striking combinations to put an individual stamp on your patio or path. Some patterns and combinations are shown on page 99.

Brick does have disadvantages, however. Cost per square foot runs higher than for most alternative materials. If you lay bricks in sand, you may have to rework the patio from time to time if frost heave (irregular buckling or swelling) raises some of the bricks. Also, you may occasionally need to spend time pulling weeds that have pushed through the joints. This problem can be reduced by laying landscaping fabric beneath the bricks. If the bricks are poorly installed, the surface can be jarringly uneven. Also, bricks in moist, heavily shaded garden areas can become slick with moss.

BRICK TYPES

Although brick's basic form and composition have remained unchanged for thousands of years, today's builder can choose from an almost bewildering variety of colors, textures, and shapes.

Bricks are made of various clay and shale mixtures that are forced through a die and cut to size with wires. The kiln-firing process, although much improved over the last century, still produces some bricks, called clinkers, that have irregularities caused by inappropriate firing. They may have an uneven surface and flashed patches from overburning. Use them for paving or as accents to give a rough cobblestone effect.

People like the familiar color and texture of common building brick. They are reasonably uniform in size and color (length may vary by as much as ¼ inch) and most economical. The rough faces of common brick create a nonglare surface with good traction. The surface is porous and readily absorbs water. As the water evaporates, it cools the air and gives a cool feeling underfoot. Unfortunately, it will just as readily absorb spilled beverages, oil, grease, and paint—all of which may be difficult to remove. In addition, in freezing climates, the moisture the bricks absorb can crack them.

Paver or hard-burned bricks are baked at a higher temperature for a longer time so are harder than common building brick. They make a metallic sound when struck by a hammer, compared to a dull, wooden sound produced by striking common brick.

Wire-cut brick is square cut and has a rough texture

LEFT: Walkway of salvaged brick curves past oakleaf hydrangea, hostas, and lady's mantle and under an arbor on the way to the backyard.
RIGHT: Brick paving laid in geometrical patterns is interplanted with creeping perennials. Flowers, ferns, and water plants soften the edges.

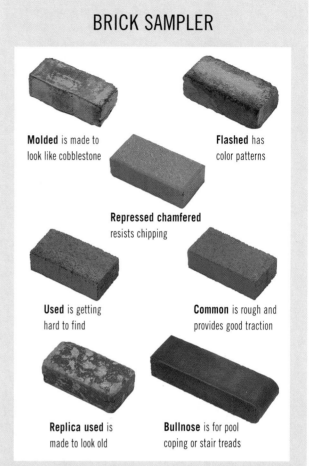

BRICK SAMPLER

Molded is made to look like cobblestone

Flashed has color patterns

Repressed chamfered resists chipping

Used is getting hard to find

Common is rough and provides good traction

Replica used is made to look old

Bullnose is for pool coping or stair treads

with little pit marks on its face. If you want a smooth surface, lay it to expose the edge. Face brick is more consistent in size and color but is also more expensive. Use them for attractive accents, edgings, and raised beds—anywhere that its smooth surface doesn't present a safety hazard.

Used brick, which may be common or face, has uneven surfaces and streaks of old mortar that can make an attractive informal pavement. Taken from old buildings and walls, these bricks are usually in short supply. Many manufacturers are now creating new bricks that look like used bricks by chipping them and splashing them with mortar and paint. Manufactured replica bricks cost about the same as the genuine article but are easier to find. They're also more consistent in quality than most older bricks.

Precut bricks in special shapes are a boon for you if you're venturing into more complicated bricklaying patterns. Tacks, quoins, bats, sinkers, traps, and spikes are just some of the traditional names for these. Expect to pay about the same price per precut brick as for a full-size brick, but keep in mind that if you had to cut bricks to these shapes, you'd need the expertise of a highly skilled mason.

BRICK SIZES

Most brick is made in modular sizes—that is, the length and width are simple divisions or multiples of each other. This simplifies planning, ordering, and fitting. The standard modular brick measures 8 inches long by 4 inches wide by $2\frac{2}{3}$ inches high. Many other modular sizes—from 4 by 12 inches to 12 by 16 inches in various thicknesses—are available. Note that all these dimensions are nominal. They include the width of a standard $\frac{1}{2}$-inch mortar joint, so the actual dimensions of the brick are reduced accordingly.

It's common for bricks to vary somewhat from specified dimensions. Different-colored bricks, even from the same manufacturer, may differ in size. Keep these variations in mind if you're planning a complicated pattern with more than one color. Your Lowe's associate can help you calculate the quantities of brick you'll need for your project.

Today, you can find many units larger or smaller than the standard dimensions that are excellent for

Generous plant pockets teeming with annuals, perennials, and herbs border the meandering brick-in-sand paths. Container plants and garden ornaments add a touch of order to the cottage-style setting.

BRICK PATTERNS

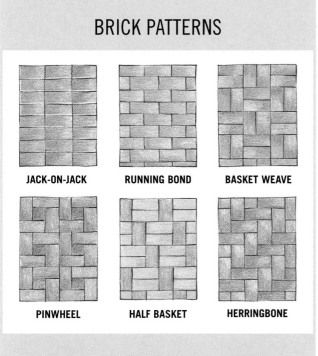

JACK-ON-JACK   RUNNING BOND   BASKET WEAVE

PINWHEEL   HALF BASKET   HERRINGBONE

A brick path or patio can harmonize with almost any style, thanks in large part to the range of patterns in which the bricks can be laid. A simple pattern, such as running bond, has a timeless, understated look. A more intricate pattern can make the surface the focal point. Intricate patterns can also add interest to the view of the project from above, such as from an upstairs window or deck.

When choosing a brick pattern, consider the degree of difficulty involved in laying it. Some require greater accuracy than others, and some more brick cutting.

After they're laid, brick pathways are virtually maintenance free. This decades-old brick path will remain for decades more.

paving. Such pavers are roughly half as thick as standard bricks. "True" or "mortarless" pavers are a standard 4 by 8 inches (plus or minus $\frac{1}{8}$ inch) and are a big help when you're laying a complex brick pattern with tightly butted joints.

BRICK GRADES
All outdoor bricks are graded by their ability to withstand weathering. If you live where it freezes and thaws, buy only those graded SX for use as pavers. Other grades recognized by the Brick Institute of America are MX, for applications where resistance to freezing is not

important, and NX, for interior applications. Bricks are also classified according to the expected traffic load. Residential paving applications usually aren't subjected to heavy traffic, so bricks classified for low traffic loads should be fine.

TIPS
- One hundred square feet of path or patio laid in running bond requires about 500 bricks.
- Running bond and jack-on-jack are the simplest patterns to lay.
- Experiment with patterns to check their look and installation.

Concrete Pavers for Paths

If your idea of a concrete paver is a gray 12-inch square, you haven't seen the new generation of these versatile paving units. Manufacturers have transformed this patio material from a functional but aesthetically limited option into an elegant choice for outdoor paving. Like brick, these precast concrete pavers are an ideal do-it-yourself material. A weekend or two of work can result in a dramatic patio or garden walkway.

Pavers are available in two types, regular noninterlocking, which have smooth edges, and interlocking, which look somewhat like puzzle pieces and fit together in almost the same way.

Noninterlocking pavers are basically like bricks, although they're usually only 1½ inches thick. They can be laid in sand, in dry mortar, or in wet mortar. Their main advantage over bricks is that they come in a wider variety of colors, shapes, and sizes.

Aside from the basic rectangular shape, you'll find circles, squares, triangles, hexagons, and specially shaped small pavers needed for complicated patterns. Small

Shaded by mature trees, this concrete-paver path and patio is an island of calm—a perfect place to while away the hours on a weekend afternoon. Concrete pavers work well in formal and informal settings.

pavers with interesting shapes can be used in combination with larger ones. Simple squares can be part of a grid or even a gentle arc. Pavers can butt together to create broad, unbroken surfaces, or they can be spaced apart and surrounded with grass, ground cover, or gravel for interesting textural effects.

Of course, you can also buy concrete pavers made to look like bricks, in classic red as well as replica used or antique finish. In many areas, they may be significantly less expensive than the real thing.

Interlocking pavers, made of extremely dense concrete that is pressure-formed in machines, have contoured edges that fit into each other. When laid in sand (sand is also used to fill the butted joints), they form a surface more rigid than bricks. No paver can tip out of place without taking several of its neighbors with it; thus,

TOP LEFT: Concrete pavers come in many styles and shapes. This group includes turf blocks, puzzle-like shapes, and interlocking kinds.
TOP RIGHT: Checkerboard path of square pavers alternating with grassy turf provides a transition from the cobbled patio to the shady border.
BOTTOM LEFT: Contemporary masonry creates an edging of interlocking pavers that match the patio floor. A compact pond mirrors the sky.
BOTTOM RIGHT: Like brick, concrete pavers can be laid in sand or mortar. They're weather resistant and work well in any region of the country.

the surface remains intact even under substantial loads.

Interlocking pavers are available in a number of colors, including tan, brown, red, and gray. Specially cut pieces are usually available to fill in the pattern at edges and corners. These modern "cobblestone" patterns are popular for casual gardens.

Offset concrete steps make a grand entry. The steps were "antiqued" with a rock salt finish, leaving irregular pits in the surface.

Subtle yet substantial, this cast concrete path is tinted to blend with stucco garden wall and border plants.

Cast Concrete and Adobe Paths

Sometimes the simplest paving options are the most effective. Cast concrete, for example, is inexpensive and can be customized to a wide variety of garden styles. Regional materials, such as adobe, which is readily available in the Southwest, are equally versatile and reflect the style of the landscape.

Cast concrete As a paving material, cast concrete is very adaptable. This mixture of sand, cement, gravel, and water is even more variable in appearance than brick. Cast in forms, it can take on almost any shape. It can be lightly smoothed or heavily brushed, surfaced with handsome pebbles, swirled, scored, tinted, painted, patterned, or cast into molds to resemble other paving materials. If you get tired of the concrete surface later on, it provides an excellent foundation for brick, stone, or tile set in mortar.

Concrete does have some disadvantages. In some situations, it can be a harsh, hot, and glaring surface. Smoothly troweled concrete can be slick when wet. If you're planning to lay concrete yourself, remember that creating a top-quality, good-looking cast concrete patio that will wear well and not crack is more difficult than it may appear. The concrete must be mixed carefully to exact specifications; there's little room for error. After the ingredients are combined and water added, work must proceed quickly and accurately; mistakes will require extensive, and perhaps costly, removal and replacement. If the concrete isn't cured correctly or if drainage needs are ignored, the surface may buckle and crack.

Concrete paths are typically given some type of surface treatment, both for appearance and for traction. Washing or sandblasting concrete paving exposes the aggregate, or you can embed colorful pebbles and stones in it. Other ways to modify the standard smooth surface include color-dusting, staining, masking, acid-washing, and salt-finishing. Concrete can also be stamped and tinted to resemble stone, tile, or brick.

Adobe The Southwest's version of the mud brick, adobe is one of the world's oldest building materials. With its warm, earthy color, adobe creates a friendly, informal

A rustic stepped walkway combines red adobe blocks with railroad ties. The ties hold the blocks in place; sand fills in the joints.

FANCY FINISHES

Finish the surface of a concrete patio to give it a personalized look that is tailored to its function. Here are some options: 1) Semismooth texture is achieved with a wooden float. 2) Smooth, troweled surface is appropriate for covered areas where it won't get wet and slippery. 3) Broomed surface provides maximum traction. Popular decorative finishes include: 4) Rock salt. 5) Travertine. 6) Seeded aggregate. Coloring concrete, either alone or in combination with other decorative finishes, adds a distinctive note.

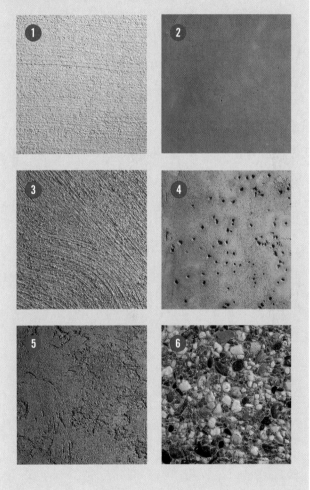

tone in an outdoor living area the way few other paving materials can. Because the blocks are large, laying the paving proceeds quickly, and your efforts yield immediate results. Adobe looks best when used in generous, open gardens, where the large size of the bricks will be in scale.

If set on a sand base and spaced with 1-inch-wide joints packed with sand or earth, adobe makes an excellent outdoor floor. Plant low-growing ground covers and moss in the joints to further soften the paving and blend it with the surrounding garden.

Today's adobe bricks are stabilized with Portland cement or asphalt emulsion that keeps them from dissolving over time. Blocks stabilized with asphalt have a darker color than traditional adobe blocks; those stabilized with Portland cement are closer in color to the original mud-and-straw bricks.

Adobe bricks used for building are generally 4 inches thick by 16 inches long, with widths varying from $3\frac{1}{2}$ to 12 inches. The most common block is 4 by $7\frac{1}{2}$ by 16 inches. Blocks can weigh 12 to 45 pounds. In addition, a nonstandard block has been designed specifically for paving use. Available in face sizes of 12 by 12 inches or 6 by 12 inches with a $2\frac{1}{2}$-inch depth, paving blocks may contain more stabilizer than is used for blocks in walls.

A circular gravel path, edged in brick, leads strollers to a lattice summerhouse tucked into a corner of the backyard. The brick edging keeps the gravel from scattering into the nearby flowerbeds.

Loose Materials

For economy, good drainage, and a more casual look, pea gravel, bark, or wood chips are good alternatives.

You needn't opt for the large, uninteresting expanses that can give these materials a bad name. Gravel can be raked into patterns or used as a decorative element with other paving materials. You can set off different gravel types with dividers. Or combine gravel or wood chips with concrete pads, concrete pavers, or other stepping-stones. Because gravel or other loose material complements plants, it can also be used effectively in transition zones between patio and garden.

The main problem with loose paving materials is that they're loose; that is, they move around, into planting beds and even indoors. Lightweight organic materials may wash away or relocate during downpours, and any organic material will need periodic replenishing.

Wood chips and bark Wood chips and shredded bark, byproducts of lumber mills, are springy and soft underfoot, generally inexpensive, and easy to apply. They're ideal for informal paths that get light use, and they can create an earthy, casual look and feel. These come in a wide variety of colors and textures. To work successfully on a path, wood chips and bark should be confined inside a grid with headers. Wood chips also make a good cushion under swings and slides in children's play areas.

Choose a material that fits its environment—a bark-mulch path in a woodland landscape or pine needles through a planting of evergreens, for example.

Rock Gravel is collected or mined from natural deposits. Crushed rock is mechanically fractured and then graded to uniform sizes. If the rock surface has been naturally worn smooth by water, it's called river rock. Frequently, gravels are named after the regions where they were quarried.

The irregular shapes of crushed rock allow it to pack well and make a firm surface that can easily support a wheelbarrow. Gravel with rounded edges resists packing, making wheelbarrow navigation—and even walking—more awkward.

When making a choice, consider color, sheen, texture, and size. Take home samples, as you would paint chips. Keep in mind that gravel color, like paint color, looks more intense when spread over a large area.

LEFT: Resembling a dry streambed, this walkway is a winning mix of coarse gravel, river rocks, and drought-tolerant native plants.
TOP RIGHT: In a woodland garden, shredded bark makes a natural paving material that blends perfectly with the shady surroundings.
BOTTOM RIGHT: A river of adobe-colored gravel flows through curving flowerbeds overflowing with ornamental grasses, perennials, and shrubs.

Stone Paths

This durable, natural material, which comes in many forms, blends well with almost any paving project. Flat flagstones and cut stone tiles are ideal for formal paving, while irregularly shaped rocks or cobblestones create a more informal, relaxed setting.

Granite is an example of volcano-formed rock; these are usually the toughest, longest-wearing options. Limestone, sandstone, and other sedimentary stones are more porous and usually have a chalky or gritty texture. Dense, smooth slate, on the other hand, is a fine-grained metamorphic rock. Imitation stones come in many types and offer an inexpensive but attractive option where stone is hard to come by. The selection of rock available depends on your area.

Generally, preparing stone for use as paving is a labor-intensive process—it takes a lot of time and effort to quarry, trim, haul, and store it, so the price to cover a given area may be higher for stone than for other

Mortared flagstone path bordered by easy-care purple-flowering catmint, mounding lavender cotton, and pink- and white-flowering Santa Barbara daisies result in colorful and low-maintenance garden.

LEFT: Rules don't exist when designing a stone path. This one includes flagstone, two colors of old brick, and blue tiles.

CENTER: A smooth cobblestone path resembles a bubbling stream. The slightly raised planting beds add to the illusion.

RIGHT: Flat stones form landings surrounded by low-growing burgundy alyssum and herbs. Pink petunias and geraniums echo stones' color.

materials. However, stone's beauty, elegance, and permanence make it well worth the extra expense.

Flagstone Technically, flagstone is any flat stone that's either naturally thin or cut from a rock that splits easily. Flagstone works in almost any setting. Its natural, unfinished look blends well with plants, and it's one of the few paving materials that can, if thick enough, be placed directly on stable soil. Its subdued colors—buff, yellow, brownish-red, and gray—add warmth to a patio, and its irregularly shaped slabs contribute pleasing texture.

Flagstone does have some less-favorable attributes. It is much more expensive than brick or concrete, and because of its irregularity, it's not a good surface for outdoor furniture, games, or wheeled toys. Snow removal can also be challenging. Also, some types of stone are easily soiled and are difficult to clean. Ask your Lowe's associate about the characteristics of the flagstone you're considering.

Flagstones generally range in thickness from $1\frac{1}{2}$ to 2 inches. They must be laid out so there are no uneven spots and the final pattern is pleasing. Without proper planning, including dry-laying the stones, the finished look may be an unattractive patchwork.

Stone tiles Many types are available, from precut to rectangular shapes. You can also find hand-cut squares and rectangles in random sizes. Slate, which is available in many colors, and granite are both popular, though expensive, choices.

Other stones Fieldstone and river rock offer alternatives to the high cost of flagstone. These waterworn or glacier-ground stones produce rustic, uneven paving that makes up in charm what it may lack in smoothness underfoot.

River rocks are available in a wide range of shapes and sizes. They are impervious to weather, and are virtually maintenance-free. Smaller stones can be set or seeded in concrete; large stones can be laid directly on the soil as raised stepping-stones. An entire surface can be paved solid with cobblestones set in concrete or tamped soil.

Keep in mind, however, that natural stones, like river rock and smaller kinds, are smooth and can be slippery, especially in wet weather. Because their shapes are irregular, they may be uncomfortable to walk on—this is especially true of rounded cobblestones.

Laying the surface, particularly when you're working with small pebbles and stones in mortar or concrete, is a slow process. Confine this surfacing to a limited area.

Wooden paths can't be beat for uneven terrain or special situations, such as spanning this man-made waterfall and stream. Here, the walkway also blends well with the traditional gazebo.

Making Paths of Wood

Few materials can match the natural, informal quality of wood. Its warm color and soft texture bring something of the forest into your landscape, and if stained or painted, wood can hold its own in even the most formal company.

A wooden pathway provides a solid, relatively durable surface requiring little or no grading and a minimum of maintenance. Because wood decking is raised above the ground and can dry quickly, it's a natural choice wherever drainage is a problem. For even less maintenance and a lower environmental impact, consider decking that's made from recycled materials (see page 77). You'll still need wood or another material for structural members, but such decking is an option for pathways that won't be subject to heavy traffic.

Whether new or old, natural or man-made, a wooden path feels right at home in almost any setting.

Wood can link a house and garden at flower-head height, smoothing out bumps and riding over drainage problems that may preclude masonry paving.

Keep in mind that codes require any walkway more than 30 inches above the ground to have a railing or similar barrier. Beyond safety, railings contribute an important design element, too. Use them to frame or block a beautiful view. Fill gaps with vertical slats, safety glass, or screening.

TOP LEFT: A boardwalk built over marshy ground provides access to a larger part of the garden. Flowers are allowed to spill over the planks.
TOP RIGHT: Wooden boardwalk offers clean, secure footing even in wet weather. Varying the direction of the boards on the meandering path adds to the dramatic design.
BOTTOM LEFT: In this small, narrow garden, a diagonal walkway divides the garden in half, making the space seem larger than it really is.
BOTTOM RIGHT: Mixing paving materials, as in this winning mix of wooden decking and tile steps, makes this path more interesting.

Massive stone slabs match the natural materials and follow the curve of the adjacent boulder-strewn watercourse. Planting pockets give plants a place to sprawl and blend into the landscape.

Landscape Steps

ON A PATIO OR DECK, YOU'LL LIKELY NEED THEM

In addition to their obvious practical function as a transition between different levels or from one garden feature to another, steps set the mood for an entire landscaping scheme. Most dramatic are wide, deep steps that lead the eye to a garden focal point. A set of stairs can also double as a retaining wall, a base for planters, or additional garden seating space.

Materials influence step styles. Poured concrete and masonry block usually present a formal, substantial look. Unglazed tiles and concrete pavers have a similar effect. Natural materials, such as stone and wood, add informality and fit into a less-structured garden.

Matching steps to the material used for a patio or garden wall helps unite a garden's overall landscaping. On the other hand, contrasting materials draw attention to the steps and the areas of the garden they serve. Combining materials can create a transition between unlike surfaces; for example, steps of concrete treads (horizontals) and brick risers (verticals) can link a brick patio to a concrete walk.

To soften the edges of a series of steps and help walkers find them without difficulty, place containers or flower beds along their borders. You can even add planting pockets within a wide series of tiers, as long as the greenery won't impede smooth travel.

Regardless of the material you use, put safety first. Treads should give safe footing in wet weather, and steps should be adequately lit at night with unobtrusive non-glare path lights or fixtures built into risers or adjacent step walls.

Scale is another important consideration. Your home's entry requires steps that are inviting and that allow several people to climb them at one time. Service-yard steps (ones not used by visitors), on the other hand, can be scaled down to fit a more limited space.

Your landscape layout and the steps' function will influence decisions about width. Simple utility steps can be as narrow as 2 feet, but 4 feet is usually recommended for outdoor steps. To allow two people to walk side by side, steps should be at least 5 feet wide.

When designing steps, make the sum of the tread depth plus twice the riser height equal 25 to 27 inches. The standard dimensions are a 6-inch riser and a 15-inch tread. These dimensions can vary somewhat, but don't make risers lower than 5 inches or higher than 8 inches and don't make treads narrower than 11 inches. Besides getting the tread-riser relationship right, it's important to make all the risers and treads in any one flight of steps the same. To design your steps, work out a detailed plan on graph paper. Try different combinations of risers and treads, widths, and configurations to achieve the necessary change of level. You'll find more details about building steps on page 238.

If your slope is too steep even for 8-inch risers, remember that steps needn't attack a slope head-on: Sometimes the most appealing solution is an L- or U-shaped series of multiple flights of steps. Consider placing a wide landing between flights, using the transition for a reading nook, a rose bed, or a wall fountain.

Rarely will the steps fit exactly into an existing slope. You may need to cut and fill to accommodate them. If you have questions about your site or if your steps will be connected to a building or touch a public access area, such as a sidewalk, check with your building department.

LEFT: Mortared brick steps have a formal look, but these are softened by a curved layout and flat adobe edgings that support potted plants.
TOP RIGHT: Wide wooden steps, flanked by exuberant and colorful annuals, easily accommodate two walkers side by side.

BOTTOM RIGHT: The beautiful grain and warm color of plantation-grown teakwood enhances this simple yet elegant walkway and steps.

Play Areas
SATISFYING KIDS' NEED FOR FUN

Kids love the outdoors and need a place to expend their energy. Yet young children (and somewhat older ones) have little sense of danger, so play areas must be as safe as they are fun. The first decision to make when planning a play yard is where to place it. Preschoolers feel safer—and can be more easily watched—if the play area is close to the house. You may prefer to corral older, noisier children father away, although still within view.

Take into account sun, wind, and shade. Hot sun increases the risk of sunburn and can make metal slides, monkey bars, and concrete walks burning hot. Instead, install slide surfaces facing north. If your property is in the path of strong winds, locate the play yard inside a windbreak of fencing or dense trees. Dappled shade is ideal. If you have no spreading foliage, position the play yard on the north side of your house, construct a simple canopy of lath or canvas, or somehow plan to shade a portion of the structure.

Many public playgrounds feature metal or plastic play structures rather than timber, because wood rots and breaks. Still, wood is a warmer and friendlier material—and a good-quality wooden structure will last as long as your children will be using it.

Gangplanks, turrets, and ramparts, all coated in electric colors, ensure plenty of fun. Forgiving wood chips and ground cover link this structure with the garden. A see-through fence contains the activity.

Perhaps you'll want a play structure scaled beyond your youngster's present abilities. Some structures allow you to add or change components as your child grows. Before you buy, view an assembled structure to evaluate its safety and design. Look through the instructions to be sure you can carry out the assembly.

Allow at least 6 feet of space for a fall zone around all sides of swings, slides, and climbing structures, and then cushion it well. A 3-inch layer of wood chips is one choice; increase the depth to 6 inches under a swing. Shredded bark (¼- to 1-inch particles of Douglas or white fir bark) holds up well, even in windy areas or on slopes. Sand provides another safe landing for falls. For children, the more sand the better—a depth of 12 inches is not too much. Building a low wall around a play yard helps contain loose materials, keeping the cushion thick and reducing the cost of replenishing.

Turf grass also makes a functional play surface (but avoid mixtures that contain clover, because its flowers

LEFT: Protected from the elements by a fence, trees, and an umbrella, this handsome play space includes a sandbox at patio level.
TOP RIGHT: Play structures don't have to be elaborate. This playhouse is made from cut tree branches lashed together with rope.
BOTTOM RIGHT: Climbing ropes and a wooden pirate ship inspire the imaginations of these sailors. A soft surface underfoot prevents mishaps.

attract bees). For maximum cushioning, keep grass about 2 inches high.

If your child will be pedaling a riding toy or tricycle, plan a smooth concrete path at least 24 inches wide. Gravel paths are frustrating for kids on wheels and for very young walkers.

The need for property-line fencing is probably obvious. Securely fence the play area from the driveway, as well as from the pool, spa, or other body of water (such as a water garden). You may need to fence off sharp or heavy tools, garden supplies, and garbage cans, too.

CHAPTER 4

Creating Privacy

Your garden should be a private haven where you can relax, enjoy the view, or gather for a celebration. To build a spot for solitude, you may prefer man-made structures—such as walls or fencing—or screening from shrubs and trees. Besides providing privacy, garden structures can be stunning ways to help define your outdoor space, complement your home's architecture, block views, and provide safe boundaries for children and pets. This chapter helps you define your privacy goals and achieve a place of solitude in your own yard.

IN THIS CHAPTER
FENCES • GATES • WALLS
ARBORS AND GAZEBOS • TRELLISES
SHRUBS • TREES • VINES

Planning for Privacy
BASIC LANDSCAPING TECHNIQUES ARE YOUR BEST TOOLS

Privacy can be hard to come by, especially in neighborhoods devoid of natural separations, such as hills and woods, and in housing developments where one yard blends into the next without any interruption. But wherever you live, you can create private spaces with a little careful planning.

Rather than planting dense hedges or erecting tall fences around the entire perimeter of your garden (which will shrink the size of a garden and cover it with deep shade), study where you need privacy the most. Consider the seasonal use of each area: Perhaps a patio needs screening only in summer because it's not usable in the cooler seasons, or maybe a vegetable garden needs no screening at all in summer if you've created a private seating area behind rows of corn or sunflowers.

For each part of the garden, think about what you're seeking privacy from. Are you trying to carve out a place away from the sights and sounds of traffic, your neighbors' backyard, or an uninspiring (or unpleasant) view farther away?

Solutions can be both natural and purchased: tree canopies, awnings, umbrellas, potted plants, walls, fences, hedges, gates, pergolas, trellises, and vines. Deciduous plants become light screens in winter, fences can let the light through, hedges have openings cut into them, or low walls can allow views over them when you're standing but allow you to eat in privacy when you're seated.

A single row of bright pink crape myrtles creates a colorful partition between two driveways. Even in winter when their branches are bare, trees and shrubs can provide privacy.

LEFT: Wisteria-covered arbor transforms a simple wooden deck into a private retreat that's hidden from view and the hot summer sun.
TOP RIGHT: Stucco wall with a wooden gate screens the house front from street traffic. Plantings help blend wall into the landscape.
BOTTOM RIGHT: Tall flowering perennials against the white picket fence separate this secluded yard from neighboring houses.

Create a screen of clipped hedge to block wind and views of neighbors. Prune trunks to add height and still allow room for beds below.

Use a vine-covered arbor for overhead protection and enclosure.

Cover a berm in front of your house with low-growing shrubs, trees, and ground cover.

Place a single tree at the front corner of your driveway to block a view of the entrance.

HOUSE

Soften the appearance of a solid (but plain) barrier with plantings.

Conceal bare trunks of mature trees with low-level shrubs.

Prune shrubs and hedges to waist or chest height to form a partial screen for a pool.

Use a fence with a gate for security.

This fence encloses a vegetable garden and provides a backdrop for a flower-filled perennial garden bursting with yellow lilies. An adjoining birdhouse invites birds to take up residence in the garden.

Fence Basics

THEY COME IN MANY STYLES AND SIZES

When well designed, fences filter the sun's glare, turn a raging wind into a pleasant breeze, and help muffle the cacophony of street traffic, noisy neighbors, and barking dogs. As partitions, they divide the yard into separate areas for recreation, relaxation, gardening, and storage. Although fences serve many of the same purposes as walls, they are generally less formal in appearance, easier to construct, and—when you calculate labor costs—less expensive to build.

Most communities have regulations restricting fence height. In many places, the maximum allowable height is 42 inches for front-yard fences and 6 feet for backyard ones. Tall fences are also more difficult to build. An alternative way to gain more height is to clothe the top of the fence with a vine or to grow narrow shrubs adjacent to it and then allow them to grow beyond the height of

the fence. Before you begin construction, check the building code of your community. Some locales have height and design covenants that may affect your project.

Normally a boundary fence is owned and maintained by both neighbors. Make every effort to come to a friendly agreement with your neighbor on the location, design, and construction of the fence. (One option is a "good neighbor" fence with crosspieces mounted in alternating directions.) If you can't come to an agreement, you can circumvent the problem by building the fence entirely on your property, just a few inches inside your boundary.

Before installing your fence, check the terrain. Few lots are perfectly smooth, flat, and free of obstructions. If your fence line runs up a hill, build the fence so that it follows the contours of the land or construct stepped panels that will maintain horizontal lines.

Most fences are built entirely of wood. Wood's versatility as a fencing material is reflected in its wide variety of forms—split rails, grape stakes, dimension lumber, poles, and manufactured wood products such as plywood and tempered hardboard.

Wooden fences have three parts: vertical posts, horizontal rails (or stringers), and siding. Posts are usually 4-by-4s and should be made of pressure-treated

TOP LEFT: Low picket fence improves the view by acting as a visual barrier between the flower-filled front yard and the drab driveway.

TOP RIGHT: Rounded plaster pilasters match the house wall and provide solid support to fence of lashed, unpeeled logs.

BOTTOM: Built with natural materials, this split-rail fence with a herringbone design blends well with its surroundings.

or decay-resistant redwood or cedar heartwood. Redwood can be left to weather naturally, but fir or pine should be painted or stained. Rails are usually 2-by-4s. Fence siding can vary from preassembled picket sections to plywood panels.

Alternative materials beyond boards, slats, and timbers include vinyl, galvanized wire, plastic mesh, and ornamental iron. If wire fencing is the right choice but you don't like the look of it, plant annual vines, such as morning glories or climbing nasturtiums, for quick cover or add plantings for permanent cover.

Although the design possibilities are endless, wooden fences fall into one of three basic types: post-and-rail, picket, and solid board. Your choice depends on the fence's intended function; a board fence may be the best choice for a full privacy screen, for example.

To increase seclusion and wind protection, look to a closed design, such as solid board, face panel, or grape stake fencing. When you want to break up a large expanse, in a solid panel fence, for example, a simple oval or square window or cutout, especially when framing a view, lends a sense of mystery and discovery.

Shrubs planted along a fence also soften the look of solid fencing.

For some degree of privacy without compromising ventilation, vertical lath (narrow strips of wood) or lattice is a good choice, as long as the space doesn't require complete protection. Vines trained onto lattice trellises or wire frames can block wind and sun without destroying the airy, open feeling of your patio. Fences can also be designed to edit views; louvers, slats, lattice, or see-through trellises provide a glimpse of what lies beyond.

TIPS

- Fences that allow some wind to pass through provide more protection than solid fences that create a solid barrier.

Alternating boards of this fence screen a patio from view but allow light and air to pass through. Narrow, high-branched trees extend the height of the fence to block intruding views from the neighboring home.

Fence Styles

Whatever your choice of fencing, coordinate the fence with the style and materials of your house. A picket fence that may be too dainty for a contemporary stone-and-glass house would look wonderful with a colonial brick or clapboard structure. Louvered or board fences, however, complement a variety of house styles.

SOLID BOARD fence offers maximum privacy but requires more lumber and can create a boxed-in feeling.

POST-AND-BOARD fence encloses space with less wood and less privacy. The diagonal pattern adds visual interest.

PICKET FENCE is used with any style of house architecture, though traditionally associated with colonial.

ALTERNATING-BOARD FENCE provides privacy without compromising ventilation, and shows the same pattern on both sides

POST-AND-RAIL fence encloses space with little wood. This one features mortised posts with overlapping rails (inset).

GRAPESTAKE fence is made of the rough-split redwood stakes traditionally used in vinyards. It's suitable for hillside and curved fencing.

Bamboo poles affixed to sturdy wood frames suggest solidity and suit the garden's Asian style, matching the fencing on either side.

This moon gate serves as an attractive focal point from both inside and outside the garden. It beckons visitors from both directions.

Gate Basics

CREATING AN ENTRANCE TO YOUR PRIVATE YARD

Place a gate for access, to frame a view, or to make a design statement in tandem with the fence. You may want to build the gate in a style and material that match the fence, but you can also choose a contrasting material or design, such as a wooden or wrought-iron gate within flanking brick columns or pilasters. A low picket gate or one made of airy lath invites people in with its open, friendly appearance. A high, solid gate guards the privacy and safety of those within.

The minimum width for a gate is usually 3 feet, but an extra foot creates a more gracious feeling. If you anticipate moving gardening equipment (such as garden carts or wheelbarrows) or other equipment (such as tillers or riding lawn mowers) through the gate, make the opening wider. For an extra-wide space, consider a two-part gate or even a gate on rollers that's designed to span a driveway.

The components of a gate are shown on the opposite page: a rectangular frame of 2-by-4s and a brace running from the bottom corner of the hinge side to the top corner of the latch side. Complete it with the siding.

Choose strong hinges and latches (see page 246). It's better to select hardware that's too hefty than too flimsy. Plan to attach both hinges and latches with long galvanized screws that won't pull out and be sure to use galvanized hardware, which resists rust.

TIPS

• For maximum impact, focus on design details or finishing touches for your gate, which is the entrance to your landscape.

A Basic Gate

Pickets may have decorative tops, and posts may be capped with decorative finials.

Rails are 2-by-4 lumber.

Swing clearance between a gate and fence posts is usually ½ inch.

The footing (which the post sits in) is poured concrete, typically one-third the post depth.

A diagonal brace prevents the gate from sagging.

Hinges must be strong enough to support the gate.

A gate's frame is generally built from 2-by-4s.

A gravel base aids drainage; rock helps keep the posts from rotting.

TOP LEFT: Traditional picket gate creates a pleasing contrast with dense, gray stone wall around this informal seaside garden.

TOP RIGHT: Mixed materials, such as this rusted iron gate framed with wooden posts, make a memorable garden gateway.

BOTTOM LEFT: Massive stucco pillars frame this high wooden gate and clearly signal the entrance to the enclosed space within.

BOTTOM CENTER: Informal wooden gate welcomes family and friends with its low, widely spaced, spindles and cheerful yellow paint.

BOTTOM RIGHT: Crisp white stacked panels give a contemporary look to a traditional picket fence and are an ideal foil for the blue door beyond.

Wall Basics
THEY FORM A PERMANENT STRUCTURE

Walls bring an unmatched sense of permanence to a garden. In fact, some of the world's oldest structures are walls. After you've determined a wall's function and location, you can choose its height, width, and degree of openess. You'll also need to select materials that coordinate with the style and design of your house and existing garden structures.

Among the typical materials for garden walls are masonry units or blocks, uncut stone, and poured concrete. The easiest materials to use yourself are brick or concrete block, which are uniform units with modular proportions that you assemble piece by piece. You can choose a decorative pattern for laying the courses, incorporate a solid or openwork face, vary the thickness, and employ combinations of materials. Glass block sections let light pass through, as do upper edgings of lath, lattice, and trellises.

In the hands of an experienced mason, stone creates walls that integrate with many landscapes. Stone that's prominent in your region will look the most natural in your garden, but poured concrete offers more design possibilities because surface texture and shape are established by wooden forms. Most of the work goes into constructing and stabilizing these forms. The actual "pour," for better or worse, is accomplished quickly. Consult a contractor for any poured concrete wall more than a few feet high.

Before beginning any wall, ask your building department about regulations that specify how high and how close to your property line you can build, what kind of foundation you'll need, and whether the wall requires steel reinforcement. Many municipalities require a building permit for any masonry wall more than 3 feet high. Some may also require that the wall be approved by an engineer.

This low, lattice-style brick wall encloses a perennial garden, yet the spaces between the bricks allow air and light to pass through—and give passersby a sneak preview of the spectacular plantings beyond.

RETAINING WALLS

You can tame a gentle slope with a low retaining wall or a series of garden steps that hold the surface soil in place. But if your slope is long and steep, consider building two or three substantial walls to divide it into terraces, which you can then enhance with ornamental plants.

Engineering aside, you can build a retaining wall from any of the materials discussed in the preceding section. Wood is another easy option, whether you use various-sized boards, railroad ties, or wood timbers set vertically or horizontally.

On a low slope, uncut stones or chunks of broken concrete can be laid without mortar or footings. Fill the soil-lined crevices with colorful plantings.

New systems for building concrete retaining walls don't require that you to mix a single bag of concrete. These walls are built with precast modules that stack or lock together with lips, pins, or friction. They are ideal for 3- to 4-foot-high walls.

Where engineering is critical, poured concrete may be your only solution, but the labor required can make a concrete wall a costly project. To make concrete more interesting, use rough form boards to texture the finish or apply a surface veneer.

TOP LEFT: A low concrete retaining wall set against a bank of fragrant flowers doubles as a space-saving seat in this tiny backyard retreat.
TOP CENTER: The pleasing texture of this mortared stone wall, set into a gentle slope, blends well with the creeping flowers growing above it.
TOP RIGHT: Plain walls, if occasionally interrupted by openings, can provide a welcome sense of shelter without being overwhelming.

BOTTOM LEFT: Stone retaining wall built into a slope is as beautiful as it is functional, appearing to meld with both earth and plantings.
BOTTOM RIGHT: To save time and money, build a low wall, and then let trees and shrubs add height for privacy.

Plastering stucco creates a clean, contemporary veneer atop a concrete block wall. Apply two coats of plaster; the final coat may be precolored or painted when dry. Decorate the wall with plates and pots.

WALL FOUNDATIONS

Regardless of the type of wall you plan to raise, it requires the support of a solid foundation. Poured concrete is about the best because it can be smoothed and leveled better than other materials can. Usually, wall foundations, also called footings, are twice the width of the wall and 12 inches deep or as deep as the frost line. But, as always, consult local codes for exceptions before building.

For walls no more than 12 inches high or for low raised beds, the base of the wall can rest directly on tamped soil or in a leveled trench.

In most cases, a freestanding wall more than 2 to 3 feet high should have some kind of reinforcement to tie portions of the wall together and to prevent it from collapsing. Steel reinforcing bars, laid with the mortar along the length of a wall, provide horizontal stiffening. Placed upright (for example, between double rows of brick or within the hollow cores of concrete blocks), reinforcing adds vertical strength that can keep a wall from toppling under its own weight.

Special steel ties of various patterns are made for reinforcing unit masonry and attaching veneers to substructures. See the illustration at the far right.

Vertical masonry columns, called pilasters, can be tied into a wall to provide additional vertical support. Many building departments require that they be used at least every 12 feet. Also consider placing pilasters on each side of an entrance gate and at the ends of freestanding walls. When you're building the foundation, make the pilaster footing twice the width of the pilasters.

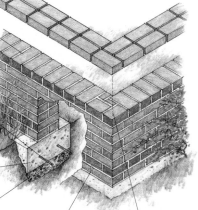

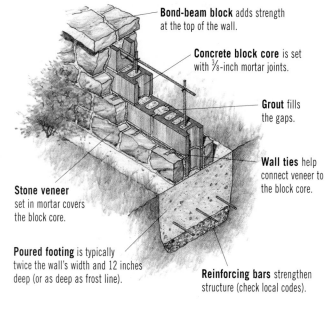

LEFT: A winding fieldstone wall encloses a broad patio. The wall's stones were applied with mortar over a base of concrete blocks.

TOP RIGHT: Exterior plaster veneer softens the plain, strict look of a concrete block core. This curved wall steps up to a bold entry gate.

BOTTOM RIGHT: Herringbone-patterned brick paving meshes easily with steps and low retaining walls that are also made of brick.

A Brick Wall

Header course (every fifth, sixth, or seventh course) spans front to back; helps lock the wall together.

Reinforcing bars strengthen structure (check local codes).

Poured footing is typically twice the wall's width and 12 inches deep (or as deep as frost line).

Gravel base ensures good drainage.

Common-bond wall has staggered joints from course to course. Double thickness is much stronger than a single row of bricks.

Corners overlap with ¾- and ¼-inch "closure" bricks.

A Concrete Block Wall

Bond-beam block adds strength at the top of the wall.

Concrete block core is set with ⅜-inch mortar joints.

Grout fills the gaps.

Wall ties help connect veneer to the block core.

Stone veneer set in mortar covers the block core.

Poured footing is typically twice the wall's width and 12 inches deep (or as deep as frost line).

Reinforcing bars strengthen structure (check local codes).

Arbors and Gazebos
PERMANENT OVERHEADS SUPPLEMENT LEAFY SHELTER

There's nothing quite like an arbor or gazebo to enhance your enjoyment of the garden. Both structures furnish shade during the day and shelter during cool evenings, yet are always open to breezes and the enticing scent of flowers. Both give you a place to sit and relax, host a party, or simply mingle with family and friends. And these garden structures play other, more practical roles, as well. They link your house to the garden, define different areas of your landscape, direct foot traffic through the garden, mask an unattractive feature, or frame a spectacular view.

Gazebos come in a variety of styles, from old-fashioned Victorian designs to contemporary or rustic motifs. Although typically built with open, airy framing, a gazebo lends a feeling of enclosure to those sitting inside because of the solid roof overhead. By contrast, arbors frame the walls and ceiling of an outdoor room and can be embellished with fragrant or colorful vines.

You can build an arbor in almost any style, from simple archways to elaborate neoclassical pavilions.

As you think about where to put a new gazebo or arbor, take a walk around your property under different weather conditions. Glance back at the house often. Look for a vantage point that marries a good view of the house with a view over the entire property. Unless the structure will conceal any unsightly areas, avoid such spaces. Also consider exposure—if your main deck or patio is in full sun, you may prefer to locate an arbor or gazebo in a shady corner. Finally, don't give up on a garden structure just because your yard is small. Tiny spaces often profit from the focus created by a small arbor or gazebo.

Late-afternoon sun warms this traditional gazebo, which was assembled from a kit. Nestled into a garden corner, the gazebo remains a private retreat, accessible only by the meandering fieldstone path.

An Elegant Gazebo

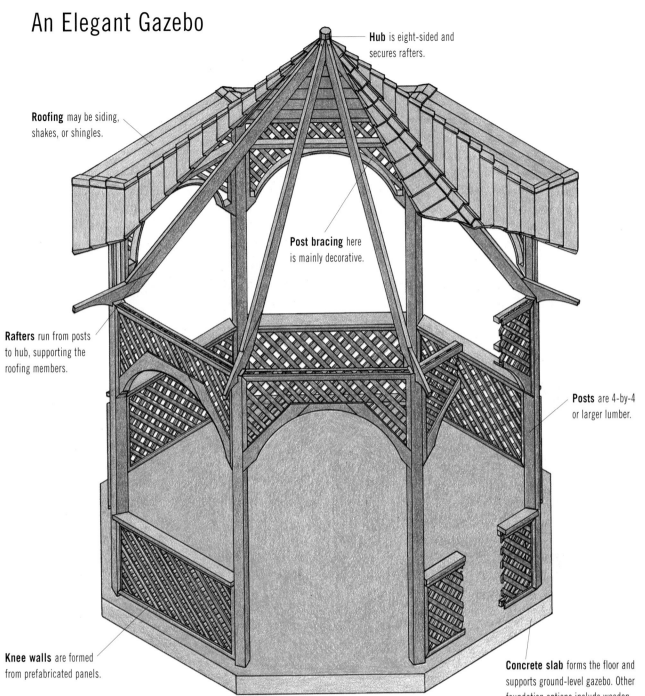

Hub is eight-sided and secures rafters.

Roofing may be siding, shakes, or shingles.

Post bracing here is mainly decorative.

Rafters run from posts to hub, supporting the roofing members.

Posts are 4-by-4 or larger lumber.

Knee walls are formed from prefabricated panels.

Concrete slab forms the floor and supports ground-level gazebo. Other foundation options include wooden framing, piers, and concrete footings.

pitched to allow water to run off. If the structure is far from the house, it's good idea to run electrical lines for lighting. Framing connections are most easily made by means of readily available prefabricated metal fasteners.

If building a gazebo from scratch seems overwhelming, consider ordering a set of plans with complete instructions or building one from a kit. The kit usually contains everything but the foundation: The gazebo must sit on a concrete slab, deck, concrete piers, or bed of crushed stone. For most gazebos, assembly will take a weekend or two and require only basic tools and skills—but it's a job for at least two people.

Trellis Know-How

USING FRAMES TO SUPPORT PLANTS

A trellis is essentially a two-dimensional frame for plants, made with verticals and horizontals fastened together. The traditional model is a rectangular wooden grid that gives plants a good foothold, allows air circulation, and holds itself together. But just about anything flat or round that stands up to the elements, supports the weight of mature plants, and can be nailed, screwed, or wired together can serve as a lightweight trellis, especially if it will be supported by a wall or fence.

Whether it flanks a patio door, props up a riot of roses, cages tomatoes or pole beans, or livens up a large, boring lawn, a trellis can add a sense of drama to any garden. Walls, fences, and arbors perform this function, too, but trellises do it with a superbly open feel—and the resulting dappled sunlight, breezes, and patches of blue sky counter any potential "prison-wall" effect.

Trellises range from humble to grand, utilitarian to sculptural. You can opt for a gridlike, symmetrical style or a more whimsical, gnarled look. What's important is that the trellis suits the rest of the garden and easily shoulders the weight of the plants you choose for it. A lightweight trellis may back a modest container plant, while a large, sturdy frame can dress up a garage wall or form a backdrop for an entire garden.

LEFT: One way to dress up a garden shed is to add a trellis over the roof. Here, roses are the crowning glory of this quaint cottage.
TOP RIGHT: Made from twisted concrete reinforcing rods, this trellis doubles as garden art. It also provides a vertical accent in the garden.
BOTTOM RIGHT: Rough and rustic fan trellis looks right at home in an informal garden. It's an ideal support for annual vines.

The trellis's scale should suit its setting. A 2½-foot-high grid may overpower a small patio container, while even a 7-foot-tall tower can look small in the center of a large, open space. The landscape also determines how finished the trellis should look. A formal landscape may call for a trellis that's sanded, filled, and painted to match the house trim. In more casual surroundings, a rough redwood cage or a frame of crooked branches lashed together may be right at home.

TOP LEFT: A permanent trellis, such as this handsome cedar lattice structure, is a focal point in the garden, even during the winter.
TOP RIGHT: Camouflaging an old shed is easy with a lath trellis. Just be sure the trellis can be easily removed for building maintenance.
BOTTOM LEFT: This neighborly fence is actually a series of trellis panels linked together down the property line. Roses bloom between the panels.
BOTTOM RIGHT: This twiggy trellis, shaped like a four-paneled screen, has horizontal grids built from birch branches screwed into the house wall.

Shrubs for Privacy
GROWING AN ENCLOSURE

Fences and walls work well between neighboring properties, but often, especially where lots are small, standard 6-foot-tall fences don't block nearby views of unsightly rooflines or a looming multistory building. In addition, building codes generally don't allow construction of anything taller than 6 feet. And these facts don't even touch on the expense and labor of building a fence or wall. This is where plants come to the rescue.

Hedges, trees, and vines define garden boundaries the same way a fence or wall does, but less rigidly and at far less expense. They can make a small space feel enclosed but also lush, and some can be clipped into narrow or creative shapes.

Shrubs are just about the most versatile group of plants in size, shape, and foliage. Some, such as roses and rhododendrons, are noted for their profusion of spectacular flowers; others, like yew and box, for their handsome foliage; and some, such as pyracantha and cotoneaster, for colorful berries.

The style and ambience of your house and garden should also be a factor in your plans. Massing large and small untrimmed shrubs can give your garden a sense of

A tall hedge provides a high degree of privacy without being as imposing as a fence of the same height. The shrubs also visually soften and cool the area and provide food and shelter for birds and butterflies.

wild, untamed nature, while neatly shaped and clipped hedges have a much more formal appearance.

Think about your needs for privacy in particular areas of your garden. Must the plant barrier be solid, or would a light screen be enough? If you wish merely to diffuse a direct view from the street to your front door, a large open shrub, such as rhododendron, may do well. But if you want to completely block the view of an outdoor sitting area that abuts a neighbor's swimming pool, a closely sheared privet hedge may be your best bet.

Shrubs are either deciduous or evergreen. What kind of shrubs you choose depends on whether privacy is desirable year-round or just during the growing season. A patio that isn't used during the cold winter months could be sheltered spring through fall by lilacs, which lose their leaves during the winter. For screening a view into a bedroom window, though, a fast-growing evergreen would be preferable.

TOP LEFT: When choosing plants for privacy, look for species with four-season interest. Pink and white flowering dogwoods are perfect.
BOTTOM LEFT: Photinias growing in 24-inch-wide pots block out the neighbor's roofline in this hillside deck garden.
RIGHT: Billowy mountain laurel protects the house's front entrance from sidewalk traffic and softens the brick wall that shelters it.

USING SHRUBS AS HEDGES

Hedges are shrubs that have been planted to form a solid barrier or define a boundary. Although hedges also have three dimensions, their primary emphasis in garden design is their height and form. Besides transforming shrubs into a linear barrier, clipping can also increase the density of the planting. Trimming the growing shoots on both sides of the hedge encourages the shrubs to grow toward each other, knitting the plants into a continuous row that can effectively block the view into or out of your garden.

TOP LEFT: A garden seems larger when some spaces are secluded from others. A clipped hedge can hide a sitting area from view.
TOP RIGHT: Screens needn't be evergreen to be effective. Here, a row of crape myrtles with lower limbs removed helps hide a neighbor's house.

BOTTOM LEFT: Removing the lower branches of common boxwood allows light and air to pass under and reveals the plants' structural qualities.
BOTTOM RIGHT: Hedge of Japanese anise divides two front yards. Behind it is a second, taller hedge of 'Nellie R. Stevens' holly.

Hedges generally come in two forms: formal and informal. Formal hedges take up less space than informal ones, making them ideal for small lots. But to maintain their more rigid shape, formal hedges require regular pruning—a chore you may not want to deal with. In general, plants with small, tight branching habits are best for formal hedges: boxwood, barberry, or holly are good choices.

Informal hedges, where plants are allowed to spread out naturally, are better suited to open spaces. Almost maintenance-free, they provide an effective easy-care screen. For an informal hedge, try viburnum, forsythia, honeysuckle, or spiraea. Higher hedges, especially dense ones, make very good insulators against street noise.

MASSING SHRUBS

Trees often are the most notable feature in a landscape, but shrubs usually provide organization, offer a sense of enclosure and give a garden its form and structure. In fact, you might think of shrubs as the skeleton of the garden.

Evergreen or deciduous A vine-covered arbor is the perfect way to obtain some overhead privacy and a bit of shade during the summer. However, a deciduous vine that loses its leaves in winter allows more sunlight to penetrate during the winter. Most deciduous vines have the added attraction of colorful foliage in the fall, and the tracery of bare stems on a stone wall can be attractive during the winter, as well.

Annual or perennial Annual vines, such as sweet peas and morning glories, can quickly create a light, colorful screen from spring to autumn. Use them to augment the screening effect of slower-growing plants. Because they die back naturally at the end of the growing season, you needn't worry about their overwhelming and stunting the growth of neighboring plants. Perennial vines, however, do not require replanting each year but likely need studier supports and occasional pruning. Examples of long-lived perennial vines are fiveleaf akebia, clematis, climbing roses, and wisteria.

Flowers and fruit Many vines are grown primarily for their flowers or fruit, but they can also serve as screens

TOP LEFT: Rugged perennial vines, such as clematis, grow bigger and better each year. Established clematis requires little maintenance.
BOTTOM LEFT: In milder climates, climbing roses can grow to great heights, smothering a trellis, arbor, or screen with fragrant flowers.
RIGHT: This wrought iron trellis, cloaked with a climbing 'Dortmund' rose, extends upward on the privacy of the wall behind it.

or adornments for privacy structures. Among vines grown for flowers are clematis, jasmine, morning glory, rose, and wisteria. The selection of vines with edible fruit is much smaller, grapes being the most outstanding example. Pole beans, such as 'Kentucky Wonder', create a lush annual screen with the bonus of delicious fresh produce.

Fast- or slow-growing Most vines are relatively fast-growing. As with other types of plants, your initial impulse may be to plant the fastest-growing kinds in order to have the most coverage in the shortest amount of time. This isn't necessarily a bad idea, but a rampant vine will continue to grow at the same rate year after year and will require a great deal of space, as well as annual heavy pruning.

CHAPTER 5

Making Your Plan

A particularly beautiful spring morning may find you sitting on your front or back steps, soaking up the sun and thinking how pleasant it is just to be outdoors. With that thought in mind, you take a long look at your yard and begin to daydream: "What can I do to make the space a little more . . . livable . . . attractive?"

Take heart. The fact is, by simply observing and dreaming, you've already started on the process of improving your landscape. On the following pages, you'll be taken step by step through a planning process that can turn your dream garden into a reality.

IN THIS CHAPTER
MAKING DECISIONS
ASSESSING WHAT YOU HAVE
PLANNING ON PAPER
LEARNING FROM PROS
FROM PLAN TO REALITY
REAL-LIFE DESIGN

Deciding What You Need

BEGIN BY ASKING—AND ANSWERING—BASIC QUESTIONS

When you want to create a beautiful and functional place for relaxing outdoors, the reality of your bare or overgrown yard may seem daunting. Before getting down to work, close your eyes and picture your dream garden. Well-designed landscapes begin with decisions made before the first spadeful of earth is turned. Do you want an elegant, formal landscape or an outdoor room for casual living and entertaining?

Do you want a plant-filled garden or a durable one that can withstand tricycle wheels and a game of tag? Do you like to read and sunbathe or play badminton or croquet? Do you enjoy gardening, or do you prefer a minimum of effort? Do you want to produce fresh fruits and vegetables? Is privacy a priority? Answering

these questions and carefully evaluating your lifestyle will help determine what you want in your outdoor space. Keep in mind that there are limits to what any landscape can include. Make a checklist of items that are essential to you and your family and include them in your plan, but be prepared to compromise on the less important elements or create a timetable for including them later.

Like most homeowners, you probably have both aesthetic and practical aims in mind. You may wish to

Picket fence encloses this welcoming entry garden, where colorful annuals and perennials mix with culinary herbs and vegetables, replacing a traditional lawn. Meandering path leads to a restful bench.

TOP: Harmony of colors is the theme of this poolside patio, where similarly toned surfaces are a foil for brightly flowering perennials. BOTTOM LEFT: Unity of design marks this drought-busting garden of grasses and stone. Path and plants echo soft blue and tan colors.

BOTTOM RIGHT: Simplicity reigns in a garden nook surrounded by shade-loving hostas. An evergreen tree shelters the sun-warmed bench.

TOP LEFT: In this formal garden, the path is an axis line that divides the lawn and symmetrically clipped hedges.
BOTTOM LEFT: An accent draws attention to itself by contrasting boldly with its surroundings, as this bright yellow chrysanthemum does.

RIGHT: Textures may be fine or coarse, delicate or bold. Here, the bold form of a variegated century plant adds variety to the garden.

The Language of Landscape Design

Whatever landscape style you choose, your plan will be most successful if you observe some simple principles of design, which in turn requires that you become familiar with the terms used by landscape professionals. Some of these terms are used throughout the broad field of design. Focal point and symmetry, for example, are used by architects, interior designers, and graphic artists alike. Other terms, such as borrowed scenery, are specific to landscape design. In this book, these terms are used to describe the features of various gardens. Knowing these terms, you'll find it easier to communicate with professionals.

TOP LEFT: A focal point, such as this jar at the end of a path, draws the eye by its placement or the distinctiveness of its features.

TOP RIGHT: Symmetry exists when matching elements, such as these crape myrtles, are balanced on either side of a central axis.

BOTTOM: Borrowed scenery incorporates views from beyond the garden to make it seem larger. See-through fence panels reveal the city.

Landscape Design Tricks

In addition to basic design principles, professionals have an array of tricks at their disposal—techniques that help overcome typical challenges or simply make the garden more attractive and livable for occupants and visitors.

Some of these ideas are very basic, such as understanding the dimensions of the human body in designing the height and size of structures in the garden. For example, the best ratio for stair risers and treads is based on dimensions that are the most comfortable for people

to climb (see page 111). Similarly, pathways are the most comfortable when they are more than 4 feet wide, and built-in seating for decks or benches should be 16 to 17 inches deep. Other techniques involve altering the perception of space by manipulating materials, colors, and

A large element in the foreground enhances depth. Framed by the cherry tree, the background appears deeper than it is. The strong forms of the conifers in the midground add perspective, as does the curving path.

BARE DIRT TO SHADY RETREAT

Eric, Mary, and their two children devoted the first year to installing the garden's bones—the brick paths, rock walls along the hill in the back, and areas of grassy lawn. These projects consumed the family's first summer in Puyallup. "For the kids, 'How I spent my summer vacation' was more like 'How I helped Dad with the yard,'" notes Eric. "This was our Disneyland."

The next year, the Holdemans planted perennials, a vegetable garden near the house, and more trees. Then came the refinements: a rockery, an arbor, stairs next to the rock wall, low-voltage lighting, a garden bench, and a sundial.

Even now, the garden continues to evolve. "I spend a lot of time just looking around the garden from different angles," Eric says. "Figuring out what to tackle next is both a challenge and a joy."

The initial work cost several thousand dollars, including bricks for the walkways, stones for the rock wall, and plants. The Holdemans' best advice to those who want to begin from scratch? "Don't be afraid to make mistakes. If a plant is not working in one place, dig it out and move it."

SOUTH SIDE YARD, BEFORE: On the back of the house, porch steps lead to an empty side yard. The proximity of the side yard to the kitchen calls for easy access to vegetable beds. Some color is needed to brighten the area beyond the porch.

SOUTH SIDE YARD, AFTER: Seen from the front, the side yard is now filled with well-mulched plants. Concrete rounds are a temporary, meeting up with brick path to the back of the house.

BACKYARD, UNDERWAY: By the end of the first year, this is what the walks and back flower border looked like. First, the owners installed a brick-on-sand walkway. The rock retaining wall at the base of the slope required almost 10 tons of rocks. A lawn went in before the owners determined which plants would grow best in the garden. Only spring-blooming bulbs were put in the ground at this point.

BACKYARD, AFTER: Ferns, bulbs, evergreen shrubs, and perennials combine in a long, narrow border above the rock retaining wall, where they offer a succession of blooms throughout the year. Beyond the lawn, shrubs and more perennials create a woodland garden beneath tall trees. Where the side yard meets the backyard, a sundial, one of the later additions, rises from surrounding leafy carpet bugle (*Ajuga reptans*).

CHAPTER 6

Landscape Plans

One of the best ways to expand your knowledge of landscaping is to tour gardens from around the country, and your nationwide tour starts here! We've collected a variety of great designs from a variety of regions.
In each, you'll find that homeowners have used many of the principles of good landscape design but in ways that are unique to their own tastes and geographic regions. In the same way, your garden and landscape should reflect your own preferences.

So enjoy the tour
and use it to pick up great ideas to use
in your own yard and garden.

IN THIS CHAPTER
SIDE YARDS • COLOR • WILDLIFE
EDIBLES • PLAY AREAS • NATIVES
SLOPES • DESERT • ROOFTOPS
SHADE • SEASONS
FRAGRANCE • TROPICAL OASIS

Taking Sides

RETHINK UNUSED SPACE

While you can recapture square footage by capitalizing on the often neglected space in your side yard, these long, narrow spaces are design challenges. In this garden, space is a premium.

The landscape designer's goal for this garden in Charleston, South Carolina, was to squeeze out every last inch of usable space. On the sunny east side of the house, the side yard measures a slim 6 feet wide, except for an alcove off the kitchen. There, the design takes advantage of the morning light and situates a cozy alfresco breakfast nook large enough for a table and a passageway.

The seating area is surfaced with sturdy water-washed flagstone. The remainder of the space is paved with brick that also matches an existing brick wall. The two surfaces are tied together by bluestone insets in the wall. To bring

foliage to eye level, raised brick planters are filled with eye-catching plants, such as bright-blooming (and shade-tolerant) impatiens. A Japanese maple (Acer palmatum 'Arakawa') provides a graceful focal point with its finely etched leaves. Large trees supply dense shade to the west side of the house, where a serene shade garden flourishes (illustrated at right).

French doors open from the living room and face symmetrical wrought-iron arches to create a mirror image. Stone fountains spout water into limestone bowls, creating the restful sound of moving water both indoors and out, while a raised bed that edges the fence overflows with lush plants, including sasanqua camellias, ferns, yaupon, and Japanese spurge. Dark green creeping fig softens the stucco wall.

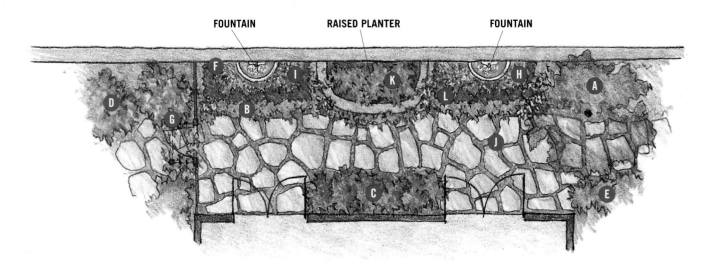

FOUNTAIN   RAISED PLANTER   FOUNTAIN

Plant List

TREES

A. Japanese maple
Acer palmatum 'Arakawa'

SHRUBS

B. Japanese boxwood
Buxus microphylla japonica

C. Sasanqua camellia
Camellia sasanqua

D. Bigleaf hydrangea
Hydrangea macrophylla

E. Yaupon
Ilex vomitoria

VINES

F. Creeping fig
Ficus pumila

G. Primrose jasmine
Jasminum polyanthemum

GROUND COVERS, PERENNIALS, AND ANNUALS

H. Japanese anemone
Anemone hybrida

I. Mother fern
Asplenium bulbiferum

J. Cranesbill
Erodium reichardii

K. Impatiens
Impatiens walleriana

L. Japanese spurge
Pachysandra terminalis

Cutting Loose

WANT COLOR? HERE'S LOTS OF IT

Imagine having freshly cut flowers at your fingertips all season long. This cutting garden provides bouquets nearly year-round, thanks to a creative selection of blooming plants and shrubs.

This Richmond, Virginia, landscape design employs traditional cut-flower favorites and supplies nontraditional flora and foliage from colorful shrubs and trees. The plantings were selected for both their in-garden beauty and their use in fresh and dried arrangements.

This garden is a seasonal color show. The flowers grow in two large beds facing the house and are separated by a grape arbor. At the back of the beds, roses help screen the raised vegetable beds from view. Beyond the beds, fruit trees, pussy willow, and flowering bulbs color the corners of the yard. Tightly trimmed feverfew defines the front of the beds.

Spring favorites include forsythia, azalea, weigela, rhododendron, lilac, French pussy willow, and flowering dogwood. Summertime features the blooms of flowering perennials: hollyhock, roses, coneflower, and yarrow. In autumn, the colorful foliage and berries of viburnum and dogwood and the curly branches of corkscrew willow supply material for inventive floral displays.

GAZEBO

▶ NORTH

Plant List

TREES

A. Flowering dogwood
Cornus florida 'First Lady'

B. Kousa dogwood
Cornus kousa 'Milky Way'

C. Pink mountain silverbell
Halesia monticola 'Rosea'

D. Himalayan pine
Pinus wallichiana

E. Autumn Higan cherry
Prunus subhirtella
'Autumnalis'

F. Sorrel tree
Oxydendrum arboreum

SHRUBS

G. Sweet mock orange
Philadelphus coronarius

H. Shrub roses
Rosa: 'Ballerina', 'Dolly
Parton', 'Chrysler Imperial',
'French Lace', 'Gold Badge',
'Graham Thomas', 'La Reine
Victoria', 'Queen Elizabeth'

I. Climbing roses
'Cl. Cécile Brunner',
'Golden Showers', 'America'

J. French pussy willow
Salix caprea

K. Corkscrew willow
Salix matsudana 'Tortuosa'

L. Mixed shrub border
Azalea, butterfly bush
(*Buddleia*), chaste tree
(*Vitex*), forsythia, lilac,
rhododendron, spiraea,
weigela, viburnum

VINES

M. 'Concord' grapes

N. Honeysuckle
Trumpet Honeysuckle
(*Lonicera sempervirens*
'Magnifica'), Goldflame
Honeysuckle (*L. heckrottii*)

O. Raspberries

PERENNIALS, ANNUALS, AND BULBS

P. Perennials
Bellflower (*Campanula*),
coreopsis, pinks (*Dianthus*),
purple coneflower
(*Echinacea*), feverfew
(*Chrysanthemum
parthenium*), foxglove,
geum, gloriosa daisy
(*Rudbeckia hirta*), false
sunflower (*Heliopsis*),
hollyhock, hosta, iris, peony,
salvia, speedwell (*Veronica*),
and yarrow

P. Annuals
Bells-of-Ireland (*Moluccella
laevis*), cosmos, heliotrope,
larkspur, scented geranium,
and zinnia

P. Bulbs
Daffodil, Dutch iris,
tulip (spring); crocosmia,
gladiolus, dahlia (summer)

Wild About Wildlife

FEED THEM, AND THEY WILL COME

Food, shelter, and water—provide these in your garden, and you'll enjoy the natural addition of color and motion as birds and butterflies flock to your yard. This wildlife garden in Madison, Wisconsin, features a smorgasbord of plant combinations that create a tasty and welcoming habitat.

Butterflies prefer sunny, sheltered spots with plenty of long-blooming, nectar-rich flowers. They also enjoy moist, damp areas and rocky places for basking. Birds need shelter (plantings as well as housing) and flowers that supply nectar, seeds, and berries. Set up nesting boxes in spring, feeders in fall, and a clean water source all year long. Water features appeal to all wildlife but particularly entice frogs, toads, and winged beauties, such as dragonflies.

To welcome wildlife, this landscape design features beds filled with colorful perennials and annuals; these flowers are attractive in their own right. At the border's edge grow the shortest plants, such as gayfeather and giant hyssop. Taller species, such as musk mallow, are used to attract butterflies that love to feed in sunny spots between 11 in the morning and 3 in the afternoon.

Like all nature gardeners, these homeowners follow three major rules: First, they don't use insecticides, which may kill desirable butterflies, caterpillars, and birds that eat insects and spiders. Second, they foil predators, such as cats, by keeping feeders and birdbaths up high or otherwise inaccessible. Finally, because the best wildlife habitats are not the most manicured, they aren't too fussy about keeping the garden neat. The less you rake under bushes, the better it is for birds. Whenever possible, leave small brush piles in out-of-the-way places for nesting and overwintering species of birds and butterflies.

NORTH

Plant Lists

For butterflies and moths

PERENNIALS

A. Yarrow
Achillea taygetea

B. Butterfly weed
Asclepias tuberosa

C. Italian aster
Aster amellus 'Violet Queen'

D. Turtlehead
Chelone obliqua

E. Blanket flower
Gaillardia grandiflora 'Mandarin'

F. Dame's rocket
Hesperis matronalis

G. Gayfeather
Liatris spicata 'Kobold'

H. Musk mallow
Malva moschata 'Rosea'

I. Garden phlox
Phlox paniculata 'Orange Perfection'

For birds

TREES

J. Saskatoon
Amelanchier alnifolia

K. Honey locust
Gleditsia tricanthos inermis 'Imperial'

L. Red pine
Pinus resinosa

M. European mountain ash
Sorbus aucuparia 'Cardinal Royal'

SHRUBS

N. Dwarf saskatoon
Amelanchier alnifolia 'Regent'

O. Redtwig dogwood
Cornus stolonifera 'Kelseyi'

P. Five-leaf aralia
Eleutherococcus sieboldianus

Q. Mapleleaf viburnum
Viburnum acerifolium

VINES

R. Japanese honeysuckle
Lonicera japonica

GROUND COVERS

S. Bearberry
Arctostaphylos uva-ursi

T. Stonecrop
Sedum 'Matrona'

PERENNIALS AND ANNUALS

U. Giant hyssop
Agastache rupestris 'Pink Panther'

V. Sunflower
Helianthus annuus 'Valentine'

W. Sweet alyssum
Lobularia maritima 'Carpet of Snow'

X. Dwarf cattail
Typha minima

The Edible Landscape
FRESH FOOD AND BEAUTY

This landscape blends beauty with good taste—literally. Every plant in this Kansas City, Missouri, garden is edible. In just 40 by 60 feet, the homeowners grow more than two dozen kinds of vegetables and herbs, as well as fruit trees and grape vines. The grassy walkways give physical and visual access to the entire garden. Overall, however, the garden's design draws visitors to its center, whether for a moment of reflection or to set up a barbecue and create a garden meal on the spot.

The garden is productive for a long season; some root vegetables and hardy greens are harvested in late autumn, and early spinach and peas may be planted as soon as the ground can be worked in spring. To save space, the dwarf apple trees, which reach only 5 to 6 feet, are espaliered. Likewise, grapes and berries are trained on trellises of 4-by-4 posts with horizontal heavy-gauge wire (2-by-2 crosspieces would also work). Concentric semicircles contain beds of perennial and annual herbs in the center, with tomatoes, eggplant, melons, and sunflowers toward the outside. Tall crops, such as corn and pole beans, grow in long beds at each corner, where they won't shade other plants. The design allows for new crops each year (last year's salsa garden could be replaced with this year's pesto garden), so the garden truly reflects the tastes of the gardeners.

A compost bin behind the apple trees converts most garden and kitchen waste to rich mulch that's lavishly spread around the beds. To make the garden easy to maintain, the double-dug mounded beds are drip-watered. In-line emitters are used for the circles, while perforated tubing is used for the straight beds.

Plant List

FRUITS AND BERRIES

A. Apples
'Cortland', 'McIntosh'

B. Berries
'Darrow', 'Northland' blueberries; 'Heritage' raspberry; 'Sweet Delight' strawberry

C. Grapes
'Marechal Foch' (red, midseason), 'Seibel de Chaunac' (blue, late season)

VEGETABLES AND HERBS

D. Bush beans
'Goldkist' (yellow), 'Provider' (green)

E. Pole beans
'Kentucky Runner'

F. Beets
'Chioggia', 'Golden Beet', 'Red Ace'

G. Carrots
'Earlibird Nantes', 'Nevis'

H. Corn
'Earlivee'

I. Eggplant
'Black Bell', 'Dusky'

J. Greens
'Buttercrunch' and 'Skyline' lettuce; 'Bright Lights' Swiss chard

K. Herbs
Basil, dill, English thyme, French tarragon, Greek oregano, parsley, purple sage, sweet marjoram

L. Muskmelon
'Earliqueen'

M. Onions
'Alisa Craig Exhibition', 'Norstar'

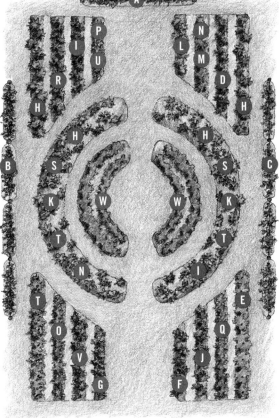

N. Hot peppers
'Big Chile'

O. Sweet peppers
'Ace' (green), 'Lipstick'
(red), 'Purple Bell' (purple)

P. Potatoes
'Kennebec', 'Yukon Gold'

Q. Radishes
'Cherriette', 'White Icicle'

R. Summer squash
'Yellow Crookneck',
'Raven' green zucchini

S. Winter squash
'Black Forest' buttercup,
'Waltham Butternut'

T. Tomatoes
'Beefmaster', 'Brandywine',
'Sweet Million' (need
staking); 'Sungem'
(bush type)

U. Turnips
'Purple-Top White Globe',
'Seven Top'

V. Perennial and late
vegetables
'Victoria' rhubarb; 'Roulette'
cabbage;
'Snow Crown' cauliflower;
'Laura' leeks

FLOWERS

W. Sunflower
'Mammoth Russian' (tall),
'Teddy Bear' (short)

NORTH

Family Garden
PLANNING FOR FUN

This landscape evolves with the family needs. Although just 55 by 65 feet, this Nashville, Tennessee, garden suits a range of family interests, minimizes maintenance, and allows for changes as the children grow.

Brick and neutral-toned washed concrete create an entry area that leads to the lawn and pool, which is fenced off from the rest of the yard for safety. The design allows an open area—a swath of lawn that's large enough for romping with kids or pets or for a summer barbecue with guests. Rimming the lawn are evergreen rhododendrons that offer cascades of blooms in late spring, while beneath the shrubs grow leafy mounds of hosta.

A long flowerbed cloaking the pool's fence is planted with sun-loving annuals and perennials. Starting in spring, this bed glows with color for nine months of the year. Framing the design are trees that have been chosen for their durability, beauty, and potential for kids to play on. The red oak is a favored climbing tree and can serve one day as a sturdy base for a tree house. The weeping mulberry offers a perfect hide-and-seek location, too.

The swing set with slide and climbing bars is close to the playhouse. When the children outgrow this area, the playhouse can be transformed into a storage shed for garden tools or sports equipment. After the kids have outgrown the swing set, the area can be tilled into a vegetable garden or landscaped with low-maintenance flowering shrubs.

Nearly indestructible rugosa roses nestle against the right side of the playhouse. During late spring and summer, these shrubs provide fragrant blooms. Bright red rose hips that grow up to an inch across make these plants equally attractive during the fall and winter.

For color where it's needed, the design incorporates containers filled with seasonal annuals or mini vegetables and fruits (such as strawberries or patio-type tomatoes) that are always ready to yield a quick snack. For fruit lovers in the family, three blueberry varieties (at least two must be planted for good fruit production) form an attractive low hedge behind the swing set. These midsize shrubs flower delicately in spring, set delicious fruit in summer, and blaze into orange and yellow glory in autumn.

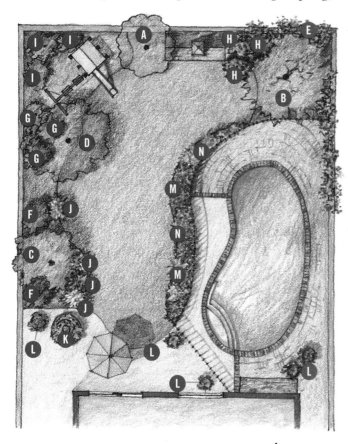

NORTH

Plant List

TREES

A. Weeping mulberry
Morus alba 'Pendula'

B. White pine
Pinus strobus

C. Sargent cherry
Prunus sargentii

D. Red oak
Quercus rubra

SHRUBS

E. Honeysuckle
Lonicera sempervirens

F. *Rhododendron* 'Blue Peter'

G. *Rhododendron*
'Boule de Neige'

H. Rugosa rose
Rosa rugosa

I. Highbush blueberry
Vaccinium corymbosum
'Jersey', 'Patriot', and
'Bluecrop'

ANNUALS AND PERENNIALS

J. Plantain lily
Hosta varieties

K. Strawberry
Fragaria 'Tri-Star' or
'Ever Red'

L. Container plants
Petunia, portulaca,
impatiens, 'Tumbler' tomato

M. Mixed annuals
Marigold, geranium, petunia

N. Mixed perennials
Coneflower (*Echinacea*), iris,
fountain grass
(*Pennisetum*), phlox, *Sedum
telephium*

Going Native
GETTING IN SYNC WITH NATURE

Go native in your landscape and reap the many benefits that hardy plants bring to any garden. Gardeners who have weathered a season of drought are easy converts to the water-saving benefits of native plants, as well as to their beauty in home landscapes. In Seattle, Washington, this garden uses predominantly local plants in settings that take their cues from nature—with stunning results.

An angled walk and gentle berm give form, privacy, and an element of surprise to the garden's shallow entry. Approached from the driveway (top of the plan), the garden reveals itself slowly. Its 35-foot-deep, 60-foot-wide area offers meandering paths, pockets packed with native plants, and a shaded private patio. The berm's natural look is created by a base of large, low boulders interplanted with the area's native multistemmed vine maples. Other Northwest native plants cover the berm to create privacy and a woodsy atmosphere.

The garden was designed with the dual purpose of viewing and cutting. Beneath the tall maples, midsize understory shrubs provide both screening and color; azaleas, lilacs, Oregon grape, and rhododendrons all offer seasonal bloom and bouquet-quality flowers. Plants offer a wide range of leaf textures—columbine, euphorbia, false spiraea, ferns, hostas, lamb's ears, sedge, and Siberian iris all provide flowers, as well as textural leaves. Lush sweet woodruff and redwood sorrel fill the spaces between.

As a contrast to the garden's soft foliage and Northwest palette, the paths are hard-edged and neutral in tone. Precast squares of buff-colored concrete are set on a bed of compacted gravel and sand.

◄ NORTH

Plant List

TREES

A. Vine maple
Acer circinatum

B. Japanese maple
Acer palmatum

C. Madrone
Arbutus menziesii

D. Flowering plum
Prunus blireiana

E. Japanese flowering cherry
Prunus serrulata 'Shirotae'

F. Douglas fir
Pseudotsuga menziesii

SHRUBS

G. *Enkianthus*

H. Lavender
Lavandula

I. Oregon grape
Mahonia aquifolium
'Compacta'

J. Azaleas and rhododendrons
Rhododendron

K. Sweet box
Sarcococca

L. Common lilac
Syringa vulgaris

GROUND COVERS AND PERENNIALS

M. Columbine
Aquilegia

N. False spiraea
Astilbe

O. Sedge
Carex

P. Common bleeding heart
Dicentra spectabilis

Q. Bishop's hat
Epimedium

R. *Euphorbia*

S. Ferns

T. Sweet woodruff
Galium odoratum

U. Hellebore
Helleborous foetidus

V. Plaintain lily
Hosta

W. Siberian iris hybrids
Iris sibirica

X. Redwood sorrel
Oxalis oregana

Y. Japanese spurge
Pachysandra terminalis

Z. Oriental poppy
Papaver orientale

AA. Solomon's seal
Polygonatum

BB. Lamb's ears
Stachys byzantina

CC. Meadow rue
Thalictrum

Taming a Slope

AN UNRULY HILLSIDE BECOMES A GARDEN

San Francisco landscape designers know a thing or two about gardening on a slope. The design of this southwest-facing hillside garden borrows heavily from the natives of California's coastal chaparral. Evergreen shrubs, such as ceanothus, flannel bush, and manzanita, dominate this ocean-influenced region of winter rains. Scrub oak is the main deciduous tree here. Existing large trees (coast redwood, magnolia, and deodar cedar) around the edges of the garden create a temperate microclimate suitable for perennial shade dwellers, such as Lenten rose.

The landscape incorporates a broad palette of California natives, as well as ones from similar climates in Europe (bush germander, herbs, salvia, and santolina) and New Zealand (*Cordyline australis*). Wide beds slope down between low retaining walls covered with a chaparral-like mix of plants that explode in alternating hues of red, yellow, and blue throughout spring and summer.

The garden's hardscape fits in as well as the native plants do. Stairs that lead from the house to the street weave between the beds, allowing a wonderful meandering walk through the garden (as well as the more practical reason of breaking up the climb). Semicircular viewing areas at the center of the walls are framed by tall *Arctostaphlos manzanita* 'Dr. Hurd'. Sandstone paves the pathways, and a coat of stucco softens the garden walls. This landscape design clearly illustrates that native plants work just as well tucked into broad beds with neatly edged walks and walls as they do in the wild land of their original homes.

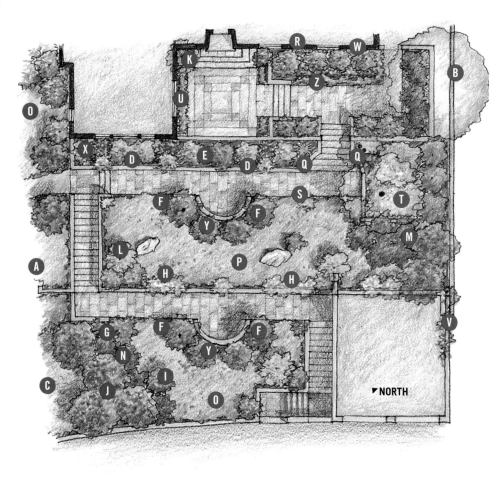

Plant List

TREES

A. Deodar cedar
Cedrus deodara

B. Saucer magnolia
Magnolia soulangiana

C. Coast redwood
Sequoia sempervirens

SHRUBS

D. Monterey manzanita
Arctostaphylos hookeri 'Wayside'

E. *Arctostaphylos* 'Lutsko Pink'

F. Manzanita
Arctostaphylos manzanita 'Dr. Hurd'

G. Fort Bragg manzanita
Arctostaphylos nummularia

H. Bearberry
Arctostaphylos uva-ursi

I. *Ceanothus maritimus*

J. Blue blossom
Ceanothus thyrsiflorus 'Skylark'

K. Dracaena
Cordyline australis

L. Pine Hill flannel bush
Fremontodendron decumbens

M. Toyon
Heteromeles arbutifolia

N. Coffeeberry
Rhamnus californica 'Seaview'

O. Evergreen huckleberry
Vaccinium ovatum

P. Shrub mix
Saffron buckwheat (*Eriogonum crocatum*); silver lupine (*Lupinus albifrons collinus*); scarlet bugler (*Penstemon centranthifolius*); *P. heterophyllus purdyi*; germander sage (*Salvia chamaedryoides*); lavender cotton (*Santolina neapolitana* 'Lemon Queen'); California fuchsia (*Zauschneria californica*)

GROUND COVERS, VINES, AND PERENNIALS

Q. *Beschorneria yuccoides*

R. *Bougainvillea* 'San Diego Red'

S. *Eriophyllum nevinii*

T. Lenten rose
Helleborus orientalis

U. Lavender
Lavandula intermedia 'Grosso'

V. Lady banks' rose
Rosa banksiae

W. Rosemary
Rosmarinus officinalis

X. California blue sage
Salvia clevelandii 'Winifred Gillman'

Y. Bush germander
Teucrium fruticans 'Azurea'

Z. Herb mix
Roundleaf, golden and common oregano; common sage; lemon and common thyme

Inviting Nature In
LET THE DESERT BE ITSELF

A selection of native plants allows this garden to blend naturally into the surrounding desert, yet the concentration of plants and the choreography of their blooming times keep the garden attractive in all seasons.

A courtyard nestled between two sections of a 1920s adobe house in Phoenix, Arizona, functions as an outdoor living room during the mild winters. To accentuate this roomlike feeling, the courtyard is paved in brown concrete, while the paths are made of compacted decomposed granite. Stone from the site was inlaid into the concrete around a simple stone bowl fountain hand carved in Mexico. Blue palo verde and Mexican bird of paradise create a floral ceiling.

Beyond the courtyard walls, plantings of creosote bush, desert ironwood, and littleleaf palo verde create pockets of shade. Their textural branch patterns make a visual transition from the oasis-like courtyard to the native desert. Below and around the trees grow flowering perennials and succulents, including Baja ruellia and sage in the courtyard and desert marigold, globe mallow, and moss verbena outside. The result is a lush garden with lots of shade and year-round color that mirrors the natural Sonoran Desert.

Plant List

TREES

A. Saguaro
Carnegiea gigantea

B. Blue palo verde
Cercidium floridum

C. Littleleaf palo verde
Cercidium microphyllum

D. Desert ironwood
Olneya tesota

SHRUBS AND GROUND COVERS

E. Woolly butterfly bush
Buddleia marrubifolia

F. Yellow Mexican bird of paradise
Caesalpinia mexicana

G. Creosote bush
Larrea tridentata

H. Texas ranger
Leucophyllum frutescens 'Green Cloud'

I. Chihuahuan sage
Leucophyllum laevigatum

J. Prickly pear
Opuntia ficus-indica

PERENNIALS

K. Smooth-edged agave
Agave weberii

L. Desert marigold
Baileya multiradiata

M. Mexican honeysuckle
Justicia spicigera

N. Baja ruellia
Ruellia peninsularis

Plant List

TREES

A. Paperbark maple
Acer griseum

B. Kentucky coffee tree
Gymnocladus dioica

C. Tulip tree
Liriodendron tulipifera

D. White oak
Quercus alba

E. Red oak
Quercus rubra

SHRUBS

F. *Daphne burkwoodii*
'Carol Mackie'

G. Oakleaf hydrangea
Hydrangea quercifolia

H. Mountain laurel
Kalmia latifolia

I. *Leucothoe walteri*
'Girard's Rainbow'

J. Oregon grape
Mahonia aquifolium
'Compacta'

K. Deciduous azalea
Rhododendron
Knap-Hill-Exbury Hybrid

L. *Rhododendron yakushi-manum* 'Yaku Princess'

M. Rhododendron 'Scintillation'

N. Tea viburnum
Viburnum setigerum

GROUND COVERS AND PERENNIALS

O. Maidenhair fern
Adiantum pedatum

P. Japanese painted fern
Athyrium niponicum
'Pictum'

Q. Bleeding heart
Dicentra spectabilis

R. Bleeding heart
Dicentra eximia
'Adrian Bloom'

S. Autumn fern
Dryopteris erythrosora

T. Bishop's hat
Epimedium grandiflorum
'Rose Queen'

U. Epimedium youngianum
'Niveum'

V. White snakeroot
Eupatorium rugosum
'Chocolate'

W. Wintergreen
Gaultheria procumbens

X. Bear's foot hellebore
Helleborus foetidus

Y. Lenten rose
Helleborus orientalis

Z. Coral bells
Heuchera 'Persian Carpet'

AA. Hosta 'Frances Williams'

BB. St. Johnswort
Hypericum calycinum

CC. Crested iris
Iris cristata

DD. Dalmatian iris
Iris pallida

EE. Japanese roof iris
Iris tectorum

FF. Virginia bluebell
Mertensia pulmonarioides

Always in Season
CHANGE AND SURPRISE THROUGH THE YEAR

You can enjoy the beauty of a garden all year long—even in climates with freezing winters. A well-chosen group of plants keeps the color show going from early spring through winter.

The Chicago, Illinois, design featured here starts with good structure. All year, two elegant evergreen pine trees provide shape and restful color. In late winter, the brave blooms of spring-blooming bulbs and early perennials start to show up in the garden. Hellebores, winter aconite, and crocus bloom, even through snow, and scented yellow flowers appear on bare witch hazel branches.

In spring, crab apple boughs swell with clouds of bloom, catkins appear on the birch, and late-season flowering bulbs spread color across the garden. Rhododendrons burst into bloom in late spring, followed by perennials that continue to flower throughout the summer. The hydrangea dresses the seasons in color as its pure white panicles mature to pinkish purple.

Come autumn, tall clumps of blue fescue brighten to gold, and red fruits cover the crab apple, hollies, and viburnum. Yellow birch leaves shower down, revealing peeling bark on the tree's trunk. The coming of winter exposes branches, berries, boulders, and statuary.

The first snow frosts the landscape into soft shapes. Snow and ice outline the evergreens and contrast with berries and bark. Year-round, the garden is easy to maintain. Evergreen ground covers minimize weeding throughout the garden, and the central lawn is large enough for a modest garden party but compact enough to mow quickly.

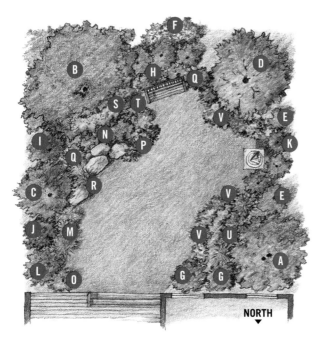

NORTH
▼

Plant List

TREES

A. River birch
Betula nigra 'Heritage'

B. Crab apple
Malus 'Donald Wyman'

C. Tanyosho pine
Pinus densiflora 'Umbraculifera'

D. Japanese black pine
Pinus thunbergii 'Thunderhead'

SHRUBS

E. Witch hazel
Hamamelis intermedia 'Arnold Promise'

F. Oakleaf hydrangea
Hydrangea quercifolia 'Snow Queen'

G. Evergreen holly
Ilex meserveae (male and female plants)

H. Winterberry
Ilex verticillata 'Red Sprite'

I. *Rhododendron yakushimanum* 'Ken Janek'

J. *Rhododendron yakushimanum* 'Bambi'

K. *Rhododendron yakushimanum* 'Yaku Princess'

L. Cranberry bush
Viburnum trilobum 'Compactum'

GROUND COVERS AND PERENNIALS

M. Blue fescue
Festuca glauca 'Elijah Blue'

N. Bear's foot hellebore
Helleborus foetidus

O. Christmas rose and Lenten rose
Helleborus niger and *H. orientalis*

P. Coral bells
Heuchera 'Palace Purple'

Q. *Hosta* 'Sum and Substance'

R. Japanese blood grass
Imperata cylindrica 'Red Baron'

S. Japanese spurge
Pachysandra terminalis

T. Sedum
Sedum telephium 'Autumn Joy'

U. Indian grass
Sorghastrum nutans 'Sioux Blue'

V. Mixed perennials and bulbs
Coreopsis 'Moonbeam'; *Aster frikartii* 'Mönch'; *Scabiosa columbaria* 'Butterfly Blue'; *Colchicum speciosum*; crocus, spring varieties; *Lilium* varieties; *Narcissus* 'Tête-à-Tête', 'Suzy', 'Barrett Browning'; *Tulipa* 'Apricot Beauty'

The Power of Scent

IT'S A PATHWAY TO THE PAST

The sense of smell is so powerful that it can make you instantaneously recall memories of the past. A single whiff of a flower in bloom can transport you back in time to the place you first encountered the fragrance. It's little wonder that fragrant plants have always ranked high among gardeners' favorites.

Where do scented plants have the most power in the garden? The obvious places are where you're most likely be on a regular basis. You can wake up to the perfume of a gardenia growing outside your bedroom window or spend a moment in noontime repose beneath a blooming Southern magnolia. And what better end to a busy day than to drift back and forth on an old porch swing and enjoy the sweet evening scents of four o'clocks?

So that you can enjoy each flower's fragrance in its own time, plan for a succession of bloom (and scent). This Birmingham, Alabama, landscape plan includes a range of fragrant favorites. Others to consider are Carolina jessamine, confederate jasmine, *Phlox paniculata*, lavender, butterfly bush, peony, sweet William, and Oriental lily.

Don't make the mistake of thinking that only flowers provide a luscious scent. Many herbs, including rosemary, thyme, lemon balm, and scented geraniums, have aromatic leaves that you'll notice as you lightly brush by. A favorite trick is planting mother-of-thyme (*Thymus praecox arcticus*) between stepping-stones so that every time you tread on their tiny leaves, their aroma envelops you.

Plant List

TREES

A. Southern magnolia
Magnolia grandiflora 'St. Mary'

SHRUBS

B. Winter daphne
Daphne odora 'Marginata'

C. Gardenia
Gardenia jasminoides 'Golden Magic'

D. Banana shrub
Michelia figo

E. Rose
Rosa 'Sun Flare'

F. Korean spice viburnum
Viburnum carlesii

VINES

G. Woodbine honeysuckle
Lonicera periclymenum 'Graham Thomas'

GROUND COVERS AND PERENNIALS

H. Grand crinum
Crinum asiaticum

I. Common ginger lily
Hedychium coronarium

J. Golden butterfly ginger
Hedychium flavum

K. Lemon daylily
Hemerocallis lilioasphodelus

L. Fragrant plantain lily
Hosta plantaginea

M. Four o'clock
Mirabilis jalapa

N. Rose-scented geranium
Pelargonium graveolens

O. Peppermint-scented geranium
Pelargonium tomentosum

A Tropical Oasis
COOL PLANTS FOR HOT TIMES

Compared to gardeners in most of the country, those in the coastal and tropical Southeast are really lucky. They can grow plants that revel in heat and humidity and that bloom nearly all year. This Miami garden shows a luxuriant backyard in south Florida awash in tropical and semitropical plants. For your landscape, select two or three to fill out a border or act as focal points.

Tropical plants include flowering banana, cabbage palm, Chinese hibiscus, canna, lily-of-the-Nile, and creeping fig. Gardeners love the lush, bold foliage that tropicals offer—either as an accent or combined with the leaves of other plants to give any garden an exotic

look. In fact, combining different shapes and sizes of leaves can be dramatic and every bit as rewarding as combining different kinds of flowers. Try juxtaposing plants that have large, coarse leaves with those having small, delicate foliage. Or pair plants with burgundy or dark green foliage to complement those with light green or variegated leaves.

Gardeners in the South can often preserve tropicals just by mulching them heavily in autumn. Northern tropical lovers can grow the plants in containers that move indoors for the winter (after all, many of these plants are used in northern climates only as houseplants).

Plant list

TREES

A. Pindo palm
Butia capitata

B. Madagascar dragon tree
Dracaena marginata
'Tricolor'

C. Flowering banana
Musa coccinea

D. Silver date palm
Phoenix sylvestris

E. Cabbage palm
Sabal palmetto

F. Golden trumpet tree
Tabebuia chrysotricha

SHRUBS

G. Mexican heather
Cuphea hyssopifolia

H. Sago palm
Cycas revoluta

I. Shower of gold
Galphimia glauca

J. Chinese hibiscus
Hibiscus rosa-sinensis
'American Beauty'

K. Yellow shrimp plant
Pachystachys lutea

L. Shrubby yew pine
*Podocarpus macrophyllus
maki*

VINES

M. Common allamanda
Allamanda cathartica

N. Creeping fig
Ficus pumila

PERENNIALS AND ANNUALS

O. Lily-of-the-Nile
Agapanthus 'Peter Pan'

P. Shell ginger
Alpinia zerumbet 'Variegata'

Q. Canna 'Red King Humbert'

R. Parrot heliconia
Heliconia psittacorum
'Suriname Sassy'

S. Impatiens, New Guinea
hybrids

T. Dwarf mondo grass
Ophiopogon japonicus
'Gyoku Ryu'

U. Golden bamboo
Phyllostachys aurea

V Coleus
*Solenostemon
scutellarioides*
'Alabama Sun'

W. Peace lily
Spathyiphyllum 'Tasson'

X. Persian shield
Strobilanthes dyerianus

CHAPTER 7

Laying the Foundation

Designing your landscape isn't just
a matter of making decisions about
structures and plantings. It's also about
grading, drainage, and irrigation needs.

If you're lucky, you can add new elements
to your landscape with minimal
disruption to the shape of the land. But
you will likely need a drainage plan and
some kind of irrigation system.
Or perhaps you need to contour the grade
to channel water away from a problem
area, or to create a level
spot for a new patio.

IN THIS CHAPTER
GETTING STARTED • GRADING
DRAINAGE BASICS
SPRINKLERS AND DRIP-WATERING
SYSTEMS

Getting Started
WORKING WITH CODES, CONTRACTORS, AND RENTAL YARDS

Before your plans are too far along, consult the local building department for any legal restrictions. These include applying for a building permit and complying with building code requirements. Also be aware of zoning ordinances, which may govern regulations, such as whether a deck can be built and where it can be located.

BUILDING A GOOD WORKING RELATIONSHIP

- Search for a contractor by collecting recommendations from friends and neighbors who are satisfied clients.
- Before you meet with one, write down all your questions.
- If a magazine or brochure photograph captures what you're aiming for, bring it to the meeting.
- Have some idea of your budget, both for consultations and for the entire project. Keep in mind that professional help need not be costly, especially if you hire on a short-term basis.
- Be as precise as you can about your expectations.
- Look for evidence that the contractor listens carefully to your ideas and respects your needs.
- Ask for references so that you can see some of the person's work and talk to former clients.

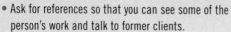

Building permits Before you put shovel to soil, get the needed permits. Have the building department check the plans before construction begins to ensure that you don't get off to a substandard start. Negligence may come back to haunt you. Officials can fine you and require that you bring an illegally built structure up to standard or dismantle it entirely.

Building codes Code requirements vary from region to region. They set minimum safety standards for materials and construction techniques: depth of footings, sizes of beams, and proper fastening methods, for example. Code requirements help ensure that any structures you build will be well made and safe for your family and any future owners of the property.

Zoning ordinances These municipal regulations restrict the height of residential buildings, limit the proportion of the lot a building and other structures may cover, specify how close to the property lines you can build, and—in some areas—stipulate architectural design standards.

Variances If the zoning department rejects the plans, you can apply for a variance at the city or county planning department. It's your task to prove to the department that the zoning requirements would create "undue hardship," and that the structure you want to build will not negatively affect neighbors or the community. If you plead your case convincingly, you may be allowed to build.

Deeds Your property deed can also restrict the project's design, construction, or location. Review the deed carefully, checking for easements, architectural restrictions, and other limitations.

WORKING SAFELY
Although the garden is not generally a hazardous place, any time you pick up a tool, climb a ladder, or start moving heavy materials, you can injure yourself—or someone else. If you're planning to carry out any of the landscape projects shown in this book follow the guidelines given here.

For protection from flying particles of dust or rock when cutting stone or brick, wear safety goggles or a full face mask. Look for comfortably fitting, fog-free types made of scratch-resistant shatterproof plastic. Dry portland cement is irritating to the eyes, nose, and mouth; wear a dust mask when mixing concrete.

Wet concrete and mortar are caustic to the skin, so wear heavy rubber gloves and tuck sleeves into them. If you must walk in the concrete to finish it off, wear rubber boots.

When working with lumber, protect your hands from wood splinters with all-leather or leather-reinforced work gloves. If you're sanding wood, wear a disposable painter's mask. For work with solvents, finishes, or adhesives, wear disposable rubber or plastic gloves. If you're using a rental equipment, be sure to ask the staff about safe operation first and read printed instructions carefully.

RENTAL YARD SAVVY

Renting gives you the chance to use professional-grade tools and tackle projects you couldn't otherwise. Rental companies offer a wide range of specialized tools, such as tractors, trenchers, and rotary tillers.

To make sure the process goes smoothly, think through the project carefully. Assemble everything you need to complete the job. If you have to stop work and run out for supplies, you risk either not finishing or not getting the tool back on time, which will cost you a late charge.

Resist the impulse to rent more elaborate tools than you can safely handle. Rental yards will review safe use and run you through operation, but they will assume you're capable. They won't prevent you from renting any kind of equipment.

MAKING A CONTRACT

Make sure you sign a written contract with any landscape professional. You'll be better protected if the contract is specific about what you expect, so make sure your contract includes the following:

THE PROJECT AND PARTICIPANTS Include a general description of the project, its address, and the names and addresses of both you and the professional.

CONSTRUCTION MATERIALS Identify the grade of materials, the quality of fasteners, and, in the case of lumber, the species and grade. Indicate brand and model number of any accessories, such as lighting systems. Avoid the clause "or equal" that will allow for substitution of other materials.

WORK TO BE PERFORMED Specify all major jobs from preliminary grading to finishing.

TIME SCHEDULE The contract should include both start and completion dates.

METHOD OF PAYMENT Payments are usually made in installments as phases of work are completed. You want to insist on a fixed price bid, although some contractors want a fee based on a percentage of labor and materials costs. Final payment is withheld until the job receives its final inspection and all liens are cleared.

WAIVER OF LIENS If subcontractors aren't paid for materials or services delivered to your home, in some states they can place a mechanic's lien on your property, tying up the title. Protect yourself with a waiver of liens, signed by the general contractor, subcontractors, and major materials suppliers.

EXHIBIT "A" It's a good idea to attach a copy of the property's site plan, drawn to scale.

If you don't have a truck or a trailer hitch on your car, you may need large tools delivered. Most rental yards will deliver and pick up, for a fee—$50 is typical.

Rental prices vary widely, but expect to pay about $65 a day for a large, rear-tined garden tiller and about $200 for a trencher or small backhoe/loader.

Be prepared to pay a cash or credit card deposit plus the tool-rental fee. Most rental companies require two forms of identification, such as a driver's license and a credit card. Most won't charge you for typical wear but will charge if they see obvious signs of abuse when you return the equipment. If you expect to give the tool extra-hard use, ask about damage coverage, usually covered by a 10 percent surcharge.

Grading

RESHAPING THE LAND

Moving soil from one place to another so it's at the proper height and slope ensures adequate drainage. More specifically, grading adds contours to flat landscapes and provides the necessary foundation for walks and patios.

Start with a plan, being sure to take into account drainage and any paving you're adding. If your house isn't connected to a sewer, locate the septic tank and drainage field.

THREE STAGES OF GRADING

The work of grading progresses hand in hand with the other aspects of installing your landscape. The first step, rough grading, brings the areas of your yard to the desired finished level. Then, after the completion of underground systems and any construction projects, you'll need to reestablish the rough grade. The final stage is the finish grading.

A layer of crushed gravel is used to level this site in preparation for paving. The front-end loader comes in handy for excavation and hauling soil, stone, and gravel.

Adequate surface drainage requires a minimum slope of 1 inch per 8 feet of paved surface, and 3 inches per 10 feet of unpaved ground.

Rough grading The goal is to remove or add enough soil in each area of your lot to bring the soil surface to the height and slope you want. Rough grading can include reshaping the soil and making mounds and berms, as well as digging foundations for patios and walks. Be advised though, that it is always preferred to install paving of any kind on firm, undisturbed soil. Fill soil, no matter how carefully tamped, will settle.

Start by eliminating high and low spots. Save the soil you remove in two separate piles—one for topsoil (the top 2 to 6 inches) and one for subsoil—so that it can be reused. Then dig foundations for patios, walls, and other paving. You may be able to use the soil from these excavations as fill in other areas. After the rough grading is complete, tamp the soil. Also tamp the soil each time you add a layer of fill soil to a deeply filled area.

Periodically reestablish the rough grade You'll probably need to do this several times while you're installing your landscape. For example, you may have to fill trenches dug for underground systems or low spots caused by the movement of heavy equipment. Mound the soil over the trench and tamp it firmly until it's at the same level as the soil around it.

your property (see page 150) to determine the soil's water-retaining characteristics. Measure water pressure and water flow rate and add the information to the plan.

As you plan your system, be sure to do the following:

Determine the hydrozones On an overlay of your scale drawing, break the planting areas that will be irri-

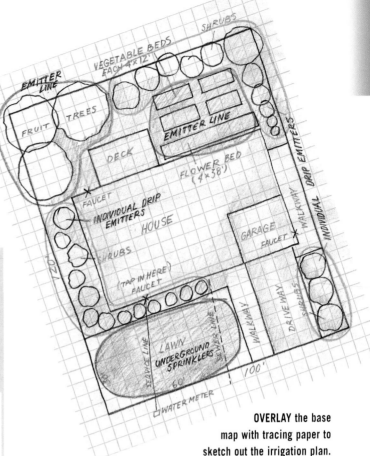

OVERLAY the base map with tracing paper to sketch out the irrigation plan.

gated into hydrozones, groups of plants that have similar moisture needs. Take into account exposure, because plants in hot, sunny spots will need more frequent watering than those in cooler, shadier locations. Also consider soil types. Plants growing in a porous container mix, for example, should be watered more often than those in clay soil. Decide on the type of watering system you'll employ for each hydrozone, for example, sprinklers or drip emitters.

When you actually plan an irrigation system, you'll be using this drawing as an aid in plotting the circuits, which are groups of watering devices connected to their own separate control valves. Only plants with the same basic watering requirements should be on the same circuit—hence the reason for initially hydrozoning your diagram. If a hydrozone is small enough, you may be able to include all of the watering devices in it on a single circuit. If your home's water supply is insufficient for all of the devices to work at the same time, you'll have to break the hydrozone into two or more circuits.

Determine your soil type Sprinkler systems work well in sandy soil and in loam. Clay soil absorbs water so slowly that low-flow sprinkler heads are needed to avoid excessive runoff. For more information about soil and soil types, see pages 300 through 303.

CONNECTING VALVES AND TIMERS

Connect control valves to a timer with low-voltage insulated cable (typically AWG-14 or 18) that's approved for direct burial. A different color wire joins each valve to a station on the timer, and another color wire (usually white) links all the valves to the timer.

Thus, if you have four valves, you'll need five-strand wire.

Run the wire underground to the timer location, leaving plenty of slack as you lay the wire; loop the wire at each valve and at turns in the trench. When you get to the timer site, bring the wire above the ground and staple it along walls, joists, and other surfaces as needed. Connect as shown at right.

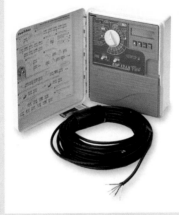

Timer, above, combines electronic and mechanical controls. Each solenoid valve has two wires. One is the common wire that connects valves (below) and the common-wire terminal. The other wire connects each individual valve to a numbered station on the timer.

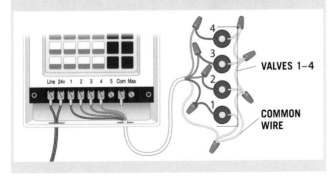

VALVES 1–4

COMMON WIRE

Check the water pressure Water pressure is measured in pounds per square inch (psi). Most sprinklers won't work efficiently if the psi is too low. To measure your house's water pressure, screw a water pressure gauge onto an outdoor faucet and, with all other water outlets turned off, turn the faucet on at full blast. Record the psi at each outside faucet location (if you have more than one), taking several readings throughout the day. Use the lowest reading as a conservative basis when calculating sprinkler output.

Check the water flow rate The flow rate, the amount of water that moves through pipes in a given period of time, is measured in gallons per hour (gph) or gallons per minute (gpm). To determine flow rate, count how many seconds an outdoor faucet takes to fill a gallon container. Divide the number of seconds by 60 to determine the gpm. (Note that for this method of measuring gpm to be accurate, the outdoor faucet must be the same diameter as the supply pipe.) Write this figure on your plan; you'll use it when plotting circuits.

Generally, the total output of a circuit of sprinklers should not exceed 75 percent of the gpm. Otherwise, the heads won't work properly and household water pressure may dip. If the sprinkler circuit requires a higher flow rate, create several separate circuits, each directed by its own control valve.

A Sprinkler System Overview

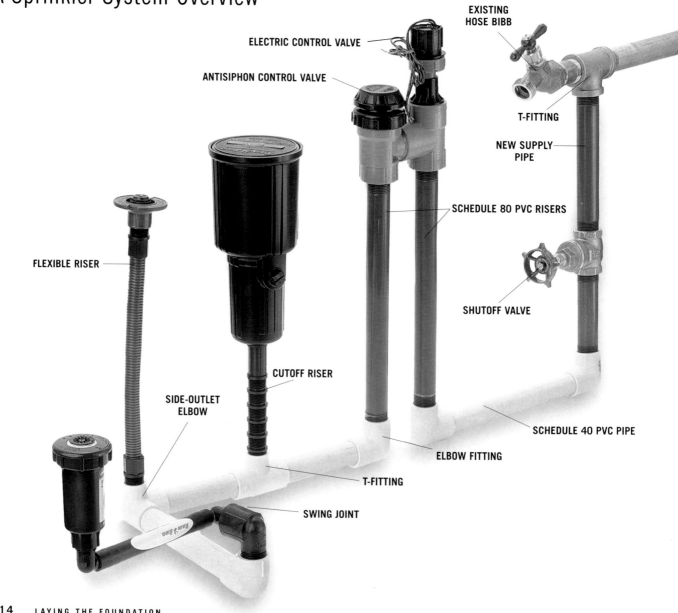

ELECTRIC CONTROL VALVE

EXISTING HOSE BIBB

ANTISIPHON CONTROL VALVE

T-FITTING

NEW SUPPLY PIPE

SCHEDULE 80 PVC RISERS

SHUTOFF VALVE

FLEXIBLE RISER

CUTOFF RISER

SIDE-OUTLET ELBOW

SCHEDULE 40 PVC PIPE

ELBOW FITTING

T-FITTING

SWING JOINT

Drip tubing is made of flexible black polyethylene. It comes in ½-inch (standard) and ⅜-inch diameters and is flexible enough (especially if warmed in the sun) to be snaked through plantings and looped around trees and shrubs. You can insert emitters directly into the tubing or install them in smaller tubing (microtubing) that branches off the main line.

Microtubing is small-diameter (usually ¼-inch), flexible polyethylene used to link individual sprayers or emitters to the larger drip tubing. Use stakes to hold microtubing in place.

Fittings connect the system. Couplings allow you to join two sections of tubing, T-fittings let you branch off in different directions, and L-shaped fittings are useful for making sharp turns. End caps close off the ends of drip tubing, and goof plugs are indispensable for sealing holes you've punched in the wrong place.

WATERING DEVICES
Most watering devices let water drip or ooze onto the root zone, while some spray water into the air like miniature sprinklers. Ooze tubing, laser tubing, and other porous tubing types double as pipes and emitters.

Drip emitters drip water directly onto the soil. Most have barbed ends that snap into the wall of the drip tubing or that push into the ends of microtubing. Drip emitters typically dispense ½, 1, or 2 gallons per hour (gph), and manufacturers color-code them to make their output obvious. For help in choosing the right emitters for your soil type and plants, see the chart below.

Microsprays are available in quarter-, half-, and full-circle patterns, as well as a bow-tie shape. These little heads are useful for covering tight or irregular spaces.

Minisprinklers, also called spinners, cover larger areas than microsprays can, throwing water in circles measuring from 10 to 30 feet across.

Misters are used to raise the humidity or to water hanging plants or bonsai. Misters are often positioned above hanging plants so that the spray is directed downward. For in-ground plants, aim misters upward.

DRIP EMITTER SELECTION GUIDE

This list provides general guidelines for the number and output of emitters for various types of plantings. The goal is to wet at least 60 percent of the root zone, so you may need to make adjustments depending on your soil type. Water tends to drip mainly downward in sandy soils but spreads wider before it goes deep in loam and clay soils (see page 390). Wherever a range is given for the emitters, choose the higher number if your soil is sandy, the lower one if it has a lot of clay. To avoid runoff on a slope, you may need more emitters of a lower output.

	OUTPUT RATE	NUMBER OF EMITTERS	PLACEMENT OF EMITTERS
Vegetables, closely spaced	½–1 gph	1	Every 12 in.
Vegetables, widely spaced	1–2 gph	1	At base of plant
Flower beds	1 gph	1	At base of plant
Ground covers	1 gph	1	At base of plant
Shrubs (2–3 ft.)	1 gph	1 or 2	At base of plant
Shrubs and trees (3–5 ft.)	1 gph	2	6–12 in. on opposite sides
Shrubs and trees (5–10 ft.)	2 gph	2 or 3	2 ft. from trunk
Shrubs and trees (10–20 ft.)	2 gph	3 or 4	3 ft. apart, at drip line
Trees (over 20 ft.)	2 gph	6 or more	4 ft. apart, at drip line

CHAPTER 8

Building Patios, Decks, and Fences

You've dreamed and planned, and now it's time to lay some bricks and pound a few nails. How do you make a pathway or a low wall? How do you build a basic deck? And what about fences and gates? On the following pages are directions for a variety of projects.

Whether you use tried-and-true materials, like wood and flagstone, or try out new products, like recycled glass tiles and colored concrete, remember that if you need help, ask for advice at a Lowe's Home Improvement Warehouse.

IN THIS CHAPTER
CONCRETE BASICS
BLOCK WALLS • STONE WALLS
PATIO PAVERS • BASIC DECK
STEPS • FENCES • GATES • PATHS

Stained and embossed concrete patio with inset boulders—also fashioned of concrete—makes an elegant space for entertaining. Fireplace and counter base are formed with blocks made of recycled plastic foam and cement.

Concrete Basics
MAKING AND SHAPING IT

Although sometimes disparaged as cold and forbidding, poured—or, more accurately, cast—concrete can be more varied in appearance than brick. And if you eventually get tired of the concrete surface you've chosen, you can use it as a foundation for a new pavement of brick, stone, or tile set in mortar.

The standard slab for pathways and patios is 4 inches thick. In addition, allow for a 4- to 8-inch base in most areas (in frost-free areas, 2 inches is sufficient). Forms for concrete are built in the same way as for wood edgings. For standard paving, you will need 2-by-4s on edge for forms and 12-inch 1-by-3s or 2-by-2s for stakes. If you leave the lumber in place as permanent edgings and dividers, use rot-resistant cedar or pressure-treated lumber. For curved forms, choose tempered hardboard, plywood, or, if edgings will be permanent, metal.

To prevent buckling and cracking, reinforce a concrete area more than 8 feet square with 6-inch welded

CHAPTER 9

Landscape Projects

In this chapter are step-by-step instructions for a variety of projects, all of which can add beauty and utility to your garden. An arbor or trellis can define space and provide a climbing structure for vines. Garden walls retain soil on a sloped site or enclose a flower bed. A pond with a fountain or small waterfall adds a tranquil note. Raised beds allow you to garden without straining your back, and they show off your plants to best advantage. A stylish compost container turns a messy process into a thing of beauty. And finally, for your kids or grandkids, a play set adds hours of fun.

IN THIS CHAPTER
ARBORS • TRELLISES
PORCH SKIRT • WINDOW BOX
GARDEN PONDS AND FOUNTAINS
RAISED BEDS
COMPOST BINS • PLAY SET

Building Arbors
A SUN SHELTER AND VINE SUPPORT

Control the degree of shade by how you attach the top boards. Here, 2-by-2 lattice is spaced 2 inches apart. Because of the roof pitch, they create more surface area to block sunlight than if the roof were flat.

An arbor can be freestanding or it can be attached to the house with a ledger board. For posts, use extra-high deck posts that rest in a concrete slab or are sunk in concrete-filled post holes.

Overhead beams support rafters. If the arbor is attached to the house, the ledger takes the place of one beam. You may want to leave rafters open so that you can train a vine over them, or you can cover them with any one of a number of materials—for example, lath, wire, bamboo, shadecloth, lattice, tree or grape stakes, woven reeds, or poles.

CHOOSING MATERIALS

A good design takes its cue from your house architectural style. Choose materials (and colors) that complement the style. If the arbor will attach to the house, consider how it will affect the view from indoors. Beams that are too low may block a pleasing view. Generally, the lowest beam should not be less than 6 feet 8 inches above the outdoor floor surface. A taller arbor gives vines room to grow and lends a spacious feel to the area. If you plan to place an outdoor dining table under the arbor, allow at least 4½ feet of clearance all around the table and provide additional room for a barbecue area.

For the longest-lasting posts, beams, and rafters, choose pressure-treated wood or naturally decay-resistant materials, such as redwood or cedar heartwood. You can use 4-by-4 posts for most arbors up to 12 feet tall. Use 2-by-6 beams and rafters for spans up to 6 feet; 2-by-8s for spans up to 9 feet.

LAYING RAFTERS AND INSTALLING POSTS

Control the amount of shade your arbor casts with the rafters. For example, running the rafters east-west provides midday shade. But if you plan on enjoying the arbor more in the early morning and the later afternoon, run the rafters north-south to maximize sun at those times.

How you attach the top boards also affects shade. If you stand 1-by-2s or 1-by-3s on edge, they will give little shade at midday when the sun is overhead, but plenty of shade in the morning and afternoon when the sun is at an angle. Lay them flat, and the result will be exactly the opposite.

If you're adding an arbor to a new deck, lengthen the deck's posts, making them tall enough to support the arbor. But when adding an arbor to an existing deck, bolt the posts to the deck's substructure, placing the posts directly above or adjacent to the deck posts.

If the arbor will span an existing patio, you can set the posts in post holes outside the edge of the patio or attach them to post anchors, as shown in step 1 on the opposite page.

Building an Arbor

The following steps give a general idea of the building sequence for a freestanding arbor. Also take a look at the more detailed step-by-step instructions for building a deck (pages 234 and 235). Constructing an arbor is a similar process, from laying out the footings to attaching the lath or other covering material, except you'll probably spend a lot more time on a ladder.

1 Cut the posts to length and set them in metal anchors embedded in concrete footings or atop precast piers. Have a helper hold each post upright and nail the anchor to the post.

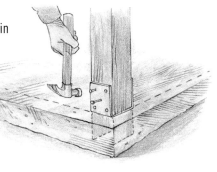

2 Check that each post is vertical by plumbing it with a level on two adjacent sides or by using a post level. With a helper holding a post in position, secure each post with temporary braces nailed to wooden stakes that are driven into the ground.

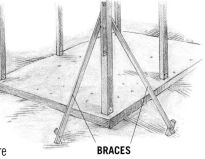

BRACES

3 Position each beam on top of the posts; you'll need a helper. Check that the posts are still vertical and the beam is level (adjust, if necessary, with shims), and then secure the beam to the posts with framing connectors or by toenailing the beam to the posts.

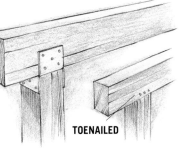

TOENAILED

4 Set and space the rafters on top of the beams.

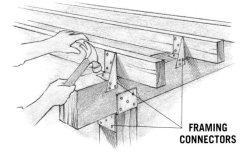

FRAMING CONNECTORS

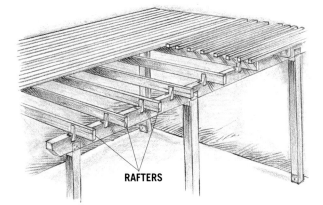

RAFTERS

5 For shade, cover the rafters with 1-by-2 or 2-by-2 lath. Space the lath to achieve a specific amount of shade.

ATTACHING AN ARBOR

Although most arbors employ the same basic components (posts, beams, rafters or joists, and some type of roofing), there are many different ways to assemble them.

To attach an arbor to a house, install a ledger, much like a deck ledger, usually a 2-by-4 or a 2-by-6. Connect it with lag screws to wall studs, to second-story floor framing, or to the roof. If your house wall is brick or stone, drill holes and install expanding anchors to bolt the ledger in place.

Set rafters on top of the ledger or hang them from it with anchors, joist hangers, or rafter hangers. If the roof will be flat, square up rafter ends. (Sloped rafters, require angled cuts at each end, plus a notch where rafters cross the beam.)

A lattice panel suspended in a sturdy frame makes a simple trellis for a raised-bed garden, next to an umbrella-shaded dining area.

Trellis-Building Basics

MAKING PRIVACY WITHOUT OVERDOING IT

A trellis is essentially a two-dimensional frame for plants, made with vertical and horizontal elements fastened together. The traditional model is a rectangular wooden grid that gives plants a good foothold and allows air circulation. But just about anything flat or round that stands up to the elements, supports the weight of mature plants, and can be nailed, screwed, or wired together can serve as a lightweight trellis, especially if it will be supported by a wall or fence.

A freestanding trellis provides both a privacy screen and a growing place for vines, and it can be moved around the garden seasonally as needed.

In many cases, you can convert a two-dimensional trellis to a three-dimensional arbor simply by building one or more matching frames, placing them parallel to each other, and bridging them with horizontal braces that create "walls" and a "roof."

CHOOSING MATERIALS

Most trellises are made from milled wood: standard dimension lumber, lattice and lath, moldings, dowels, or tree stakes. Wood is easy to work with. It's strong, and, if chosen and prepped properly, it should stand up to many years of water, wind, and summer heat.

The most durable structures are made from naturally decay-resistant woods, such as redwood or cedar heartwoods, or from pressure-treated lumber. Most trellis pieces are lightweight—typically ½- by 1½-inch lath, 1-by-2s, 2-by-2s, and sometimes 2-by-4s. Occasionally, larger freestanding frames are held up with stout 4-by-4 posts or 6-inch diameter poles. You can let redwood or cedar weather naturally, paint, or seal it with an exterior finish. Pressure-treated lumber can be hard to find in small sizes, and you'll probably want to paint or stain it to conceal its typical greenish cast.

Most trellis joinery is simple. Butt joints, such as those in the project at right, are the norm; they are held together by nails, screws, or wire, and sometimes with waterproof glue, as well. For a more formal look, some projects call for more intricate lap joints. You'll want rust-resistant galvanized fasteners and hardware for these outdoor projects.

Making a Framed Trellis

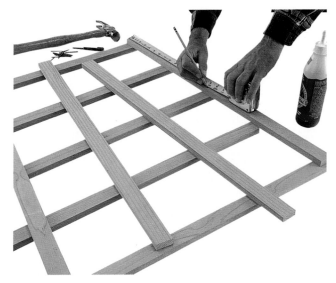

1 **Lay the uprights on a flat surface,** face down, and lay out crosspieces one at a time. This grid uses ⅝- by 1½-inch redwood pieces spaced on 8-inch centers. Before assembly, add a dab of waterproof glue where pieces cross. Then nail or screw each intersection. When the finished grid is flipped over, the nail or screw heads are out of sight.

2 **If a simple standard trellis** is all you're after, stop here. But if you'd like to add a frame, here's how. This frame has 2-by-2 verticals; the top piece was shaped from a 2-by-8. To be on the safe side, wait until you have built the grid before sizing the frame. Countersunk deck screws and glue hold sides to top piece. Don't put the bottom rail on just yet, however.

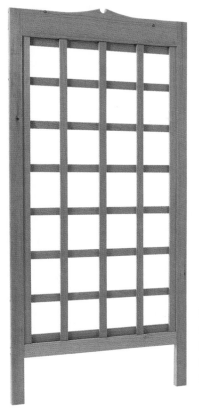

3 **Grid meets frame.** Slide the trellis grid inside the three-sided frame, and then snug the bottom 2-by-2 rail up against the grid's bottom edge. The grid is not as thick as the frame—for a nice design touch, line the backs up, leaving a reveal at the front. Screws and glue hold the bottom rail in place; more screws, driven from the outside in, keep the grid in place.

Completed trellis is distinguished by its frame with chamfered edges, and the detailed top.

Hinged lattice panels dress up the skirt of this front porch while still allowing good air circulation and easy access.

Building a Lattice Porch Skirt

IT'S A GROUND-LEVEL TRELLIS

In between cosmetic touch-ups and major renovations, you can tackle small improvements to keep a porch looking great. Here's how to handle one of the most common of all porch repairs: building a new lattice skirt.

Keep in mind that these techniques can also be adapted for replacing lattice on a deck, fence, gate, privacy screen, or trellis.

MAKING THE FRAME

First remove the old lattice with a flat pry bar. Measure the openings between the columns or posts. The completed frames must be ½ inch narrower than the overall width and 1 inch shorter than the height.

The porch shown here had five 26-inch-high openings that ranged between 8½ and 9½ feet long. The lattice panels are 8 feet long, so a vertical brace was installed in the middle of each frame to conceal the seam between the two lattice pieces. If your porch has frames that are less than 8 feet long, eliminate this center brace.

Make the four perimeter pieces of each frame out of a pressure-treated 1-by-6 trimmed down to 4½ inches; use a pressure-treated 1-by-4 for the center brace. When buying the lumber, choose the straightest, driest boards with the fewest knots. (If you can't find 1-by pressure-treated lumber, use 1-by-6 heart redwood or cedar or ⅝-by-6-inch pressure-treated decking.)

Cut the frame parts to length and assemble them face down on a flat surface. Strengthen the frame with steel reinforcement hardware. At each corner joint, install a 6-inch mending plate and a 3½-inch flat corner brace (see step 2, opposite page). Position the hardware pieces about ¼ inch from the edge of the frame and secure them with ¾-inch-long flathead screws.

Connect the center brace to the frame with two 4-inch T-plates. Be sure the leg of the T-shaped plate is centered on the 1-by-4 brace. After the frames are assembled, apply a coat of primer, followed by two coats of gloss enamel trim paint to match your porch or deck.

ATTACHING THE LATTICE

Shown is forest green, diagonal-pattern plastic lattice. Made of high-density polyethylene, it is resistant to decay, splitting, and mildew. It comes in 4- by 8-foot sheets in six colors and three basic patterns: square and basket weave in addition to diagonal. Wood lattice is widely available and also paintable so easier to match with other colors.

First cut the lattice panels down to size using a sabre or circular saw. Lay the frames face down and attach the lattice to the frame with 1-inch panhead screws driven through washers (step 4). Be sure to drill

holes slightly larger than the screw shanks so that the lattice can expand and contract without buckling. If a frame has a center brace, secure the seam between the lattice pieces with two rows of screws.

INSTALLING THE PANELS

Hang the framed lattice panels from the porch with a 3- or 4-inch strap or T-hinges. Two hinges are sufficient for a panel 8 feet or shorter, but use three hinges on one longer than 8 feet. Shown (step 6) are 3-inch galvanized T-hinges.

Screw the hinges to the frames first, and then set the panels in the openings under the porch. Slip a pry bar under the panel and raise it up tight against the porch fascia. Use a drill/driver to screw the hinge to the porch.

Check to make sure the panel swings up and down smoothly. If it drags on the ground, use a shovel or rake to remove some dirt from in front of the panel. If there's a large, uneven gap beneath the panel, add some soil, and then smooth it out to create a consistent space between the panel and ground.

① Remove the old lattice skirt with a pry bar. If necessary, first cut it into pieces with a reciprocating saw.

② Hold together each corner joint of the frame with a 6-inch mending plate and flat corner brace.

③ Use two T-plates to secure the 1-by-4 center center brace to the frame. Fasten the plates with ¾-inch screws.

④ Secure the seam between two lattice panels with panhead screws that are driven through washers.

⑤ Screw the plastic lattice to the back of the frames after drilling oversized clearance holes.

⑥ To hang the lattice panel, screw the hinge to the porch fascia; then lift and attach the panels to the hinges.

Making a Window Box

IT'LL BE THE RIGHT SIZE AND STYLE FOR YOUR HOUSE

When you want herbs and flowers close at hand, try building a window box. One big advantage to making a window box instead of buying one is that you get exactly the right size, and you can stain or paint it to match your house or trim.

Designers recommend that a window box be about the same width as the window where it will be installed, including trim. To allow enough room for plant roots, make the box about 8 inches deep (slightly less for short-lived annuals) and 8 inches wide. To be sure the box has well-drained soil, install drain holes in the bottom of the box.

BUILDING A WINDOW BOX

The box shown here is 32 inches long, 8 inches high, and about 8 inches deep. It is made from a single 10-foot, 1-by-10 board of clear white pine. Although you pay a premium for clear pine, it's a pleasure not to deal with knots that can bleed through paint finishes.

Boxes can be plain or elaborate, but remember that they'll mostly be hidden when full of plants. This box has only five pieces of wood: two sides, two ends and a bottom. The ends of the outer side are tapered at a 10° angle from 7 inches at the bottom to $8\frac{7}{16}$ inches at the top. The dimensions aren't critical. The taper makes the finished box a little more interesting to look at.

After the pieces have been cut, they are assembled with an exterior-grade glue and $1\frac{1}{2}$-inch trim-head

HANGING A WINDOW BOX

Some houses may have window sills wide enough to accommodate flower boxes. If so, set the box on spacers so water can drain freely from the bottom. More often, a window box must be attached directly to the side of the house or held in place by wire attached to the window casing.

A pair of sturdy metal brackets should be enough to support most window boxes. On houses sided with wood, attach the brackets to the house either with galvanized or stainless steel wood screws. For heavy boxes or when the siding is thin, drive screws $1\frac{1}{2}$ inches into studs beneath the sheathing. For masonry walls, wedge or sleeve anchors will safely support the weight of the box. When installing a window box, however, be careful that it doesn't trap water against the house. A wood box in direct contact with wood siding is likely to encourage rot.

Vinyl-sided houses present a special problem. The siding needs to be free to move slightly with changes in temperature. When installing brackets to the wall, enlarge the screw hole slightly, allowing $\frac{1}{8}$-inch clearance between the siding and the screw, and seal the gap with silicone caulk to keep water out. Instead of snugging the bracket tightly to the wall, allow a space of about $\frac{1}{16}$-inch so the siding can move. Another method of attachment is to set the back edge of the window box on the sill and secure it with steel cable attached to the window casing. A third option is to attach the box to the front edge of the sill with T-shaped galvanized brackets. The long edge of the bracket is screwed to the back of the box, and the short leg is attached to the sill.

screws. The box could just as easily be nailed together with galvanized box or finish nails or assembled with galvanized, stainless steel, or brass screws. When set below the surface, however, trim heads are easy to conceal with exterior putty. Choose a good-quality putty, such as a two-part polyester filler that holds up well outdoors.

One trick to making the box fit together well is to make sure that edges are square and corners are 90°.

If you want the box to last more than a couple of years, finishing it inside and out is crucial. A top-quality primer and two coats of 100 percent acrylic latex paint on the outside and a clear wood preservative on the inside protect this one. And don't forget the drain holes in the bottom. This one has three pairs of ½-inch holes spaced along its length.

1 **Tapering the fronts** of the end pieces makes the box more interesting. Mark the cut with a straightedge, then cut along the line. If necessary, smooth the cut with a block plane.

2 **Predrill to avoid splits.** Make the hole in the top piece of wood the same size as or slightly larger than the screw shank.

3 **Glue and screw** the pieces together. Screw heads should be set slightly below the surface of the wood.

4 **Fill screw countersinks** with an exterior-grade filler. After the filler has cured, sand it flush.

5 **Use top-quality primer** and paint to protect wood from the elements. A finish coat of 100 percent acrylic latex is more durable than oil-based paint.

Stones covering the edge of the finished preformed pond give it a natural appearance. Low-growing perennials and grasses complete the scene.

Making a Garden Pond

USE A RIGID LINER AND STONE BORDER

Add a pond to your garden in a day or less by starting with a preformed plastic shell from Lowe's. Installing one is easy, but it does require gloves, a good shovel, and a strong back. You dig a hole, drop in the shell, and fill it with water and plants. Edged with stones and low-growing plants, the pond becomes graceful and inviting.

Preformed pond shells come in a variety of shapes, sizes, and depths. Some have smooth, vertical sides (which discourage raccoons); others have textured walls. Some have shelves around the sides to hold containers of water plants. Despite their bulk, most shells are light-weight, made of a heavy-duty UV-stabilized polyethylene. Shapes range from tidy ovals to free-form; volume ranges from about 30 gallons to several hundred. Costs increase with size. The pond shown here is available in 42- and 85-gallon sizes.

To help keep the pond clean, you'll need a pump. Submersible models are fine for a small pond like this one. Consider a pump powered by a small photovoltaic collector, but it runs only when sunlight hits the collector.

Water plants also help keep ponds clean. As a rule, they should cover about two-thirds of the water's surface.

Position edging stones around the pond so that they hide the lip from view. Cantilever them beyond the lip of the shell, but keep most of their weight on surrounding soil, not on the lip.

Installing a Rigid Liner

1 **Select the site; trace the shell.** Open areas are better than areas beneath trees whose leaves or needles will build up debris on the pond's bottom. To install a pond in a lawn, remove the sod and keep it moist and protected in a shady area so you can reuse it later. Set the pond shell on the cleared, level site, adjusting it to face the direction you want. With a yardstick vertically against the outside edge, trace around the pond shell to outline it in the soil.

2 **Remove the pond shell** and trace the soil outline with sand (as shown) or use a hose or length of rope.

3 **Dig the hole inside the outline.** Make the hole 2 inches deeper and wider than the shell to accommodate a layer of sand. With a carpenter's level, make sure the bottom of the hole is flat. Remove protruding stones or roots, then cover the bottom with 2 inches of packed damp sand. Recheck flatness with a level.

4 **Place the pond shell in the hole** slightly higher than the surrounding ground, with the top lip level. (To check, place the level to span the pond.) Adjust the shell as necessary. Start filling the pond from a slow-running hose. Backfill around the shell with moist sand, tamping as you go. Periodically recheck that the top is level. Continue until pond and hole are filled; backfill to slope soil away from the pond's edges.

Fountains and Falls

ADD THE SOUND OF MOVING WATER TO YOUR GARDEN

Water in motion, whether spilling gently, gurgling, or tumbling energetically, is always enchanting. Both fountains and waterfalls help bring falling water's sparkle and the musical sounds into the garden.

Fountains are of two types: the kind that spray water up (in different patterns) and the kind that cascade water down (for example, from a statue or chute). In the first case, water sprays up from a nozzle screwed onto a pump. In the second, water cascades down plastic tubing running up from an outlet on the pump and to the top of the fountain. To create a waterfall, aim the tube at a pile of rocks, configured so that the water runs down them and back into the pool.

Fountains and waterfalls require a pump, which is hidden in the bottom of the pond or in a reservoir that's out of sight. An electrical cable, which can be buried in a shallow trench, extends from the submerged pump to a ground-fault interrupt (GFI) outlet. Have an electrician install a GFI outlet, if necessary, and make sure you buy a pump with a cable long enough to reach from the bottom of the pond or water reservoir to the outlet. Where the cable crosses the garden, keep it safe from the blade of a spade or any other sharp object by running it through a 1-inch PVC pipe and burying the pipe in the ground.

A Pond in a Pot

Water features don't have to be expensive. The simple one shown below cost less than $400 and took a weekend to make. Start by purchasing a concrete planter with a drain hole in the bottom. Coat the inside of the pot with water sealer to keep the concrete from absorbing water. This will prevent cracking during a freeze.

1 Set a small submersible pump in the planter and run the cord through the drain hole. Conceal and protect the cord by running it through ¾-inch plastic conduit to a grounded outlet.

2 Set the pump at the desired height, level the planter, and use a cork to plug the drain hole and hold the cord in place. Seal both sides of the hole with silicone.

3 Fill with water, and then plug in the cord. Surround the fountain with flowers and enjoy.

A Wall Fountain

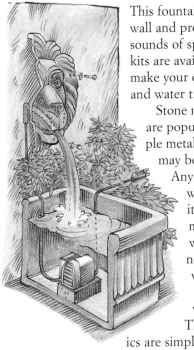

This fountain decorates a dull wall and provides the soothing sounds of splashing water. Many kits are available, or you can make your own with any spout and water trough.

Stone masks and lion heads are popular spouts, but a simple metal or bamboo spout may be easier to work with. Any kind of bowl or basin will do for a trough. If it's large, it will catch most of the fountain water, and you won't need to refill it as often when water evaporates in hot or windy weather.

The fountain's mechanics are simple: Water rises through flexible tubing from a pump in the trough up to the spout and spills back down to the trough. If you're building the wall that the fountain is to be mounted on, you can install the water delivery pipe out of site behind the wall. For an existing wall, you can hide the pipe by planting a vine around the fountain or placing a tall water plant in the trough.

The pump's electrical cable needs to be plugged into a nearby GFI outlet. The simplest arrangement is to take the cable out over the rim of the trough, hiding it in foliage.

To make a fountain like the one shown here, follow these steps:

1 **Attach the mask to the wall** below eye level with screws and expanding anchors. If you're taking the water delivery pipe up the face of the wall, mount the mask a little away from the wall on wood spacer blocks to allow room for the pipe to pass behind it.

2 **Place the pump** in the reservoir on top of a clean brick; this way, silt that collects on the reservoir bottom won't enter the pump. Attach the water pipe to the pump and take it up behind the mask into the spout. Where the pipe enters the mask, attach a right-angle connector so the pipe doesn't kink.

3 **Fill the trough with water,** plug the electrical cable into the GFI outlet, and adjust the water flow so that the water returns reliably to the reservoir. Watch the water level in the trough on windy days; it mustn't fall below the pump's water intake.

A Pebble Fountain

In a pebble fountain, water rises from a reservoir through a fountainhead nozzle on a pump, spills over a tray of pebbles, and trickles back down to the reservoir.

1 **Make the reservoir** with a black liner, a preformed shell, or any watertight container at least 15 inches deep. If the reservoir is small, you'll need to add water frequently during hot or windy weather so the water level never drops below the pump. In a windy site, choose a low, bubbling fountainhead so the water doesn't blow away.

2 **Dig a hole for the reservoir** and set it in place. Place the pump on a clean brick so silt that collects on the reservoir bottom won't enter the pump. Fit a rigid extension pipe to the pump outlet; screw the fountainhead to the top of the pipe. The fountainhead should just clear the top of the reservoir.

3 **Cut a piece of strong wire mesh** to fit over the reservoir and hold the stones in place. Overlap the surrounding area by at least 6 inches. If necessary, cut a hole in the mesh to make

room for the fountainhead. Position the mesh over the reservoir, and then cut a square out of the mesh, big enough to put your hand through comfortably, so that you can reach the pump to adjust the water flow or clear the filter screen. Cover the hole with a larger square of mesh that won't sag into the hole after it's covered with pebbles.

4 **Fill the reservoir.** Place a few large pebbles on the edges to hold it in place and cover the rest. Mark the access to the pump with a few uniquely colored or glass pebbles. Plug in the pump, check the jet spray, and adjust, if necessary, to ensure that the spray drips back into the reservoir.

Herbs thrive in two-tiered raised bed. Blooming marigolds surround basil, fennel, mint, and chives in the bed.

Building Raised Beds

MAKE GARDENING EASIER, NEATER, AND MORE EFFICIENT

A raised bed is just what the name implies: a planting bed elevated 8 to 12 inches above soil level. In its most basic form, it's simply a raised plateau of soil. More often, though, you'll encounter raised beds surrounded by a low wall of wood (such as 2-by lumber or railroad ties), concrete, brick, or stone.

Although making a raised bed takes a bit of effort, the bed gives a number of advantages. If you have problem soil—impenetrable clay, nutrient-deficient sand, a soil that's highly acid or alkaline or one that's compacted from construction—a raised bed filled with good soil may be your best shot at raising healthy plants. Particularly where drainage is slow to nonexistent, a raised bed is the easiest way to provide a well-drained root run. And even if your garden soil is good enough for what you want to grow, a raised bed may be worth installing. It will help you prepare a "powerhouse" plot for top production, a defined area where you can add topsoil, amendments, and fertilizer to make the finest possible soil.

In cold-winter regions, soil in raised beds warms earlier than that in regular garden plots, allowing you to plant and harvest earlier, as well. When it comes time to pick flowers or veggies, the elevated soil level makes the job a bit simpler. And the fact that plants and soil are contained makes the entire operation neat and tidy: Water, fertilizer, and soil remain within the bed.

When planning a raised bed, choose the site carefully. Most vegetable, flower, and herb plants are sun loving, so the bed should receive at least 6 hours of sun daily. Select a spot that has good air circulation but isn't exposed to frequent winds. Be sure, too, to locate it at some distance from trees and large shrubs; if they're too close, their roots will infiltrate the soil of the bed. Also make sure that a hose bibb or other water source is near enough to make watering easy.

To the extent that you can, loosen up the soil where

SCREENING OUT GOPHERS

If pocket gophers or ground squirrels are a problem in your area, consider a screen-bottomed bed that will prevent them from getting to your plants. Make a wooden framework as shown on the facing page, and then staple $\frac{1}{2}$-inch-mesh hardware cloth to the bottom before setting the frame into the soil. Be aware that you must dig quite carefully in screen-bottomed beds, and, of course, you can't dig below the depth of the bed. For this reason, it's best to make these beds a bit deeper—up to $1\frac{1}{2}$ feet.

the raised bed will be. This way, you'll be able to mix the existing soil with whatever you use to fill the bed, creating some transition between the native soil and that of the bed. And of course, loosening the soil below the bed will make it easier for roots to penetrate as deeply as possible.

Now you're ready to build the bed. No matter what material you use as a border, the base should extend about 2 inches below soil level. If you construct a wood frame like the one below, you can assemble it off-site and move it into place. Dimensions are important: you should be able to reach into the bed's center easily from its long sides.

With the border in place, you can fill the bed with additional soil. If your soil is good, you may just add soil from somewhere else in the garden. Another option is to use purchased topsoil. (Be aware, though, that this product varies greatly, depending on the supplier. Some topsoils are raw dirt, while others are mixtures of soil and organic amendments.) Fill the bed in stages: Add several inches of new soil and dig it into the native soil beneath, and then add several more inches and dig it into the previously dug soil.

Spread organic amendments over the soil and sprinkle on fertilizer if needed, digging these in thoroughly. The settled level of the finished bed should be about 2 inches below the top edge of the border.

1 **Cut 2-by-6 lumber** and 4-by-4 end- and midposts to length. With an electric drill make pilot holes for nails or screws.

2 **Attach boards** for one end, then set that section upright. Nail or screw on boards for the sides, being sure they cover the butt ends of end boards.

3 **Set the fully assembled bed** in place. Before installing it, loosen the soil and dig shallow trenches for recessing the sides.

4 **Use a shovel to dig** and fill to adjust bed's position. Use a level to ensure that the finished bed is properly aligned.

5 **After bed is in place** and leveled, use a sledgehammer to drive a ½-inch steel stake up against each side and end to anchor the bed in place.

6 **For a finished appearance,** cap the bed with 2-by-6 finished lumber. Miter the corners and use an electric drill to make pilot holes for nails or screws.

Compost Bins
THREE TIME-TESTED SYSTEMS

There are numerous references to compost in this book, and for good reason. It's the secret ingredient of many of the best gardens. Using it to amend soil prior to planting or spreading it around established plants as a mulch is one of the best things you can do for plants. Compost is also the most practical way to recycle garden and kitchen waste. You can read more about mulching with compost on pages 300 and 301, and more about making it on pages 393 through 395. But on these pages is how to make three of our favorite compost bins.

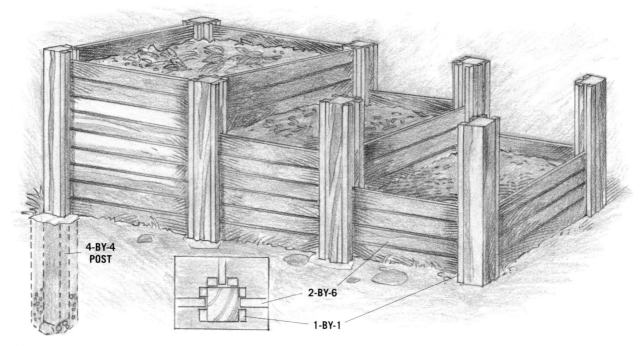

4-BY-4 POST

2-BY-6

1-BY-1

Three-Bin Composter

This classic three-sectioned container allows you to always have "fully cooked" compost on hand. The bin on the left holds new material; the one in the center contains partly decomposed material; and the bin on the right holds finished compost. Material is forked from bin to bin as composting progresses. Side boards are spaced for air penetration and slide out for easy turning and removal of compost.

1 **Dig eight post holes,** about 3 feet deep, in two rows. The holes should be about 3 feet apart. Shovel a couple of inches of gravel in each hole and set a 6-foot-long post in each hole. Use a level to check each post for plumb and brace the posts temporarily. Mix and pour concrete into the holes. Allow a day for the concrete to set.

2 **Have your lumberyard rip-cut pieces of 1-by lumber to 1¼ inches wide.** (Or rip it yourself with a table saw or radial-arm saw.) Cut the pieces so they're long enough to reach from the top of a post to the ground. Attach them to the posts, as shown, by drilling pilot holes and driving 1⅝-inch deck screws. There should be a 1-inch gap between the 1-by pieces.

3 **Cut pieces of 1-by-6** to fit loosely between the posts, so you can easily slide them in and out. Attach a 1-by-2 spacer to the bottoms of the 1-by-6s to give the compost breathing room.

Single Bin with Removable Frame

A compost maker need not be complicated; all you really need is a container with plenty of ventilation and a removable side so that you can easily mix the ingredients with a spading fork.

Construct four frames out of 2-by-2s, all the same size. Cut and

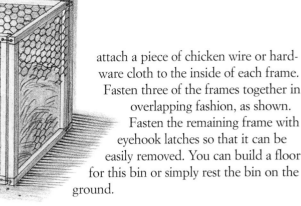

attach a piece of chicken wire or hardware cloth to the inside of each frame. Fasten three of the frames together in overlapping fashion, as shown. Fasten the remaining frame with eyehook latches so that it can be easily removed. You can build a floor for this bin or simply rest the bin on the ground.

Stackable Compost Bins

This design is simply five 36-inch-square boxes without bottoms. Set one box on the ground, perhaps with another box stacked on top, and start the compost pile by filling it. Stack on the other sections as you add more compostable material. You'll have a load of finished compost in about six weeks.

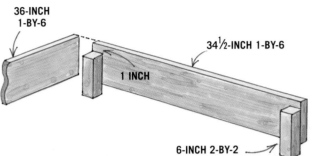

36-INCH 1-BY-6

34½-INCH 1-BY-6

1 INCH

6-INCH 2-BY-2

1 **Saw ten 1-by-6s** into 36-inch lengths and ten to 34½-inch lengths; saw twenty 2-by-2s into 6-inch lengths. Lay each of 34½-inch boards over two 2-by-2s, with one 2-by-2 flush with each end but offset from the top edge by 1 inch. Drive two screws through the 1-by-6s into each 2-by-2.

2 **Place one 34½-inch board** upside down with 2-by-2s extending upward. Place a 36-inch board against one end, flush with the top, bottom, and outside edge. Attach with two woodscrews through the 1-by-6 into the 2-by-2. Add a second 34-inch board at the other end of 36-inch board. Complete the section with other 36-inch board, making a 36-inch square. Repeat the process for each of the remaining four sections. Apply two coats of wood sealer.

Climbing up or skidding down, a gang of kids turns this simple structure into a perpetual-motion machine.

Building a Backyard Gym
TWO KID FAVORITES COMBINE: SANDBOX AND SLIDE

This modest gym takes up little space but provides a variety of activities for young ones. Not only can they slide, climb, and play in the sandbox, but the area below the platform makes an ideal hideout.

At Lowe's, you'll find an array of gym components, including slides (plastic or metal), ladders, rope swings, monkey bars, and net ladders. These parts can be bought separately or in kits that save money and come with complete instructions.

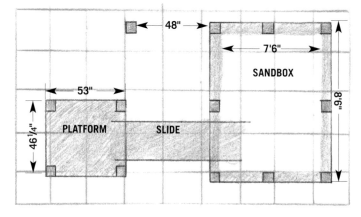

In the plan, each square equals approximately 2 feet, and the dimensions apply to the pictured gym. Your plan will vary if you use a manufactured slide, for instance, or you may customize the gym in other ways. Once your own plan is established, carefully plot out post placement and mark each one's location with a stake before digging.

1 **Determine the positions of all the posts** (see the diagram, facing page). Check that everything is square. Dig post holes at least 3 feet deep. Set the posts in the holes, brace them so that they are plumb, and check again that they are square in relation to each other. Pour concrete into the holes and allow the concrete to set for a couple of days. Use a level to mark and cut the posts to height; you may want to add a decorative post cap or decorate the posts tops yourself with bevel cuts.

2 **To build the platform,** install the front and rear joists at the correct height for the slide you have chosen, using ⅜-by 3½-inch lag screws with washers. Add the remaining joists and attach them with 3-inch deck screws. Cut 2-by-6 deck boards to fit and anchor them with two 3-inch deck screws driven into each joist.

3 **Set one ramp support** against the platform at the desired angle, scribe the angle onto the face of a 4-by-4 ramp support, and cut along this line. Cut a matching angle in the other 4-by-4 ramp support. Cut twelve or so 2-by-6 ramp boards to 46½ inches and attach them from behind with ⅜-by-3½-inch lag screws. Screw the ramp boards to the supports, and then attach three 2-by-6 ramp cleats for easy climbing.

4 **For the sandbox,** attach 1-by-8 sides to each post with three 3-inch deck screws. Miter-cut 2-by-6s for the top trim. Attach the slide to the platform, following the manufacturer's instructions.

5 **Attach 2-by-6** horizontal rails about 3 feet above the platform. Taper-cut 2-by-4s to serve as railing uprights. Space them evenly, about 5 inches apart, and attach them with 3-inch screws.

6 **For the hanging bar,** have a 1-inch galvanized pipe cut to length. Anchor it at the desired height (depending on the size of your children) with a pipe flange at either end.

7 **Sand all the edges** smooth and apply a coat of sealer to all surfaces. Fill the sand box with playground-grade sand.

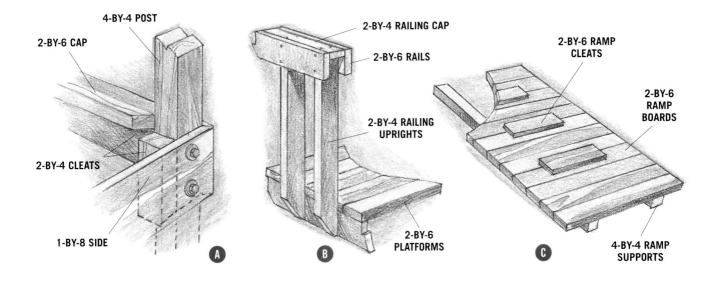

2-BY-6 CAP

4-BY-4 POST

2-BY-4 CLEATS

1-BY-8 SIDE

A

2-BY-4 RAILING CAP

2-BY-6 RAILS

2-BY-4 RAILING UPRIGHTS

2-BY-6 PLATFORMS

B

2-BY-6 RAMP CLEATS

2-BY-6 RAMP BOARDS

4-BY-4 RAMP SUPPORTS

C

LEFT: An antique hand pump turns a simple barrel into an easy-to-manage water garden.
RIGHT: Gently circulating water overflows cast-in-place concrete container and falls into catch basin hidden beneath rocks. 'Regal Mist' deer grass provides shelter, and penstemon an accent.

reflection pool. For the best reflections, find a container with an extra-wide opening at the top and a dark interior. Aluminum and glazed ceramic containers are beautiful because they gleam when wet. Stone and unglazed bowls develop an interesting patina with age.

Experiment to find the best places in your garden for water bowls. Set up a bowl somewhere and check the reflection as you approach it along the path or look down on it from the deck. If it's too cumbersome to keep filling and emptying the bowl as you move it around the garden, test the reflection by simply putting a mirror across the top of the bowl in different locations.

After the bowl is in its final position, use a carpenter's level to check that the rim is perfectly even before filling the bowl with water. If it isn't, adjust it by shimming up the container or moistening the soil underneath it and screwing the container into the ground until the rim is level. Fill the bowl with water only then. When a bowl is full, even a slight tilt will be evident in the water line, and a large container will be too heavy and awkward to reposition.

See pages 262 through 265 for information about more fountains and ponds like these that you can make.

GROWING WATER LILIES

A 30-inch glazed and watertight ceramic pot makes a simple, handsome water feature. Fill it about two-thirds full with water,

then add plants—each in its own pot (set plants on bricks to raise them). The size of the container dictates the number of plants you need. Start with water lilies and water irises. After they're in place, fill the tub with water. To control mosquitoes, add mosquito fish or goldfish. They'll also feed on algae. A 30-inch-diameter tub can accommodate about six fish.

Once a year, without emptying the water, scrub the plant pots and the inside of the tub with a stiff brush. Remove loose algae. Drain when 2 inches of decomposed matter accumulates on the bottom (every few years). Scrub the inside surfaces and divide plants.

TOP LEFT: Frozen in time, sculpted birds are a winter focal point.
BOTTOM LEFT: Terra-cotta beehive and glass hurricane lamps add light and a pleasing touch to a patio.
RIGHT: Tilted containers show off hydrangeas, licorice plant, and petunias.

Artful Touches
INTRIGUING GARDEN ACCESSORIES

A garden's personality comes from more than its plants and structures. Much depends on the gardener's knack for adding finishing touches—a copper lantern, a brightly glazed pot, a collection of folk-art birdhouses. From a teak bench to a lacy hammock or a well-placed boulder, these decorative elements can create a focal point, complement a grouping of foliage and flowers, or simply delight the eye.

The traditional pineapple symbol of welcome in Colonial Williamsburg still appears in many gardens, but you can opt for more obvious and personal invitations. Place a carved stone or painted wood or metal sign at the main entrance to your garden or use a sign to point the way to a more hidden path. Don't be afraid to add a little humor or fun to your garden, either. Just the right personal touch makes the garden your own.

Fasteners on the garden gate, finials on the fence posts, or brass hose guides can add a pleasing touch. Or your details may be less evident, such as the careful selection of just the right flat stones to place at the end of a downspout, the use of a section of old iron fence as a trellis for a pea vine, or the choice of a translucent dragonfly that floats on a copper stake above a perennial bed.

By definition, details are not the focal point of the garden, but they can provide great pleasure when selected in thoughtful counterpoint to a garden's themes. Searching for just the right detail can continue the adventure of gardening long after the main plan is accomplished.

Luckily, garden accessories have never been as plentiful and as varied as they are today. Furniture is available in a variety of styles, umbrellas come fitted with lights or with canvas walls that block the wind, and birdbaths range from rustic to sculptural in form. Resourceful gardeners are turning humble boulders into striking sculptures and adding flair with birdhouses, statuary, outdoor lighting, and painted fences. Giving your garden a distinctive look is as simple as letting your imagination lead the way.

In style, spirit, and materials, you have a tremendous choice of garden décor.

Whatever ornaments you use, they will look best if they're part of a unified and harmonious design based on principles similar to those for interior décor.

In a unified design, plants, structures, and decorative objects all share one style and character, and all work together to convey the garden's mood. No one plant, structure, or object stands out too much; rather, all of the parts work together to establish a sense of unity.

Ornaments in the garden must also be to scale if they are to be blended attractively. A monumental sculpture will tend to overwhelm a small garden, just as a towering tree will. Conversely, a small stone figure will look lost in a spacious setting. Generally, the ornaments you choose should be in proportion to the house, the plantings, and any nearby garden structures. You can give a smaller object or statue more importance by placing it atop a pedestal or other support. This will usually look best if the support is surrounded by foliage or flowers that mask the distance between the ground and the ornament.

LEFT: Cast-stone pineapple finial marks the axis point of clipped boxwood hedges.
RIGHT: Gazing globe reflects golden daylilies.

For the Birds

ATTRACTING THOSE SPECIAL GARDEN VISITORS

To entice birds to your yard, you'll need to provide them with the three elements they need most: food, water, and shelter. These necessities of life will be supplied in part by your selection of plants (see page 58), but you can make your garden irresistible by supplementing the natural resources the plants provide.

Supplemental feeding increases your garden's powers of attraction simply because nature can't usually match the concentrated supply of food that you can provide. Birds often remember where they had a good meal many months before, and they will return to the same spot for more.

Whether birds flock to your feeders seasonally or year-round, catering a banquet for them can be wonderfully satisfying, bringing life and color to the garden.

Most people assume birds need supplemental feeding most in the winter, especially where winter is snowy. But it turns out that bird feeding is less an act of charity than indulgence, like raising a perfect rose.

SORTING OUT BIRDSEED

For vegetarian birds, seeds are nutritious meals, conveniently packaged. The oil in the seeds helps birds maintain body fat to sustain themselves in winter weather and furnishes calories for their constant activity. Seed protein is important for birds' strenuously worked muscles.

Sunflower seeds delight seed-eating birds almost anywhere, but other seeds vary in appeal from one locality to another. To find out what the birds in your neighborhood like best, experiment with small amounts of different seeds to see what disappears first.

TOP LEFT: Satellite-style feeder offers sugar water to hummingbinrds.
TOP LEFT CENTER: Nut feeder captures attention of a tufted titmouse.
TOP RIGHT CENTER: Spring-loaded perches deter raiding squirrels and large birds.
TOP RIGHT: Goldfinch feasts on black oil sunflower seeds.
BOTTOM LEFT: Western scrub jay dines at dressed-up platform feeder.
BOTTOM RIGHT: Concrete feeder includes sculpted versions of visitors.

FEEDER BASICS

Locate feeders at varying levels to attract different birds, close enough to cover to allow escape from predators but not right next to shrubs where cats could lie in wait. Use feeders designed to protect seed from rain, snow, and garden sprinklers. Situate them where the wind won't blow seed away and birds will be protected from winter's chill. Keep suet out of direct sun, especially in warm weather, or it may turn rancid.

You can choose traditional feeders of wood or more modern designs of sleek acrylic or lightweight metal—and all sorts of design styles, from whimsical to high tech. Just keep in mind the kind of food you'll be offering and the species of birds you want to attract (or discourage). Some feeders are designed for certain birds; by offering more than one type of feeder, you're bound to attract a wider clientele.

When selecting a feeder, evaluate how easy it will be to fill and clean it. Keeping feeders clean is imperative for the health of the birds you'll be feeding, so you want feeders that open easily for cleaning.

Platforms The most basic kind of feeder is a platform or tray—a flat surface on which food is scattered. This is a good way to begin, because this type of feeder is quickly noticed by birds and appeals to many species, thus giving you a good snapshot of the birds in your neighborhood.

Platform feeders need frequent cleaning because seed hulls and bird droppings are deposited on the surface. Large birds tend to dominate these feeders, and birds are more vulnerable to predators on an open platform.

Hoppers, tubes, and globes A longtime favorite, the hopper feeder has a storage bin so that seed automatically flows as it is needed. This kind of feeder attracts a varied following of bird species. Some hoppers have separate bins for different kinds of seed, or suet or fruit holders in addition to seed bins.

The tube feeder, usually plastic, is a popular way to dispense black oil sunflower seed or thistle (niger) seed, depending on the size of the holes. Tube feeders attract small birds, such as finches, chickadees, and nuthatches. Don't fill them with mixed birdseed—the

unwanted kinds of seeds will just be discarded. Tube feeders with metal perches and openings are the most durable.

A globe feeder attracts small clinging species, like chickadees and titmice, giving them their own private diner, because larger birds can't get a toehold on the feeder.

Other feeders Acrylic seed feeders that attach to windows with suction cups are fun to watch from indoors, although they usually have limited capacity. Most are best suited to small birds. Window feeders for suet and hummingbird nectar are also available. Some window feeders have one-way backs so that birds can't see through and won't be frightened away by indoor bird-watchers—or you can buy a separate sheet of one-way screening material.

SUET WITH NUTS

BLACK OIL SUNFLOWER SEED

THISTLE (OR NIGER) SEED

SEED MIXTURE

SAFFLOWER SEED

LEFT: A robin and brown-headed cowbird share a drink and a dip in terra-cotta bath with glazed bottom.
RIGHT: English birdbath fountain of cast stone is fitted with a plug-in pump. Water bubbles out from the bowl's top.

THE LURE OF WATER

Water holds a powerful attraction for birds. By offering a place where they can drink and bathe, you'll greatly increase the number of resident and visiting birds in your garden. Birds will happily frolic in a puddle, but a birdbath in the right spot—kept full and clean—is the ultimate backyard watering hole for all kinds of feathered friends.

The vessel itself isn't critical, as long as it's shallow, slopes gently, and has a roughened surface to give birds a good foothold. Even an upside-down garbage can lid or a simple terra-cotta plant saucer can make a fine birdbath.

Birdbaths can be made out of practically anything—concrete, glazed ceramic, metal, plastic, terra-cotta, stone, fiberglass, even wood. Plastic and metal withstand lots of weather variations, but surfaces can be slippery, and some plastic cracks with age. Metal should be rust-resistant.

Provide a gradual transition from shallow to deeper water—no more than 3 inches deep.

A birdbath might deepen from the edges to the center or from one end to the other. A bird won't plunge into water of unknown depth but will instead wade in until it finds a level to its liking. If the bath has steep sides, birds may have difficulty judging the water's depth, so position a flat rock or two in the center.

To allow room for more than one bird at a time, choose a bath that's at least 24 inches in diameter.

To create the necessary traction in slick-bottomed baths, you can add gravel to the bottom, although that does make cleaning more difficult. Lightweight birdbaths need secure pedestals to keep them from being tipped over.

For your own enjoyment, position a birdbath where you can see it from your house or patio. For the birds' sake, choose a location sheltered from strong winds where the bath will get morning sun but midday shade (so the water doesn't get too warm).

NESTING STRUCTURES

Birds can suffer from a housing shortage, especially in developed areas where natural vegetation has been removed and gardens aren't mature enough to provide desirable nesting sites. Even rural farmland may not be hospitable: As woods are cut, brush is cleared, and tree crops are tended, the number of good nesting areas is reduced. Man-made nesting structures can provide a remedy—and lure birds into your garden.

Only cavity-nesting birds (those that nest in holes in trees) use birdhouses; these include chickadees, nuthatches, wrens, bluebirds, and some swallows, among other backyard birds. To accommodate species such as barn swallows, robins, and phoebes, that don't nest in cavities, you can put up nesting shelves. These open-sided structures offer a bonus—they let you observe the activities of your tenants.

All birdhouses aren't created equal, and different kinds of houses appeal to different birds. House dimensions, the size of the entrance hole, and the mounting height need to be tailored to the particular species you're trying to attract. These aren't hard-and-fast rules, but your odds of attracting tenants will be improved if you come close to following them. Remember that even though a birdhouse may be designed for a wren, chickadee, or bluebird, it will be fair game for any bird of similar size.

Nowadays, you'll find an abundance of decorative birdhouses representing a range of materials and artistic fancies. Such houses make fine garden art, but they may not work as living spaces for birds. Most functional nesting boxes are made to handle all sorts of weather, and they're usually unpainted—birds tend to shy away from the cute, colorful houses that attract humans.

Whether you're buying or building, wood is the old standby and has good insulating properties, but you can also find birdhouses made of ceramic, metal, acrylic, PVC pipe, gourd, and other materials. Aluminum purple martin houses are popular and easier to hoist than wooden versions.

In bird real estate, as in the human kind, location is everything. Know the kinds of birds that frequent your locale and tailor your accommodations to their habitat preferences.

Keep birdhouses away from feeders—mealtime bustle makes nesting birds nervous. If you put up more than one nest box, keep houses well separated and out of sight of one another—nesting birds like privacy. Face house entrances away from prevailing weather. To keep nest boxes safe from raccoons and cats, mount them on metal poles. If you want to put a birdhouse in a tree, hang it from a branch that's partially protected from the elements and the watchful eyes of predators.

BIRDHOUSE BASICS

Make sure your houses are installed in plenty of time for the nesting season. Migrant birds start returning in some areas as early as February and look for nest sites soon after they arrive. Also keep the following pointers in mind:

- Remove any perch that came with your birdhouse—it's unnecessary, and house sparrows may use it to heckle birds inside.
- Birdhouses should be made from materials that insulate well, like wood that's at least ¾ inch thick.
- One side or the top should open for cleaning (before the next nesters arrive) and monitoring the nest box, and there should be drain holes on the bottom and ventilation holes high up on the sides.
- Add a textured surface on the inside wall below the entry to allow hatchlings to climb to the hole.
- Angle the roof and extend it well beyond the entry, both to keep rainwater out and to discourage predators. Double-thick entry holes help keep predators, such as raccoons, from reaching in.
- If you hang a birdhouse, keep the chain short to minimize swinging.

VICTORIAN-STYLE NESTING BOX

CEDAR BLUEBIRD HOUSE

BLUEBIRD OR TREE SWALLOW HOUSE

ALUMINUM PURPLE MARTIN CONDO

CEDAR WREN HOUSE

CHAPTER 11

Choosing the Right Plants

When properly placed, plants have a chance
to show off their unique qualities. Perennials
brighten beds and borders. Silvery foliage
soothes strong color combinations.
A redbud brings dappled shade to a patio
and a burst of vibrant color in spring. But
choosing plants is more than just making
sure they're functional and pretty.
They must also be well adapted to the area
where you live and the conditions around
your home—low winter temperatures,
shade, hot and bright summers, or dry
periods. This chapter helps you choose plants
that will not only look good but also grow
well after they're planted.

IN THIS CHAPTER
USDA ZONES • TREES • PALMS
SHRUBS • GROUND COVERS • VINES
PERENNIALS • ANNUALS • ROSES
LAWNS • BULBS • HERBS • GRASSES
VEGETABLES • WILDFLOWERS • NATIVES

Where Plants Grow

IT'S MOSTLY DETERMINED BY LOW TEMPERATURES

Quirky octopus cactus takes the heat in this Tucson, Arizona, garden, but northern winters would surely kill it.

When you're trying to determine if a certain plant will grow in your garden, begin by thinking about your typical winter minimum temperatures. While it's not the only factor that determines a plant's hardiness, it's usually the most crucial. But while winter cold is a key consideration, other climatic features are just as important.

WHAT'S YOUR ZONE?

Gardeners have a variety of plant zone maps they use to determine whether plants are well adapted to the climate in which they live. While none is perfect, the one used most widely is the USDA Plant Hardiness Zone Map. Based on average annual minimum temperatures, it indicates the ability of plants to withstand cold temperatures. The plants described in this chapter include the USDA zones in which they can be grown.

But cold hardiness is not all that influences plant adaptation. Heat, humidity, intensity of summer sunshine, and many other factors also determine how well a plant will grow in a given area. While most garden centers carry only plants that are adapted locally, investigate regional sources (garden books and cooperative extension bulletins, for example) that offer more precise information about how plants perform in your area and the growing conditions under which they grow best.

Some areas are perpetually windy; in others, windy weather is associated only with certain seasons. Wind dries out plants and soil, and it's hard on plants with delicate foliage and flowers. You may be able to compensate by providing windbreaks and extra water and by choosing plants that withstand wind successfully.

Many plants are accustomed to receiving a certain amount of rain at a particular time of year, depending on the conditions prevailing in their native regions. In general, the eastern half of the United States has rainy summers, while summers in the West are dry (though early summer can be wet in the Pacific Northwest). Many plants native to the East require extra summer water if planted in the West; conversely, some western natives will die in eastern gardens, drowning in the summer rain. (For an example, of these differences and how they affect zone recommendations, see "Plant Samplers" on the opposite page.)

Mountains interfere with basic wind patterns and the movement of air masses. Depending on their height and alignment, they either block the wind's progress or direct it. They also cause moist air to rise and cool, so that more rain is deposited on one side of a mountain than on the other. If you live near hills or mountains, your climate may differ from that of a neighbor living on the opposite slope. You may live on the west side of a mountain

Many deciduous shrubs survive ice, snow, and temperatures below –30°F.

USDA ZONES

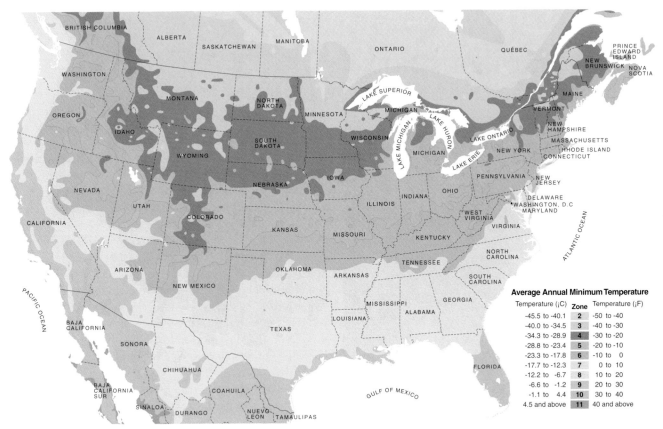

Average Annual Minimum Temperature

Temperature (°C)	Zone	Temperature (°F)
-45.5 to -40.1	2	-50 to -40
-40.0 to -34.5	3	-40 to -30
-34.3 to -28.9	4	-30 to -20
-28.8 to -23.4	5	-20 to -10
-23.3 to -17.8	6	-10 to 0
-17.7 to -12.3	7	0 to 10
-12.2 to -6.7	8	10 to 20
-6.6 to -1.2	9	20 to 30
-1.1 to 4.4	10	30 to 40
4.5 and above	11	40 and above

and receive 40 inches of rain per year, for example, while someone on the eastern side, just 20 miles away, gets only 12 inches.

If you live near the ocean or a large inland body of water, your climate will differ from the climate at the same latitude some miles inland. In Buffalo, New York, for example, the nearby Great Lakes produce extremely snowy winters. In San Francisco, California, the Pacific Ocean makes for cool, overcast summers. You'll need to account for these conditions in choosing plants for such ocean- or lakeside regions.

Microclimates also affect plant adaptation. Around your house or neighborhood are small areas that, due to factors such as elevation, shade from buildings or trees, or reflected light, differ from the general climate of the region you live in. For more details about identifying and exploiting these microclimates around your house on pages 152 and 153.

TIPS

- Choose long-lived plants, such as trees and shrubs, known to be both winter- and summer-hardy in your area.

PLANT SAMPLERS

Descriptions of plants and advice on their care is in the plant sampler sections. Each entry begins with the plant's common name (if it has one), followed by its botanical name in italics. Plants are listed alphabetically by their more standard botanical name. The index, beginning on page 424, includes both common and botanical names. The information varies slightly according to the needs of the particular group of plants. Usually you find a reference to the type of plant, such as "evergreen" (meaning it has green leaves all year) or "deciduous" (meaning leaves fall or the plant dies to the ground in winter).

In all cases, you'll find a recommendation of USDA Zones where the plant grows well, and those zone numbers, from 2 through 11, refer to the map shown above. Because zones 9 through 11 in the mild-winter West are different from those in the South, the recommended zones for that region follow in parenthesis. An example is the zone recommendations for Japanese maple on page 310: "...zones 5–8 (5–11W)."

Improving Your Soil
DEVELOP GOOD SOIL BY ADDING ORGANIC MATTER

A rich brown color, crumbly texture and sponge-like ability to hold moisture are sure signs of good soil. Create it by adding organic matter before planting and by periodically adding an organic mulch.

While you can't do much to change the climate you live in, you can improve the soil in which your plants will grow. In fact, the most important task you can undertake to ensure the health and longevity of your new landscape is to properly prepare the soil before you plant.

AMENDING YOUR SOIL
Most gardens have soil that provides a less-than-ideal environment for many plants. Perhaps the soil is rocky or scraped bare from new construction; perhaps it's too claylike or too sandy to suit the plants you want to grow. While changing a soil's basic texture is very difficult, you can improve its structure—making clay more porous or sand more water retentive—by adding amendments.

The best amendment for soil of any texture is organic matter, the decaying remains of plants and animals. As it decomposes, organic matter releases nutrients that are absorbed by soil-dwelling microorganisms

and bacteria. The combination of these creatures' waste products and their remains, called humus, binds with soil particles. In clay, it forces the tightly packed particles apart, so drainage is improved and the soil is easier for plant roots to penetrate. In sand, it lodges in the large pore spaces and acts as a sponge, slowing draining water so that the soil stays moist longer.

You want organic matter to make up at least 5 percent of your soil. Commonly available organic amendments include compost, well-rotted manure, and soil conditioners (composed of several ingredients). These and others are sold in bags at many full-service nurseries or in bulk (by the cubic yard) at supply centers. Byproducts of local industries, such as rice hulls, cocoa bean hulls, or mushroom compost, may also be available.

Finely ground tree trimmings (wood chips) and sawdust are also used, but because they are high in carbon will use nitrogen as they decompose, taking much-needed nitrogen from the soil. To make sure your plants aren't deprived of the nitrogen they need, add a fast-acting nitrogen source, such as ammonium sulfate, along with the amendment (use about 1 pound for each 1-inch layer of wood chips or sawdust spread over 100 square feet of ground).

Although the particular organic amendment you choose is often decided by what's available at the best

What Is Soil?

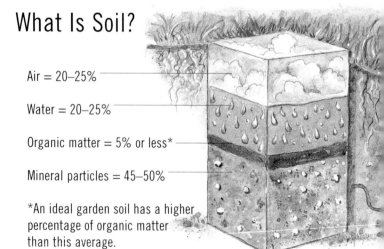

Air = 20–25%

Water = 20–25%

Organic matter = 5% or less*

Mineral particles = 45–50%

*An ideal garden soil has a higher percentage of organic matter than this average.

Adding Organic Soil Amendments

① Spread amendment layer evenly over surface of soil.

② Mix amendments into soil, using either a rotary tiller or spade.

③ Rake tilled soil smooth to break up clods, remove stones, and level surface.

price, many experts favor compost over all other choices.

Amend new beds before you put any plants into the ground. For long-term benefits, choose an amendment that breaks down slowly. Shredded bark and peat moss hold their structure the longest, taking several years to decompose. Include compost in the mix, as well; although it breaks down in just a few months, it bolsters the initial nutrient supply available to soil microorganisms—and these will contribute humus to the soil, increase the soil aeration, or amount of air in the soil, and help protect your new plants from certain diseases.

In beds earmarked for vegetables and annual flowers, amend the soil before each new crop is planted. Compost and well-rotted manure are preferred by most gardeners, because they dramatically improve the soil's structure, making it hospitable to the fine, tiny roots of seedlings. Unamended soil may dry into hard clods that small roots can't penetrate, and plants may grow slowly, be stunted, or die as a result. Manure and compost break down rapidly—manure in a few weeks, compost in several months—so be sure to replenish these amendments before you plant each crop.

To add amendments to unplanted beds, spread the material evenly over the soil, and then work it in by hand using a spade or with a rotary tiller to a depth of about 9 inches. If your soil is mostly clay or sand, spread 4 to 5 inches of amendment over it; after you work this in, the top 9 inches of soil will be about half original soil, half amendment. If the soil is loamy or has been regularly amended each season, add just a

2- to 3-inch layer of amendment; you'll have a 9-inch top layer of about three-quarters original soil, one-quarter amendment.

Permanent or semipermanent plantings of trees, shrubs, or perennials benefit from soil amendments, too, but you need to do the job without damaging plant roots. It's often sufficient simply to spread the amendment over the soil surface as a mulch; earthworms, microorganisms, rain, and irrigation water will all carry it downward over time, gradually improving the soil's top layer. If the plant isn't shallow-rooted (that is, if it doesn't have many roots concentrated near the soil level), you can speed up the improvement process by working the amendment into the top inch or so of soil, using a three-pronged cultivator. In a lawn use a core aerator to pull plugs of soil out. Then refill the holes with compost. (See page 413.)

If your climate is generally mild and winters are rainy, amend the soil around established plantings annually after fall cleanup. In cold-winter regions with spring and summer rainfall, do the job as you begin spring gardening.

TIPS

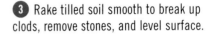

- Amend soil before planting.
- If you suspect your soil is poor ask your cooperative extension service how to get it tested.
- If you need more than a few bags of amendment, buy in bulk.

Solving Soil Problems

DRAINAGE AND ACID-ALKALINE BALANCE ARE COMMON ONES

Improving soil structure is important, but you may also need to correct other problems if your garden is to thrive. Soil may drain poorly, it may be too acid or alkaline, it may suffer from chlorosis or excess salts, or it may be underlain by a cementlike layer of hardpan. This section describes these conditions and offers solutions.

POOR DRAINAGE

Poor drainage causes myriad problems. If water simply stands in the soil's pore spaces rather than draining away, not enough air is available for roots and beneficial soil-dwelling microorganisms, and both may die. The reduced root structure can't adequately support the plants' leaves and stems, and the resulting stress makes plants more susceptible to insect infestation or disease. Below ground, molds develop and the normal balance of fungi is disrupted, so the weakened root structure is more prone to invasion by water-mold fungi.

Fortunately, many drainage problems are easily solved once you become aware of them. Keep your soil's texture in mind. If the poor drainage is due to heavy clay soil, amend it thoroughly with organic matter. You may

also want to mound the amended soil slightly, and then grow plants on the mounds. This can be pleasing to the eye as well as beneficial to plants.

Many gardens drain poorly only in some spots. To pinpoint problem areas, inspect your garden after a heavy rain to see where water is standing. You may be able to simply slope the soil in those areas so that water drains away. If that doesn't do the trick, you may need to dig a sloped trench, install drainage pipe perforated along the top and sides, and refill the trench. When heavy rain comes, water should flow down through the soil, go into the pipe, and be carried away.

If certain areas in your garden are always slightly boggy and don't lend themselves to structural change, your best tactic is to give in graciously. Accept the situation and choose water-loving plants for those locations.

LEFT: Create raised mounds of soil above grade for sensitive plants where drainage is poor.
RIGHT: Dig a 2-foot-deep hole and fill it with water to check drainage. After it drains, refill it. If the second filling drains in an hour or less, drainage is good.

ACID OR ALKALINE SOIL

The pH scale indicates acidity or alkalinity. A soil with a pH number below 7 is acidic, while one with a pH above 7 is alkaline. Garden plants typically grow best in neutral or slightly acidic soil, with a pH 7 or slightly below. Most won't thrive in highly acidic or highly alkaline soil, although a few have adapted to such extremes. Certain nutrients can't be efficiently absorbed by plant roots if the soil pH is too high or too low.

Local climate gives you a clue to the likely soil pH. In high-rainfall areas, soils are often acidic, and you tend to find acid-loving plants like azaleas, rhododendrons, camellias, and blueberries. Alkaline soils, in contrast, are typically found in low-rainfall areas. Many of the plants popular for waterwise gardens—plants that need little water after they are established—do well in alkaline soil. The olive, native to the Mediterranean basin, is one example of a plant that thrives in alkaline soil; oleander (*Nerium oleander*) and pomegranate also perform well.

If you're not sure about your soil's pH, you can test it yourself with a kit that tells whether your soil is alkaline, acidic, or neutral. Some also test for nutrients, such as nitrogen, phosphorus, and potassium.

To raise the pH of your soil, use ground dolomitic limestone. Look for the kind formulated into small pills; it is much easier to handle and apply accurately. The amount needed depends on the soil texture (more is needed for clay than for sandy soil, for example) and other factors.

Common sulfur is the least expensive material available that will lower pH. Ferrous sulfate is sometimes recommended instead. Ferrous sulfate, which also adds iron to the soil, is of the most help to plants that show yellow leaves as well as overall poor health. You can also lower the pH of alkaline soil over time by regularly applying organic amendments, such as compost and manure.

To determine how much of these products to add, follow the advice included with your test results. Also, if your soil is extremely acidic or alkaline and you need to change the level by more than one point on the pH scale, check with a professional.

If amending the soil just isn't feasible, choose only native plants that thrive in the kind of soil that you have. You can also build raised beds and fill them with problem-free, well-amended topsoil.

TOP RIGHT: To use a pH test kit, mix a small amount of soil with the provided solution and compare to color chart.
BOTTOM RIGHT: Most plants grow best in neutral or slightly acidic soils, where pH is just below neutral.

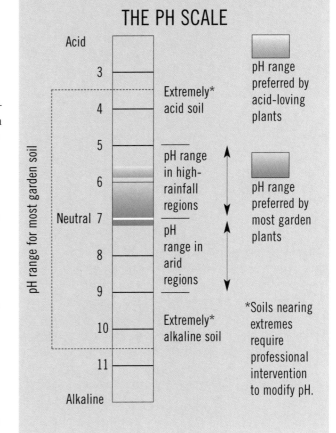

THE PH SCALE

Acid

3

4

5

6

Neutral 7

8

9

10

11

Alkaline

pH range for most garden soil

Extremely* acid soil

pH range in high-rainfall regions

pH range in arid regions

Extremely* alkaline soil

pH range preferred by acid-loving plants

pH range preferred by most garden plants

*Soils nearing extremes require professional intervention to modify pH.

Create an instant colorful border with annuals and perennials. To experiment with color combinations, arrange blooming plants over the planting area while still in their nursery containers.

Creating Planting Beds
GETTING PLANTS STARTED RIGHT

Garden beds are of two basic types. Some are dug directly in the ground, while others are located in frames that sit on the soil surface (see pages 266 and 267).

When making new in-ground beds, some gardeners always raise them, even if just by a few inches, using decorative stones, bricks, or benderboard as an edging. These gardeners will tell you that by time they amend the bed's soil, it's "fluffed up" higher than its original boundaries anyway. The raised soil gives plant roots a few more inches of growing room, and the edging keeps the soil in place.

Other gardeners make mounds as they dig. In this case, the bed's edges are close to the original soil surface, while the center is elevated; plants can grow both on top of the mound and on its sides. You may want to create several mounds, adding large decorative stones for accents so that the mounding forms part of the landscaping. As is true for slightly raised beds, the mounded soil ensures plenty of depth for root growth as well as excellent drainage.

When you're getting ready to dig, the soil should be neither too wet nor too dry: A handful squeezed in your fist should form a ball that crumbles apart, yet still feel moist. If you dig into soil that's too wet, you'll compact it

Removing Seedlings from Containers

Turn cell-packs upside down and press on the bottom to push rootballs out.

Hold rootball around stem with fingers, and turn individual pots over. Tap lightly if necessary.

Use a putty knife to cut through soil and roots of flat-grown plants, and to lift them out.

(making it difficult for air to penetrate throughout the soil after it dries) and destroy beneficial microorganisms. You can't work amendments evenly into wet soil, either. If the soil is too dry, water the area thoroughly.

When you dig, clear most of the debris from the soil. Then use a sharp, square-bladed spade or a spading fork to break up the soil to a spade's depth—typically 8 to 12 inches. Don't turn each spadeful completely over; if you do, roots and debris remaining on the soil surface may form a one-spade-deep barrier that cuts off air and water. Instead, turn the loosened spadefuls of soil only onto their sides. After you've broken up the soil, change to a round-point shovel for mixing in amendments and evening the surface.

If you're digging a large bed, consider using a power-driven rotary tiller. If the soil hasn't been worked in a long time, go over it first with the blades set to a shallow level. Spread amendments over the surface, then rotary till again with the blades set deeper into the soil.

After a bed is ready for planting, don't walk on it. Following this rule will be simpler if you can easily reach all parts of the bed from its borders; if it must be wider, add board paths or stepping-stones to control foot traffic.

Select your plants wisely and plant them correctly, and you'll be on your way to a successful landscape. Many kinds of plants—annuals, vegetables, and some perennials and ground covers—are sold as seedlings in small containers or in flats during the growing season. Larger plants, such as shrubs, trees, and certain vines and perennials, are offered in various ways: as bare-

root plants during the dormant season; in 1-gallon, 5-gallon, or larger containers at any time during the growing season; or with the rootball enclosed in burlap from late fall to early spring. In this section, you'll discover how to choose and plant each type.

SELECTING AND PLANTING SEEDLINGS

Nurseries offer young seedlings of both annuals and perennials, giving you a head start over sowing seeds yourself. Frost-tender summer annuals, such as marigold and petunia, and warm-season vegetables, such as tomatoes and peppers, should be planted after the last spring frost in your area. Hardy annuals, including pansy and calendula, and cool-season vegetables, like lettuce and broccoli, can be set out three to four weeks before the last frost date. They also can be planted in late summer and will provide flowers and vegetables in fall or (in mild climates) in winter. Plant perennials from pots or cell-packs in spring or early fall.

At the nursery, choose stocky plants with good leaf color. It may be tempting to buy plants already in bloom, but younger ones perform better in the long run. Be sure to keep the plants moist until you're ready to set them out. Soil should be moist but not soggy.

TIPS

- Shop for freshest plants. Ask your nursery when new plants are delivered.
- Add compost or fertilizer to soil before planting; mulch afterward.
- Fertilize annuals again six to eight weeks after planting.

Landscape plants, meaning long-lived trees, shrubs, ground covers, and vines, are available bare-root, balled-and-burlapped, and in containers. Here's what you need to know to get each kind off on the right start.

PLANTING CONTAINER PLANTS

Plants in containers are popular and convenient—and in fact, many kinds of shrubs and trees are sold only this way. Such plants offer certain advantages. They are sold throughout the growing season, they are relatively easy to transport, and, unlike bare-root and balled-and-burlapped plants, they don't have to be planted immediately. Furthermore, these plants can be purchased with their flowers, fruit, or autumn leaf color on display, letting you see exactly what you're getting.

When selecting these plants, look for healthy foliage and strong shoots. Check the leaves and stems to be sure no insects are present. Inspecting the root system is more difficult, but healthy roots are vital to successful establishment of container plants. A relatively small plant in a 5-gallon container may not be well rooted, usually because it has recently been moved to the larger container from a 1-gallon pot. If you buy such a plant, keep it growing in the container until it develops a good root system.

A plant that looks large for the size of its pot is often rootbound. Try to avoid such plants, but if you do buy one, loosen its roots before planting.

Container plants are available in several sizes, with 1- and 5-gallon the most common. Which of these you buy depends on how much immediate impact you want the plant to have and on how long you're willing to wait for it to grow. Keep in mind, though, that smaller plants grow

① Dig a rough-sided, bell-shaped planting hole twice as wide as the original rootball. Fill hole twice with water to check drainage (see page 302).

② Set plant and container in the hole; lay a shovel handle across the hole to check rootball height. One-gallon plants should be about ½ inch above grade.

③ Fill the hole with water to soak the surrounding soil, then knock the plant out of its container, loosen tightly knit roots, and set the plant in the hole.

④ Fill the hole halfway with backfill, then water. Finish backfilling; water again. Double-check the elevation of the rootball top.

quickly; within three years of planting, a 1-gallon plant will usually have reached the same size as a 5-gallon one set out at the same time.

PLANTING BALLED-AND-BURLAPPED PLANTS

Some woody plants and evergreens have root systems that won't survive bare-root transplanting or just can't be bare-rooted. Such plants are dug from the growing field with a ball of soil around their roots, and the soil ball is then wrapped in burlap or a synthetic material. These are called balled-and-burlapped (or B-and-B) plants. Some deciduous trees and shrubs (large ones, in particular), evergreen shrubs (such as rhododendrons and azaleas), and conifers are sold this way in fall and early spring.

When buying B-and-B plants, look for healthy foliage and an even branching structure. The covering should be intact so that the roots aren't exposed, and the rootball should feel firm and moist. If you have any doubts about the condition of the rootball, untie the covering and check for healthy roots and a solid, uncracked rootball.

When moving the plant, always support the bottom of the rootball. Don't pick the plant up by the trunk or drop it, which may shatter the rootball. Because a B-and-B plant is usually quite heavy, have the nursery deliver it or have a friend help you load and unload it in a sling of stout canvas. At home, slide the plant onto a piece of plywood and pull it to the planting spot.

PLANTING BARE-ROOT PLANTS

Retail nurseries and mail-order companies sell these plants in late winter and early spring. Many deciduous plants are available including fruit and shade trees, flowering shrubs, roses, grapes, and cane fruits.

Look for strong stems and fresh-looking, well-formed root systems. Avoid plants with slimy roots or dry, withered ones; also reject any that have already leafed out.

Plant as soon as possible after purchase. If bad weather delays planting, plant them in a temporary trench in a shady spot and cover the roots with moist soil. The day before planting, soak the roots overnight in a bucket of water. Just before planting, cut off any damaged roots.

Planting B-and-B Plants

1 **Measure the rootball** from top to bottom. The hole should be a bit shallower than this distance, so that the top of the rootball is about 2 inches above the surrounding soil. Adjust the hole to the proper depth; then set in the plant.

2 **Untie the covering.** Burlap will eventually rot and need not be completely removed (remove synthetic material entirely). If planting in a windy site, drive in a stake beside the rootball. Fill the hole to within 4 inches of the top, and then water.

3 **Continue to fill the hole,** firming the soil as you go. Make a berm of soil to form a watering basin; then water the plant. If you staked the plant, tie it loosely to the stake. As the plant becomes established, keep the soil moist but not soggy.

Planting Bare-Root Plants

1 **Make a firm cone** of soil in the planting hole. Spread the roots over the cone, positioning the plant at the same depth as (or slightly higher than) it was in the growing field. Use a shovel handle or yardstick to check the depth.

2 **Hold the plant** as you firm soil around roots. When backfilling is almost complete, add water to settle soil and eliminate air pockets. If the plant settles too low, raise it to the proper level while the soil is saturated .

3 **Finish filling** the hole with soil; then water again. Don't water again until soil dries. Later, make a ridge of soil around the hole to form a watering basin; water only when the top 2 inches of soil are dry.

Landscaping with Trees

FOR SHADE, BEAUTY, AND PERMANENCE

Whether they are palms rustling near California beaches or sugar maples coloring New England mountain slopes, trees help define the general character of a landscape. They serve so many purposes—both aesthetic and practical—that few homeowners would consider doing without them. Trees offer cooling shade, provide shelter, and establish perspective. They can also frame special vistas and block out unattractive ones. Trees can make dramatic statements, enhance the landscape with sculptural effects, and be the dominant feature of a landscape.

Although trees are often the most expensive individual plants to buy, they can be relied on to give permanence to any landscape. Not surprisingly, they are particularly valued in new housing developments.

Often overlooked is the role trees play in a house's energy conservation. For example, a tree-shaded house will require less air conditioning in summer than an

Grand old sycamores shade this California house through hot summers, but let in sun during winter.

STAKING

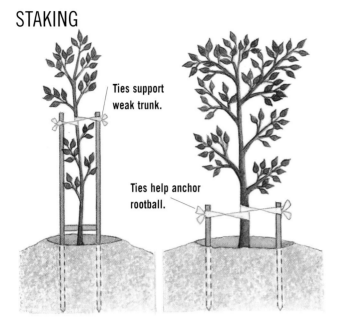

Ties support weak trunk.

Ties help anchor rootball.

Stake a young tree if it is planted in an extremely windy location or if the main trunk is too thin to stay upright. Use wide strips of canvas or rubber that won't bind or cut into the bark, and fasten around the tree and stakes in a figure-8 pattern. Tie at the lowest height at which top remains upright, and remove once no longer necessary.

exposed one. And if deciduous trees, which lose their leaves in winter, are planted around the south side of a house, the warmth of winter sunshine will be able to penetrate the interior of the house, helping to reduce heating and lighting costs.

Your choice of trees will be determined largely by their purpose in your landscape. To block the sun, for example, select only trees that develop widely spreading branches. If you need a screen, look for trees that produce branches on their lower trunks, or combine shrubs or walls with trees that have bare lower trunks. For a focal point, choose a tree that displays flowers or fruits or one with attractive foliage, bark, or a striking winter silhouette.

Trees usually live for decades, even centuries. Each year, new growth springs from a framework of last year's branches to form a gradually enlarging structure. Tree silhouettes vary greatly from one species to another, and a tree's ultimate shape is usually not obvious in young nursery specimens.

Although the range of shapes is enormous, all trees are classified as either deciduous or evergreen. Most deciduous types produce new leaves in spring and retain them throughout the summer. In the fall, leaf color may change from green to warm autumnal tones, and the trees then drop their foliage for the winter, revealing

bare limbs. Broad-leaved evergreens, such as many magnolias, have wide leaves similar to many deciduous trees, but these cover the plant year-round. (Older leaves drop, however.) Needle-leafed evergreens include trees with needlelike foliage—firs, spruces, and pines, for example—and those with leaves that are actually tiny scales, such as cypresses and junipers. Because they keep their foliage in winter, conifers retain their appearance throughout the year, although their colors may change slightly during cold months.

TRAINING

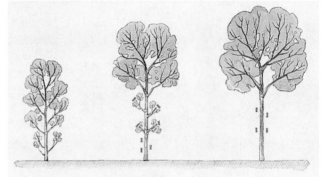

A young tree develops a strong trunk faster if its lower branches are removed gradually. At first, allow lower branches to grow (left). Gradually shorten lower branches as the tree matures (center) and ultimately remove them (right).

STAKING AND TRAINING YOUNG TREES

Avoid trees that are too weak to stand upright on their own. If you have such a tree, cut it back so that a new, stronger shoot is encouraged to develop. In general, staking prolongs the time a tree is too weak to stand on its own. The type of staking depends on the size of the tree. For trees with trunks up to 2 inches thick, place two stakes on either side of the tree, and secure the tree to them at about breast height (as shown at top left). Use three stakes to support trees that have trunks 2 to 4 inches thick.

In a windswept site, a young tree's roots may need anchoring to keep them in firm contact with the soil; use stakes and ties only a foot above ground level for this kind of staking (top right). In both cases, sink stakes at right angles to the prevailing wind. Remove them after about a year or as soon as the tree appears to be self-supporting.

TIPS

- Look for a tree with a strong, slightly tapered trunk.
- Allow lowest branches to remain the first year or two; they'll add strength to the trunk.

A Sampler of Deciduous Shade Trees

Japanese maple (*Acer palmatum*) Red maple (*Acer rubrum*) Eastern redbud (*Cercis canadensis*)

Japanese maple (*Acer palmatum*)
Zones 5–8 (5–11W), 5–25 feet,
depending on variety. Regular water.
Small, graceful tree with diminutive
habit and bright red, orange, or yellow fall color. Excellent for small
spaces and pots. Prefers some shade
in hot summer areas. Many named
varieties are available, including
those with lacy foliage, red or variegated leaves, or weeping habit.

Red maple (*Acer rubrum*) Zones
3–9, 50–70 feet. Regular to moderate
water. Fast growing, upright tree
with lobed leaves that turn glorious
shades of red in fall. 'Armstrong',
'October Glory', and 'Red Sunset'
are popular varieties. Good shade
tree over a wide range of growing
conditions.

**Red horsechestnut (*Aesculus
carnea*)** Zones 4–8, 30–40 feet.
Regular water. Round-headed with
large, dark green leaves that cast
dense shade. Bears 8-inch-long
plumes of soft pink to red flowers

in late spring. Useful as a specimen
tree. Popular varieties include
'Briotii' and 'O'Neill Red'.

Silk tree (*Albizia julibrissen*)
Deciduous, zones 6–9 (6–10W),
30–40 feet. Regular water. Finely
divided, fernlike foliage folds up at
night. Flat-topped, spreading canopy
makes it a good patio tree. Fragrant
fluffy pink flowers bloom from late
spring through summer. Hardier
variety 'Rosea' has darker flowers.

Serviceberry (*Amelanchier*) Zones
3–7, 20–40 feet. Regular to moderate
water. A graceful, airy tree with
drooping clusters of white or
pinkish flowers in early spring followed by edible berries. Foliage
casts light shade and turns fiery
orange to red in autumn. Bark is
smooth and silvery.

River birch (*Betula nigra*) Zones 3–9
(3–11W), 40–80 feet. Ample water.
Bark is pinkish on young trees,
brown and flaky on older ones.

Bright yellow autumn foliage.
Tolerates poor or slow drainage
and hot, humid climates. Good
shade tree, which is usually sold in
multitrunk clumps. 'Heritage' is a
popular variety.

**European white birch (*Betula pen-
dula*)** Zones 2–6 (2–11W), 30–40
feet. Ample water. Upright growth
with weeping side branches on
mature trees. Casts light shade
and has yellow fall foliage. White
bark on trunks and main limbs.
'Dalecarlica' has deeply cut leaves
and a weeping habit, 'Purpurea'
purplish twigs and leaves.

Eastern redbud (*Cercis canadensis*)
Zones 5–9 (5–11W), 25–35 feet.
Regular water. Attractive horizontal
branching and round-headed habit.
Pink to white early-spring flowers,
depending on variety. Yellow
autumn foliage. 'Forest Pansy'
has purple foliage on reddish
branches. An excellent patio or
specimen tree.

Flowering dogwood (*Cornus florida*)   **Hawthorn (*Crataegus viridus* 'Winter King')**   **Ginko (*Ginkgo biloba*)**

Chitalpa (*Chitalpa tashkentensis*)
Zones 6–9 (6–11W), 20–30 feet.
Moderate to little water. Clusters of
frilly pink, white or lavender trumpet-shaped flowers from late spring
to fall. Good in desert areas and as a
patio tree where it casts light shade.
Varieties include 'Morning Cloud'
and 'Pink Dawn'.

Flowering dogwood (*Cornus florida*)
Zones 5–9, 20–30 feet. Regular
water. Horizontal branching with a
flat crown. White or pink flowers in
spring followed by red berries. Red
fall foliage. Many named varieties
offered differing mostly in flower
colors. Best in small spaces and in
partial shade.

Hawthorn (*Crataegus*) Zones 4–8,
15–30 feet, depending on species.
Moderate water. Small trees known
for pretty white, pink, or red flower
clusters in spring and for showy,
small applelike fruit that persist into
winter. Many species are available,
most are multi-trunked and have

thorny branches, and orange to red
or purple autumn foliage. The eastern U.S. native green hawthorn
(*C. viridis*), is one of the best.

Russian olive (*Elaeagnus angustifolia*)
Zones 2–8, 20 feet. Regular to little
water. Fast-growing tree with silvery-
green foliage that tolerates seashore
and dry conditions. Often thorny and
can be pruned into an excellent hedge
or barrier. Fragrant, small greenish
yellow flowers in early summer. Can
be invasive.

Green ash (*Fraxinus pennsylvanica*)
Zones 3–9, 50–60 feet. Regular to
moderate water. Moderately fast-
growing shade trees that tolerate hot
summers and cold winters. Oval to
upright pyramid shape and glossy
divided leaves. Varieties include
'Marshall', 'Patmore', and 'Summit'.
In the West, use *F. oxycarpa*
'Raywood.'

Ginkgo (*Ginkgo biloba*) Zones 4–8
(4–11W), 35–80 feet. Regular to

moderate water. Fan-shaped leaves
turn gold in autumn. Form and
growth rate vary by variety from
narrow and upright to broad and
spreading. Trouble-free for use as a
street tree or in lawns. Good varieties include 'Autumn Gold',
'Fairmount', and 'Princeton Sentry'.

**Thornless honeylocust (*Gleditsia
triacanthos inermis*)** Zones 4–9,
35–70 feet. Regular to moderate
water. Grows quickly upright with
spreading branches. Bright green,
fernlike leaves cast light shade.
Tolerates a wide range of growing
conditions. Good varieties include
'Shademaster' and 'Skyline'.

**Goldenrain tree (*Koelreuteria
paniculata*)** Zones 5–9, 30–40 feet.
Regular to moderate water. Open
branching pattern and 15-inch-long
divided leaves provide light shade.
Very showy, fragrant yellow flower
clusters appear in early to midsummer followed by lantern-like fruits
that mature from red to buff or

A Sampler of Deciduous Shade Trees

Crape myrtle (*Lagerstroemia indica*)

Flowering crabapple (*Malus*)

Tupelo (*Nyssa sylvatica*)

brown. Chinese flame tree (*K. bipinnata*) is showier but hardy to zone 8.

Crape myrtle (*Lagerstroemia indica*) Zones 6–9, 20 feet, but variable. Moderate water. Habit varies from shrublike to tree depending on variety and pruning. All have dark green leaves, which often turn orange or red in fall, and clusters of crinkled, crepe-papery white, pink to purple, or red flowers. Smooth bark is attractively mottled.

Sweet gum (*Liquidambar styraciflua*) Zones 5–9 (5–11W), 60–75 feet. Regular to moderate water. Narrow and erect when young, becoming more rounded with age. Lobed leaves turn purple, yellow, or red in autumn. Attractive branching pattern and bristly fruits add winter interest. Plant where shallow roots won't interfere with lawn or raise pavement. 'Cherokee' doesn't make seedpods; 'Burgundy' and 'Palo Alto' offer bright red fall color.

Tulip tree (*Liriodendron tulipifera*) Zones 4–9 (4–11W), 60–90 feet. Regular water. Straight, columnar trunk with spreading branches that form a tall pyramidal head. Tuliplike flowers appear in the branches in late spring. Glossy green leaves turn bright yellow in autumn. Useful as a shade tree.

Saucer magnolia (*Magnolia soulangiana*) Zones 4–9, 20–30 feet. Regular water. White, pink, or purple goblet-shaped flowers bloom before the large leaves unfurl in early spring. Late frosts frequently damage buds and blossoms. Choose late-blooming varieties such as 'Alexandrina' or 'Lennei'. Star magnolia (*Magnolia stellata*) has spreading star-shaped flowers and grows up to 20 feet tall. Many varieties.

Flowering crabapple (*Malus*) Zones 4–8, 6–40 feet, depending on variety. Regular to moderate water. White, pink, or red spring flowers and persistent red to yellow fruit make these

valuable for specimens, lawn trees, and street trees. Hundred of varieties exist, some with reddish foliage. Growth habit ranges from weeping to round-headed to column-shaped. Choose disease-tolerant varieties, such as 'Donald Wyman', 'Profusion', or 'Snowdrift'. Sargent's crabapple and Japanese flowering crabapple are natural dwarfs, growing only about 8 to 10 feet tall and spreading up to twice as wide.

Tupelo (*Nyssa sylvatica*) Zones 4–9, 30–50 feet. Regular to moderate water. Pyramid-shaped when young, becoming spreading and dramatic with age. Glossy dark green leaves turn yellow and orange, and then bright red in autumn. Birds enjoy the small fruits. Excellent specimen or shade tree.

Chinese pistache (*Pistacia chinensis*) Zones 7–9 (7–10W), 30–60 feet. Moderate water. This broadly rounded tree has good

Flowering cherry (*Prunus serrulata*)   **Pin oak (*Quercus palustris*)**   **Little-leaf linden (*Tilia cordata*)**

orange to red fall color even in mild climates and tolerates a wide range of soils, including alkaline types. Very drought tolerant after it's established. A reliable choice for street, lawn, or patio plantings.

London plane tree (*Platanus acerifolia*) Zones 5–8 (5–11W), 30–70 feet. Regular water. Smooth, cream-colored bark on upper trunk and limbs look handsome in winter. Grows somewhat slowly and tolerates city conditions, but drops messy fruits. Disease-resistant varieties include 'Columbia' and 'Liberty'.

Flowering cherry (*Prunus*) Zones 4–9 (varies with species), 10–50 feet (also variable). Regular to moderate water. Prized for glorious spring blossoms; many also have attractive horizontal branching habits and mahogany red bark. Many kinds are available. Popular flowering cherries include sargent (*P. sargentii*), Japanese (*P. serrulata*), and Higan (*P. subhirtella*).

Purpleleaf plum (*Prunus cerasifera*) Zones 5–9, 15–30 feet. Regular water. Popular for its purplish red leaves and small light pink to white flowers. Form varies from upright to round to spreading. Common varieties include the dwarf 'Purple Pony' and dark-leaved 'Krauter Vesuvius'.

Flowering pear (*Pyrus calleryana*) Zones 5–8 (5–9W), 25–50 feet. Regular water. Horizontal branching, white flowers in early spring and glossy green leaves that turn purplish red in fall combine to make this a popular street and shade tree. Best varieties include 'Aristocrat' and 'Chanticleer'. Evergreen pear (*P. kawakamii*) has drooping branches and white flowers in late winter. It grows to 12–30 feet in zones 9–11.

White oak (*Quercus alba*) Zones 3–9, 50–80 feet. Regular water. Pyramidal in youth, then grows slowly to a round-headed or widely spreading form. Leaves with

rounded lobes turn red to brown in autumn. Other popular landscape oaks include scarlet oak (*Q. coccinea*), which has bright autumn foliage, pyramid-shaped pin oak (*Q. palustris*), and narrow-leaved willow oak (*Q. phellos*).

Golden trumpet tree (*Tabebuia chrysotricha*) Deciduous to partly evergreen, zones 9–11, 25–30 feet. Regular water. Showy, trumpet-shaped flowers in clusters appear in spring. Use as patio or specimen trees. Pink trumpet tree (*T. heterophylla*) blooms later and is sometimes grown as a large shrub.

Little-leaf linden (*Tilia cordata*) Zones 3–8, 60–70 feet. Regular water. A popular shade and street tree that forms a dense pyramid of deep-green leaves. Fragrant white flowers in early summer. Very tolerant of city conditions; takes pruning to form large hedges. Improved varieties include 'Chancellor', 'Glenleven', and 'Greenspire'.

A Sampler of Evergreen Trees

Deodar cedar (*Cedrus deodara*)   Leyland cypress (*Cupressocyparis leyandii*)   Southern magnolia (*Magnolia grandiflora*)

White fir (*Abies concolor*) Needled evergreen, zones 4–8 (4–11W), 50–70 feet. Regular to moderate water. Symmetrical, pyramid-shaped tree with 2-inch-long, bluish green needles. Good large screen. Best in cold-winter climates.

Deodar cedar (*Cedrus deodara*) Needled evergreen, zones 7–8 (7–11W), 40–80 feet. Moderate water. Fast growing with a spread of up to 40 feet at ground level. Graceful pyramid shape with soft texture. Needles may be green or have a blue, gray, or yellow cast. Suitable for hot, humid climates.

Citrus (*Citrus*) Broadleaf evergreen, zones 9–11, 6–20 feet, depending on variety. Regular water; full sun. One of the finest ornamental edibles for mild climates. Fragrant, white spring flowers are followed by colorful, edible fruit that hangs among deep green foliage. Choose from oranges, mandarins, grapefruit, lemons, and limes, depending on local adaptation.

Useful small trees for the patio. Excellent in containers. Can be clipped as hedges. Plant in well-drained soil and fertilize regularly.

Leyland cypress (*Cupressocyparis leylandii*) Needled evergreen, zones 6–10, 60–70 feet. Regular to moderate water. Very fast growing with an upright form. Useful for hedges and screens. Varieties offer differing foliage colors.

Arizona cypress (*Cupressus arizonica*) Needled evergreen, zones 7–9 (7–11W), 40–50 feet. Moderate water. Broad pyramid shape with green to blue-gray or silvery scale-like leaves. Thrives in hot, dry climates. Useful windbreak and screen. Italian cypress (*C. sempervirens*) grows very tall and narrow and is useful in formal gardens.

Gum (*Eucalyptus*) Broadleaf evergreen, zones 9–11 (varies with species), 20–80 feet (also varies). Regular to little water. Fast-growing

trees for hot climates. Many are drought tolerant. Species with attractive flowers include coral gum (*E. torquata*) and red-flowering gum (*E. ficifolia*). Many have aromatic ornamental foliage, including silver dollar tree (*E. cinerea* and *E. polyanthemos*) and willow-leaf peppermint (*E. nicholii*).

American holly (*Ilex opaca*) Broadleaf evergreen, zones 5–9 (5–10W), 40–50 feet. Regular water. Slow-growing pyramid to round-headed tree has dark green leaves with spiny margins. Bright red berries appear on female trees and persist into winter. Use as a specimen tree or large screen. Hundreds of varieties exist, some with variegated leaves or yellow berries.

Southern magnolia (*Magnolia grandiflora*) Broadleaf evergreen, zones 6–9 (6–11W), 60–80 feet. Regular water. Large, glossy, green leaves and huge, fragrant, white flowers offer year-round beauty. A

Colorado blue spruce (*Picea pungens glauca*)   **Eastern white pine (*Pinus strobus*)**   **Japanese black pine (*Pinus thunbergiana*)**

popular tree that varies in shape from spreading to upright, depending on variety. Its shallow roots and dense shade may defeat lawn grasses.

Colorado blue spruce (*Picea pungens glauca*) Needled evergreen, zones 3–7 (3–9W), 30–60 feet. Regular to moderate water. Stiff, horizontal branches spread up to 20 feet across at the base forming a broad pyramid. Needle color ranges from dark green to steely blue. The related dwarf Alberta spruce (*Picea glauca* 'Conica') has softer, greener needles and grows to only 7 feet.

Eastern white pine (*Pinus strobus*) Needled evergreen, zones 3–7, 50–100 feet. Regular water. Fast growing with 4-inch-long, blue-green needles and horizontal branching that give the tree a soft texture. Becomes broad and irregular with age. Intolerant of salt and air pollution. Some varieties remain dwarf or have weeping habits.

Japanese black pine (*Pinus thunbergiana*) Needled evergreen, zones 5–8 (5–10W), 20–40 feet or more. Regular to little water. Spreading branches form a broad, conical tree that becomes irregular and picturesque with age, often with a leaning trunk. Dwarf varieties are suitable for containers and bonsai. Tolerates seacoast conditions.

Southern live oak (*Quercus virginiana*) Broadleaf evergreen to partly deciduous, zones 8–10, 40–80 feet. Regular water. Heavy-limbed crown may spread twice as wide as the tree's height. Commonly used as a street tree and in parks and estates throughout the South. Sheds old leaves in spring before new leaves emerge. Tolerates salt spray.

Coast redwood (*Sequoia sempervirens*) Needled evergreen, zones 7–9 (7–11W), 60–90 feet or more. Regular water. Forms a symmetrical pyramid of soft-looking, feathery foliage. Straight trunk with

horizontal limbs that curve up at tips with drooping branchlets.

English yew (*Taxus baccata*) Needled evergreen, zones 6–7, 25–40 feet. Regular to moderate water. Soft, flat, dark green needles on wide-spreading branches that form a low crown. Tolerates shade and pruning; useful for hedges and screens. Other common yews include cold-hardy Japanese yew (*T. cuspidata*) and many hybrids. Tall varieties include 'Capitata' and 'Fastigiata'.

Eastern arborvitae (*Thuja occidentalis*) Needled evergreen, zones 3–7, 40–60 feet. Regular to moderate water. Feathery juvenile foliage becomes flat and scale-like, forming sprays with age. Trees have scaly brown bark and an open, rounded canopy. Use for large screens or prune into tall hedges. Western red cedar (*T. plicata*) grows taller and retains its dark green color through winter.

Palms

SIGNATURE TREES OF THE TROPICS AND NEAR-TROPICS

Compared to tall, single-tunked palms, clump-forming European fan palm is low and graceful.

Although palms aren't suited to every landscape, they can shine in the right setting. They can line an avenue, shade a deck, serve as accents, or form an evergreen backdrop. Some, such as lady palm and European fan palm, stay shrublike for many years, thriving under taller trees as well as in entryway plantings, mixed borders, and courtyards.

Palms are especially effective near swimming pools, because they don't drop leaves and their roots don't buckle paving. Fronds, whether fanlike or feathery, reflect beautifully in the water, as do the curved trunks of the Senegal date palm, which creates an atmosphere reminiscent of the tropics.

When carefully placed, palms produce dramatic effects. Night lighting, in particular, shows off their stateliness and spectacular leaves. You can backlight them, shine spotlights up on them from below, or direct lights to silhouette them against a pale wall. Sunlight also casts evocative shadow patterns onto walls.

So many different palms exist for the garden, it's hard to keep up with them all. The modest array here represents tried-and-true choices for just about anywhere palms can be grown.

Palms are one of the few plants that can be easily transplanted as large, mature specimens. Even tall plants can be dug up, placed in relatively small boxes, and transplanted with almost certain success. Planting specimen palms still usually requires heavy equipment and expert help, but it's one of the best ways of instantly converting an empty garden into a tropical paradise. Although expensive, it may be worthwhile around a large new pool or patio or as a stunning focal point in the front yard.

Few plants reflect the mild climates of Florida and California the way that palm trees do. But except for cabbage palm in the Southeast and a few others, most of the palms you see aren't native to the United States. Canary Island date palm, for example, comes from the islands off northern Africa.

Surprisingly, many palms are cold-hardy. Windmill palm, one of the hardiest, tolerates temperatures as cold as 5°F. Many others can withstand brief periods of freezing temperatures, making them good candidates not only for Florida and southern California, but also in milder areas of the deep South and northern California.

KING PALM

TIPS

- The best time for planting palms is in late spring or early summer.
- When removing dead leaves, cut just above leaf base and take care to not cut into the trunk.

A Sampler of Palm Trees

King palm (*Archontophoenix cunninghamiana*)   Canary Island date palm (*Phoenix canariensis*)   Windmill palm (*Trachycarpus fortunei*)

King palm (*Archontophoenix cunninghamiana*) Zones 10–11, 20–40 feet but may grow up to 60 feet in mildest climates. Eight- to 10-foot dark-green leaves; purple flowers. Fast growing. Takes some frost when established. Grows best out of wind; needs abundant water. Not suited to desert landscapes.

Bamboo palm (*Chamaedorea*) Zones 10–11, 5–10-feet. Several species, most with clumping, bamboolike growth. All grow slowly. Frost tender; needs ample water and a shady spot.

European (or Mediterranean) fan palm (*Chamaerops humilis*) Zones 8–11, 20 feet. Blue-green or silver-green leaves make this palm outstanding. Forms clumps if not pruned; endures baking sun and drought. Grows slowly. Leaf stems carry sharp spines.

Chinese fan palm (*Livistona chinensis*) Zones 9–11, 15 feet. Strongly drooping, dark green leaf tips resem-

ble a fountain. Remains trunkless for years; develops a broad head. Makes a fine patio palm when sheltered from the wind and hot afternoon sun.

Canary Island date palm (*Phoenix canariensis*) Zones 9–11, 60 feet. Big, heavy-trunked plant with gracefully arching fronds that form crown up to 50 feet wide. Young plants do well in pots.

Senegal date palm (*Phoenix reclinata*) Zones 9–11, 20–30 feet. Clumps grow from offshoots, with several curving trunks. Remove offshoots for single-trunked tree.

Pygmy date palm (*Phoenix roebelenii*) Zones 9–11, 6–30 feet. Soft, feathery leaves; stem grows slowly to 6 feet. Wind resistant but tender and suffers below 28°F. Silver date palm (*P. sylvestris*) is similar in shape, but hardier and grows to 30 feet.

Lady palm (*Rhapis*) Zones 9–11, 5–18 feet. Multiple stems bear dark

green, glossy leaves. Makes good screen but grows slowly. Requires little pruning. *R. excelsa* grows 5–12 feet; *R. humilis* to 18 feet. Prefers rich, moist soil and protection from sun and drying winds.

Cabbage palm (*Sabal palmetto*) Zones 9–11, 90 feet. Single-trunked and slow growing. Dense, round head formed by leaves 5–8 feet across. Tolerates wind, salt spray, and sand; ideal for coastal gardens in the South.

Queen palm (*Syagrus romanzoffianum*) Zones 9–11, 30–50 feet. Lush plumelike leaves 10–15 feet long. Grows quickly. Shelter from winds; needs abundant water and fertilizer.

Windmill palm (*Trachycarpus fortunei*) Zones 7–11, 30 feet. Stiff, upright shape; hairy brown trunk. Reaches 30 feet in warm-winter areas; shorter elsewhere. Looks best in groups of three or more. Fronds get shabby in wind and must be trimmed.

Deciduous azaleas and rhododendrons combine with spring-flowering bulbs in a showstopping Pacific Northwest garden.

Shrubs

THE GARDEN'S BACKBONE

Just as a large sofa or bulky upholstered chair fills a room, shrubs can add weight and substance to a landscape. They are permanent fixtures, altering traffic flow and framing views. Planted near a wall, they create attractive backdrops; set close together, they form a living fence.

Like trees, shrubs are either deciduous or evergreen. They grow in a variety of rounded, tapered, or fountain-like shapes. Many shrubs, with their showy flowers, fruits, or autumn foliage, offer seasonal appeal. Some, however, have decorative foliage throughout the growing season. Others, such as daphnes, lilacs, and viburnums, are valued primarily for their fragrance.

With hundreds of shrubs available, one key to success is to select only ones that suit your landscape's climate, soil conditions, available sunlight, and water resources. Azaleas and rhododendrons, for example, thrive in semishade and in acidic soil that both retains moisture and drains excess water fast.

MAINTAINING SHRUBS

Prune most flowering shrubs after their blossoms fade. For example, prune a May-flowering lilac in June. Other deciduous shrubs bring forth long stems each year from the base and benefit from an early-spring removal of some older stems. Most evergreens, however, can be pruned at any time of year; exceptions are bloomers, such as camellias, and pines such as mugho pine.

Shrubs that grow directly from the base, sending up stems from the roots, can withstand severe pruning. These include glossy abelia (*Abelia grandiflora*), barberry (*Berberis*), forsythia, oleander, mock orange (*Philadelphus coronarius*), spiraea, and common privet (*Ligustrum vulgare*). Cut all growth back to the ground before new spring growth begins. If the treatment is successful, the plant will usually achieve its normal height within several years. If you're not sure whether a shrub can take such drastic pruning, carry out a four-year program. Do no cutting the first year—just water and fertilize well to make the plant as healthy as possible. Over the next three years, remove about a third of the oldest stems in spring, pruning them back to the ground just before growth begins.

SALVAGING OLD SHRUBS

If you move into a house with a landscape filled with overgrown shrubs, try a salvage operation before just taking them out.

Transform a large shrub with upright main stems (left) into a multi-trunked small tree (right) by removing side stems.

If a shrub has one or more upright stems and a framework of side branches, convert it to a small tree by removing the lower side branches. Remove side stems on the trunk up to the point where you want the branching to begin, and then thin those that remain to form an uncluttered crown. If the shrub has several good stems, you can leave them all.

If you don't want to transform an overgrown shrub into a tree, you can lower it. Each year, cut about a third of the highest branches back halfway. Most will sprout new growth at the lower level. After you've achieved a smaller shrub with vigorous young growth, thin out any weak, badly placed, or crowding shoots.

TIPS

- Maintain best flowering of most shrubs by selectively removing a few of the oldest stems each year.
- Prune spring-flowering shrubs after flowers fade.
- Prune summer-flowering shrubs in early spring.

Pruning a Mock Orange

1 **Shrub** is overcrowded and needs thinning to remain vigorous.

2 **Cut out the oldest** and weakest stems at their base, in spring after flowering.

3 **Remove least productive** canes every year, and the shrub will produce more flowers and be more attractive.

A Sampler of Shrubs

Japanese barberry (*Berberis thunbergii*) **Butterfly bush (*Buddleia davidii*)** **Lemon bottlebrush (*Callistemon citrinus*)**

Glossy abelia (*Abelia grandiflora*)
Evergreen to semievergreen, zones
6–9 (6–11W), 5–10 feet. Regular
water; full sun to light shade. White
to light pink flowers in summer and
fall. Small, oval, glossy leaves cover
graceful, arching branches. Use in
borders and near houses.

Japanese aucuba (*Aucuba japonica*)
Evergreen, zones 7–10 (7–11W),
6–10 feet. Moderate water; shade to
deep shade. Grown for its attractive
green or variegated gold leaves and
ability to grow in deep shade, even
under trees. Useful in patio tubs or
indoors. Popular varieties include
'Gold Dust' and 'Mr. Goldstrike'.

**Japanese barberry (*Berberis
thunbergii*)** Deciduous, zones 4–8
(4–11W), 4–6 feet. Regular to moderate water; full sun to light shade.
Slender arching branches are
covered with sharp spines and small
oval leaves that turn yellow to crimson in autumn. Red berries persist
into winter. Many varieties with

differing leaf colors and growth
habits, such as golden 'Aurea' and
bronze 'Crimson Pygmy'.

Butterfly bush (*Buddleia davidii*)
Deciduous, zones 5–9 (5–11W),
5–15 feet. Regular to moderate
water; full sun to light shade. Spiky
6- to 12-inch clusters of small, fragrant, white to purple blooms
appear in midsummer, attracting
many butterflies. Vigorous with wil-
lowlike leaves. Many varieties,
including 'Nanho Blue'.

**Japanese boxwood (*Buxus micro-
phylla*)** Evergreen, zones 5–8
(5–11W), 15–20 feet. Regular water;
sun or shade. One of the most widely
planted shrubs for formal hedges and
edging. Dense foliage of lustrous,
dark green oval leaves. Many varieties and hybrids, including 'Winter
Gem' and 'Winter Green'.

**Lemon bottlebrush (*Callistemon citri-
nus*)** Evergreen, zones 8–11, 10–15
feet. Regular to moderate water; full

sun. Massive shrub that can be
trained into a small tree. Bright red, 6-
inch-long brushy flower spikes attract
hummingbirds throughout the year.

Scotch heather (*Calluna vulgaris*)
Evergreen, zones 4–7, 1–3 feet.
Regular water; full sun. Spikes of
purple, pink, or white flowers from
summer to fall. Foliage color is
mostly dark green, but can vary.
Many varieties turn reddish in cold
winters. Prefers cool, moist summers
and acidic soils. Can be used as a
ground cover.

Camellia (*Camellia japonica*)
Evergreen, zones 7–9 (7–11W), 6–12
feet. Regular to moderate water;
light shade. Large showy blooms
from autumn through spring and
leathery, deep green glossy foliage
make these very popular shrubs for
patio containers and display gardens.
Many species and thousands of varieties with differing flowers and
growth habits. Especially useful are
the sasanqua camellias (*C. sasanqua*),

California lilac (*Ceanothus* 'Julia Phelps')   Flowering quince (*Chaenomeles*)   Redtwig dogwood (*Cornus stolonifera*)

upright or spreading plants that bloom from fall into winter. Flower form and color are similar to Japanese camellia. Use low-growing varieties as ground covers.

Natal plum (*Carissa grandiflora*)
Evergreen, zones 10–11, 2–7 feet. Little to regular water; full sun to light shade. Dependable flowering shrub for mild-winter areas. Star-shaped, fragrant, white flowers bloom nearly year-round, followed by edible bright red fruit. Can be used as a low hedge or ground cover. Varieties differ in habit and height.

Bluebeard (*Caryopteris clandonensis*)
Deciduous, zones 4–9 (4–11W), 2–3 feet. Moderate water; full sun. Compact, mounding shrub with a long season of summer flower color in various shades of blue that lasts into fall. Some varieties have grayish leaves. Fine as a small border or mixed with perennials. Keep plant compact by cutting back to 6 inches in winter.

California lilac (*Ceanothus*)
Evergreen, zones 9–11W, 1–12 feet or more, depending on species. Little or no water; full sun. Mostly California natives valued for their blue or white spring flowers, dark green foliage, and ability to thrive with little water. Excellent for slopes and native gardens. Many species and varieties to choose from. Shrubby types include 'Dark Star', (6 feet high, rich blue flowers), 'Joyce Coulter', (5 feet high), and 'Julia Phelps' (7 feet tall, dark indigo flowers).

Flowering quince (*Chaenomeles*)
Deciduous, zones 5–9, 3–10 feet. Regular water; full sun. One of the earliest shrubs to bloom in spring. Mostly red or pink flowers are borne on upright, thorny bare branches. Can be clipped as a hedge. Many varieties to choose from, varying in height and flower color.

Rockrose (*Cistus*)
Evergreen, zones 9–11W, 2–5 feet, depending on species. Moderate to little water; full sun. Carefree shrubs that bloom profusely in spring and require little water. Tolerant of seaside and desert conditions.

Redtwig dogwood (*Cornus stolonifera*)
Deciduous, zones 2–7 (2–9W), 7–9 feet. Regular water; full sun to light shade. Vigorous, bright-red stems contrast in winter with snowy landscape. Creamy white flowers in summer, bluish fruits, red autumn foliage. Good for informal borders and barriers. Some varieties have yellow stems or variegated leaves.

Smoke tree (*Cotinus coggygria*)
Deciduous, zones 4–10 (4–11W), 12–15 feet, sometimes taller. Moderate to little water; full sun. Tiny green flower clusters transform into purplish puffs, giving the whole plant the look of a cloud of smoke in summer, hence the name. Most varieties also have purplish foliage that turns yellow, orange, or red in fall. Usually grown as a tall, upright shrub but can be kept small.

A Sampler of Shrubs

Parney cotoneaster (*Cotoneaster lacteus*)   **Slender deutzia (*Deutzia gracilis*)**   **Heath (*Erica cinerea*)**

Parney cotoneaster (*Cotoneaster lacteus*) Evergreen, zones 7–9 (7–11W), 8–10 feet. Moderate water; full sun. Graceful, arching habit with dark green leaves, clusters of white flowers, and persistent red fruit. Use as informal hedge or screen.

Winter daphne (*Daphne odora*) Evergreen, zones 7–9 (7–11W), 4–8 feet. Regular to moderate water; full sun with midday shade. Prized for fragrant clusters of pink to red flowers and neat growth habit. Narrow glossy leaves. 'Aureo-marginata' has gold-edged foliage.

Slender deutzia (*Deutzia gracilis*) Deciduous, zones 5–8, 2–5 feet high. Moderate water; full sun to light shade. Showy, fragrant, white flowers on gracefully arching stems in spring. Can be clipped as a hedge. 'Nikko' bears double flowers on a dwarf shrub and has burgundy fall color.

Hop bush (*Dodonaea viscosa*) Evergreen, zones 8–11W, 12–15 feet.

Regular to little water; full sun to light shade. Rugged, dependable shrub with a billowy habit. Most widely grown are purple-leaved varieties, such 'Purpurea', which need full sun to retain color. Can get by with little water. Very useful screen or accent.

Silverberry (*Elaeagnus pungens*) Evergreen, zones 6–9 (6–11W), 6–15 feet. Regular to little water; full sun to part shade. Gray-green leaves with wavy edges on spiny branches. A tough shrub useful in containers and hot, windy areas. Several varieties have variegated foliage.

Heath (*Erica*) Evergreen, zones 4–8, 6–18 inches. Consistent, careful watering; full sun except in hottest climates. Small, needlelike leaves and abundant small flowers throughout the year, depending on species. Many hardy, low-growing varieties good for borders and ground covers. Larger species range in size up to 10 feet or more.

Escallonia (*Escallonia exoniensis*) Evergreen, zones 7–11W, 5–10 feet. Regular water; full sun in cool summer climates, part shade in warmer areas. A colorful shrub particularly useful in coastal areas of the western United States. Rosy pink flowers appear among glossy, dark green leaves almost year-round. Can be trimmed as a hedge. 'Frades' and other varieties have more compact habit, rarely growing over 6 feet tall.

Evergreen euonymus (*Euonymus japonicus*) Evergreen, zones 7–9, 8–10 feet. Regular to moderate water; full sun. Very glossy, small, leathery, deep-green leaves. Upright growth often pruned into formal hedges. Many varieties with varying leaf color and size, such as 'Microphylla Variegata' and 'Silver King'. Evergreen wintercreeper (*E. fortunei*), has a creeping or low shrubby habit and is hardy to zone 4. Many varieties with yellow or white variegated leaves like

Burning bush (*Euonymus alatus*) **Forsythia (*Forsythia intermedia*)** **Oakleaf hydrangea (*Hydrangea quercifolia*)**

'Emerald 'n' Gold'. Some turn purplish in fall and winter.

Burning bush (*Euonymus alatus*)
Deciduous, zones 4–8, 15–20 feet. Regular to moderate water; full sun. Stems have corky ridges, leaves turn flaming red in autumn. Growth is upright with horizontal branching. Use for hedges, screens, near houses. 'Compacta' stays smaller and more compact. Can be invasive.

Forsythia (*Forsythia intermedia*)
Deciduous, zones 4–8 (4–9W), 7–10 feet. Regular to moderate water; full sun. Fountain-shaped shrubs are covered in bright yellow flowers in early spring. Use in informal borders and for screens. Many varieties with varying hardiness. Most cold-hardy include 'Meadowlark' and 'Northern Sun'.

Gardenia (*Gardenia augusta*)
Evergreen, zones 8–10 (8–11W), 1–8 feet. Regular water; light shade. White, intensely fragrant flowers

contrast with shiny, dark green leaves. Grow in pots on patios and in greenhouses. Popular varieties include 'Golden Magic' and 'Mystery'.

Witch hazel (*Hamamelis intermedia*) Deciduous, zones 5–9, 12–15 feet or more. Regular water; sun to light shade. Delicate, wonderfully fragrant, yellow to sometimes reddish flowers appear on bare branches in early spring. Leaves turn gold in fall. Looks best with a dark green background. Plant where the fragrance can be enjoyed.

Tropical hibiscus (*Hibiscus rosa-sinensis*) Evergreen, zones 10–11, 4–15 feet. Regular water; full sun. Showy trumpet-shaped flowers in all colors produced throughout the summer. Glossy dark green foliage in all seasons. Use for hedge or accent planting. Hundreds of varieties. Deciduous rose of sharon (*H. syriacus*), has smaller flowers and is hardy in zones 5–8.

Garden hydrangea (*Hydrangea macrophylla*) Deciduous, zones 6–9 (6–11W), 4–12 feet. Regular water; full sun to part shade. Large, thick, coarsely toothed leaves and rounded growth habit. Round or flat-topped pink, blue, or white flower clusters up to 12 inches across. Many varieties available for containers and landscape accents. Oakleaf hydrangea (*H. quercifolia*) grows 3–6 feet and has very attractive oaklike foliage that turns crimson in fall.

Chinese holly (*Ilex cornuta*)
Evergreen, zones 7–9 (7–11W), 6–20 feet, depending on variety. Regular to moderate water; full sun to partial shade. Leathery, glossy leaves with spines and large, bright red, long-lasting berries. Varieties that produce berries without a male pollinator include 'Burfordii', 'Dazzler', and 'Dwarf Burford'. Many varieties and hybrids with differing growth habits, hardiness, berry abundance and color, and foliage. Popular hybrids include

A Sampler of Shrubs

Winterberry (*Ilex verticillata*)   Juniper (*Juniperus chinensis*)   Wax leaf privet (*Ligustrum japonicum*)

'Foster's', 'Nellie R. Stevens', and the Meserve varieties 'Blue Girl' and 'China Girl' (zone 4). Other important species lack spiny leaves, including Japanese holly (*I. crenata),* yaupon holly (*I. vomitoria),* and inkberry (*I. glabra).*

Winterberry (*Ilex verticillata*)
Deciduous, zones 3–9 (3–8W), 6–10 feet. Regular water; full sun to light shade. Large crops of very showy red berries persist on female plants into winter and are prized by birds. Tidy oval, dark green leaves. Plant one male for every few female shrubs and choose varieties adapted to your climate. Good female varieties include 'Afterglow', 'Sparkleberry', and 'Winter Red'.

Juniper (*Juniperus*)
Needled evergreen, zones 2–9 (2–11W), 1–10 feet. Regular to moderate water; full sun to light shade. Widely used and diverse group of landscape shrubs prized for ground covers, borders, planting near houses, and large groupings. Many kinds with varying foliage color and growth habits. Popular shrubs include Chinese juniper (*J. chinensis*) 'Hetzii', 'Old Gold', 'Pfitzerana', and 'Sea Green'; Rocky Mountain juniper (*J. scopulorum*) 'Wichita Blue'; and singleseed juniper (*J. squamata* 'Blue Star'). Columnar types grow strongly upright and narrow and include *J. chinensis* 'Spartan' and *J. virginiana* 'Skyrocket'.

Wax leaf privet (*Ligustrum japonicum*)
Evergreen, zones 7–9 (7–11W), 10–12 feet. Regular water; full sun to partial shade. Compact growth and thick, glossy leaves make it useful for hedges and screens. Deciduous privets (*L. amurense, L. ovalifolium,* and *L. vulgare*) are popular hedge plants in zones 4–7. Growth habit and leaf color varies. Vicary golden privet (*L. vicaryi*) has yellow leaves.

Chinese fringe flower (*Loropetalum chinense*)
Evergreen, zones 7–9 (7–11W), 5–10 feet. Regular water; full sun to part shade. Neat, compact habit with arching tiered branches. Delicate-looking white flower clusters appear throughout bloom season, especially in spring. Variety 'Rubrum' has pink bloom and purplish leaves.

Oregon grape (*Mahonia aquifolium*)
Evergreen, zones 5–9 (5–11W), 3–6 feet. Moderate to little water; full sun to shade. Long, spiny-toothed leaves turn purplish to bronze in winter. Clusters of flowers mature to edible blue-black fruit. 'Compacta' grows to only 2 feet but spreads into broad colonies.

Wax myrtle (*Myrica cerifera*)
Evergreen, zones 8–11, 10–20 feet. Regular water; full sun to partial shade. Glossy, dark green leaves are aromatic. Waxy grayish white berries used for candle-making. Deciduous bayberry (*M. pensylvanica*) is similar, but hardy in zones 3–6. Use for hedges and screens.

Mock orange (*Philadelphus virginalis*)   **Japanese pieris (*Pieris japonica*)**   **Mugho pine (*Pinus mugo mugo*)**

Heavenly bamboo (*Nandina domestica*) Evergreen, zones 6–9, 6–8 feet. Regular to moderate water; sun or shade. Lightly branched, canelike stems and fine-textured, lacy foliage. Excellent leaf color from pink to red when young, soft green changing to bronze and purple in fall. White flower clusters in early summer. Dwarf purple 'Nana', variety grows only 1–2 feet tall.

Oleander (*Nerium oleander*) Evergreen, zones 8–11, 8–12 feet. Regular to little water; full sun. Narrow, 4- to 12-inch-long, dark green leathery leaves are attractive year-round. White, yellow, pink, and red flower clusters from spring into autumn. Many varieties. Use for screens, borders, and containers. All plant parts are poisonous.

Sweet olive (*Osmanthus fragrans*) Evergreen, zones 9–10, 6–10 feet. Regular to moderate water; full sun to partial shade. Tiny white, powerfully fragrant flowers in spring to

early summer. Glossy, oval- to holly-shaped 4-inch leaves. Forms a broad, dense hedge or screen with pruning. Also good in containers.

Mock orange (*Philadelphus virginalis*) Deciduous, zones 4–8, 6–8 feet. Regular to moderate water; partial shade in hottest areas. White, very fragrant flowers in early summer. Fountain-shaped growth habit with medium green foliage. Use as background plant or choose smaller variety, such as 'Dwarf Snowflake', for foundation plantings.

Red tip photinia (*Photinia fraseri*) Evergreen, zones 7–9 (7–11W), 10–15 feet. Regular to moderate water; full sun. Five-inch, bright bronzy oval new leaves mature to dark green. Valuable as a foliage plant and for clusters of white flowers.

Japanese pieris (*Pieris japonica*) Evergreen, zones 5–8, 9–10 feet. Regular water; shade, especially in

afternoon. Whorls of leathery narrowly oval leaves are red to bronze when new, maturing to green. Drooping clusters of white to nearly red flowers emerge from red buds. Use in containers and shady woodland landscapes. Varieties include 'Mountain Fire' and 'Temple Bells'.

Mugho pine (*Pinus mugo mugo*) Needled evergreen, zones 3–7 (3–11W), 4–20 feet, depending on variety. Regular water; full sun. Stiff, 1- to 2-inch-long needles densely cover the branches of this slow-growing mounded shrub. Use in containers and borders.

Tobira (*Pittosporum tobira*) Evergreen, zones 8–11, 10–15 feet. Regular to moderate water; full sun to partial shade. Leathery, narrowly elliptical, shiny dark green leaves form dense whorls. White flower clusters in spring. Tolerant of seacoast conditions. 'Variegata' has gray-green white-edged foliage.

A Sampler of Shrubs

Cinquefoil (*Potentilla fruticosa*)

Firethorn (*Pyracantha*)

Rhododendron (*Rhododendron* 'PJM')

Yew pine (*Podocarpus macrophyllus maki*) Evergreen, zones 8–11, 6–8 feet. Regular to moderate water; full sun or partial shade. Grows slowly into a dense, upright form. Narrow 3-inch leaves. Excellent in containers and for low hedges.

Cinquefoil (*Potentilla fruticosa*) Deciduous, zones 2–6 (2–9W), 1–4 feet. Moderate water; afternoon shade in hot climates. Yellow, pink, or white single or double roselike flowers bloom from late spring to early fall. Trouble-free shrub with divided, green to gray-green leaves. Popular varieties include 'Abbotswood' (white), 'Floppy Disc' (double pink), and 'Goldfinger' (yellow).

English laurel (*Prunus laurocerasus*) Evergreen, zones 7–10, 5–12 feet but often taller. Regular water; full sun to partial shade (in hot summer areas). Very useful hedge, screen, or background plant with clusters of small, fra-grant, white flowers and rich green leaves. Bears small black fruit. Dwarf varieties, like 'Nana' and 'Otto Luyken', are most widely grown.

Firethorn (*Pyracantha*) Evergreen, zones 5–9 (5–11W), 2–15 feet (both zone and height depending on variety). Moderate water; full sun. Grown for its spring flowers and bright red, orange, or yellow fruits and its deep green foliage. All forms have small, glossy leaves, and most have needlelike thorns. Cold hardiness varies, so ask before pur-chase. Grow or train against a wall or fence.

Indian hawthorn (*Rhaphiolepis indica*) Evergreen, zones 8–9 (8–11W), 3–5 feet. Regular to mod-erate water; full sun to light shade. Clusters of small, white to pinkish blooms from early winter to late spring. New growth is bronzy red, maturing to glossy dark green. Grow as a low hedge.

Azaleas and rhododendrons (*Rhododendron*) Evergreen and deciduous, zones 3–9 (3–10W), 2–15 feet. Regular water, filtered shade. A large and variable group that includes more than 800 species and countless varieties. All are grown for their spectacular clusters of blooms in white and many shades of pink, red, purple, yellow, salmon, and peach. Evergreen types have thick, glossy leaves. Deciduous species often have red to orange fall foliage. Nearly all demand moist, acidic soil. Grow in containers, near houses, and in woodland landscapes.

Roses (*Rosa*) Many roses make excellent landscape shrubs which are useful in borders, and as edgings and hedges. For more information, see page 354.

Rosemary (*Rosmarinus officinalis*) Evergreen, zones 7–8 (7–11W), 2–8 feet. Moderate to little water; full sun. Dense, needlelike, 1-inch-long highly aromatic leaves are useful in

Spiraea (*Spiraea vanhouttei*)   **Lilac (*Syringa vulgaris*)**   **Viburnum (*Viburnum plicatum tomentosum*)**

cooking. Trailing to upright growth habit varies with variety. Useful as a ground cover, low border, or hedge, depending upon variety.

Sweet box (*Sarcococca*) Evergreen, zones 6–8 (6–11W), 1–5 feet. Regular to moderate water; partial to full shade. Prized for handsome dark green, waxy foliage and tiny but very fragrant white flowers that bloom in late winter to early spring. Slow growing and needs rich soil. Useful in shaded areas under trees and house overhangs, or on the north side of your house.

Spiraea (*Spiraea*) Deciduous, zones 3–8 (3–10W), 1–6 feet, variable. Regular to moderate water; full sun to light shade. Popular for clusters of white, pink, or reddish flowers in spring, summer, or sometimes, fall. Bridal wreath forms have long, arching branches covered with white flowers. Mounding types form lower, rounded shrubs. Most common species are *S. japonica* and *S. van-*

houttei. Popular varieties include 'Anthony Waterer', 'Froebel', 'Goldflame', 'Little Princess', and 'Shirobana'.

Lilac (*Syringa*) Deciduous, zones 3–9, 6–20 feet. Regular water; light shade in hot areas. Multistemmed shrubs cherished for showy, usually fragrant flowers clustered at stem tips in early to late spring. French lilac (*S. vulgaris*) has hundreds of varieties differing in cold- and heat-hardiness, flower color, and bloom period. Lilacs with smaller leaves and more compact habits include meyer (*S. meyeri*), littleleaf lilac (*S. microphylla*), and 'Miss Kim' (*S. patula*). In mild winter regions of California, choose Descanso hybrids.

Viburnum (*Viburnum*) Deciduous and evergreen; zones and height variable. Regular water; full sun or part shade. A large and diverse group, including more than 150 evergreen and deciduous species and countless varieties. All bear

clustered, sometimes fragrant flowers often followed by brightly colored fruits. Some have attractive horizontal branching or colorful autumn foliage. Useful near patios and as screens, hedges, and specimens. Popular deciduous species include Burkwood viburnum (*V. burkwoodii*), Korean spice viburnum (*V. carlesii*), Japanese snowball viburnum (*V. plicatum*), doublefile viburnum (*V. plicatum tomentosum*), tea viburnum (*V. setigerum*), and dwarf cranberry (*V. trilobum* 'Compactum'). Evergreen species include sweet viburnum (*V. awabukii*), leatherleaf (*V. rhytidophyllum*), and laurustinus (*V. tinus*).

Xylosma (*Xylosma congestum*) Evergreen, zones 8–11, 10–12 feet tall. Moderate water; full sun to partial shade. Attractive foliage shrub with bronzy-green new growth that gradually turns shiny light green. Arching natural habit makes an attractive screen; can be clipped as a hedge.

Vines

FOR TRELLISES, ARBORS, AND WALLS

Cloaking brick walls of Ivy League colleges or low stone walls around a house, Boston ivy is noted for brilliant fall colors.

Whether framing an entry, draping a pillar, or just rambling along the ground, vines can bring dazzling color to any landscape. The fast growth of many vines makes them ideal plants for temporary screens and permanent structures alike. They can cover a large area, such as a fence, or weave a delicate tracery on a wall in a small garden. Trailing vines can be planted in hanging containers on a small deck or balcony to shield the space from view. And because many vines are evergreen or feature variegated foliage and decorative fruits, they can provide year-round interest.

Not only do vines have a softening effect on walls, but they also greatly improve the appearance of other landscape structures, such as arbors, gazebos, and spa surrounds. Keep in mind that plants climbing on

vertical supports need less frequent pruning than those that are trained horizontally. The latter tend to bloom more heavily, however, because their stems are more exposed to sunlight.

Other than the fact that all have long, pliable stems (when they're young, in any case), vines differ greatly. They may be evergreen, semievergreen, or deciduous; they may be modest in size or rampant enough to engulf trees or scale high walls. Many grow well in ordinary garden soil with an annual springtime application of fertilizer, but a few need rich, well-amended soil and regular fertilizer throughout the growing season. Some require ample moisture, but a great many perform well with little additional water after they're established.

Climate preferences vary, too, so always match your climate zone (see page 299) to the vines you want to grow. Many are native to semitropical parts of the world and cannot tolerate cold temperatures. Some remain lush and green all year where winters are mild, but drop their foliage or die to the ground during winter in colder areas. Some vines are well behaved in temperate zones but grow with great vigor in warmer regions, overwhelming their support (and possibly the entire garden).

HOW VINES CLIMB

The particular way each vine climbs determines what sort of support you'll need to provide.

Twining vines As these vines grow, their stems twist and spiral. They coil too tightly to grasp large supports, such as posts, so give them something slender, such as cord or wire. To cover a wood fence with fiveleaf akebia (*Akebia quinata*), for example, string wire up and down the fence through eyescrews attached at 6- to 8-inch intervals.

Vines with tendrils or coiling leafstalks Tendrils are specialized plant parts growing from the end of a leaf or the side of a stem. They grow straight until they contact something they can grasp—wire or cord, another stem on the same vine, another plant—then reflexively contract into a spiral and wrap around the support. Vines that climb by tendrils include grape and sweet pea (*Lathyrus odoratus*).

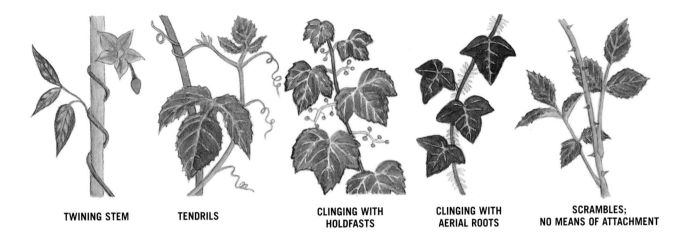

TWINING STEM   **TENDRILS**   **CLINGING WITH HOLDFASTS**   **CLINGING WITH AERIAL ROOTS**   **SCRAMBLES; NO MEANS OF ATTACHMENT**

Clinging vines If any kind of vine gives the whole group a bad name, it's the clinging sort, which adhere tenaciously to almost any flat surface. Specialized structures let them grip their supports. Some, such as trumpet vine (*Campsis*) and ivy (*Hedera*), have stems equipped with aerial rootlets; others, like Boston ivy (*Parthenocissus tricuspidata*), have tendrils that terminate in tiny suction cup-like disks called *holdfasts.*

Scrambling vines Some vines have no means of attachment; they climb only in the sense that their stems will proceed on a vertical path if secured to a support. Left to themselves, they'll simply mound, sprawl, and scramble, although a few, such as climbing roses and most bougainvilleas, can hook their thorns through adjacent shrubs or trees. To provide appropriate attachment, many gardeners cover flat surfaces with eyescrews and wire, and tieing the plant in place at various points as it grows.

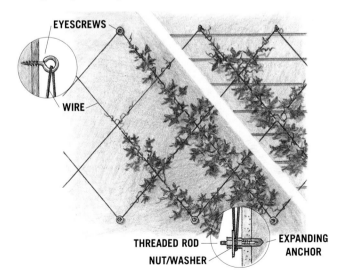

EYESCREWS

WIRE

THREADED ROD — EXPANDING ANCHOR

NUT/WASHER

Attach wires for training vines to wooden walls with eyescrews or to masonry walls with expanding anchor bolts.

TRAINING AND PRUNING VINES

Until a vine gets a firm hold on its support, you may need to tie it in place with twine or plastic garden tape. For heavy vines, you can use thin rope or strips of canvas or rubber. For clinging vines, you might tack plastic mesh over the stems until you see the aerial rootlets or holdfast discs adhering. After the stems of twining and scrambling vines gain some length, you can weave them through any openwork support, such as a trellis or wire fence.

To encourage bushy growth on young vines, pinch out the stems' terminal buds. If you want just a few vertical stems, though (for a tracery of growth around a column, for example), don't pinch. Instead, remove all but one or two long stems at the base.

After a vine is established, you'll need to prune it periodically to keep it in bounds or to clear out unwanted or dead growth. The job is often done late in the dormant season, just before new growth begins, although you may want to wait to prune early-spring bloomers, such as Carolina jessamine (*Gelsemium sempervirens*), until flowering has finished. Some vines are so vigorous they can pruned at any time.

Vines that twine, climb by tendrils or coiling leafstalks, or scramble are pruned by similar methods. Start by removing dead and damaged growth. If the stems are so tangled that can you can't tell what to remove, snip through the mat of stems here and there; later on, remove those that have died. If the problem is really severe—if the vine is such a haystack of growth that you can hardly find the support, for example—make heading cuts low enough to reduce the vine's length by half. After you've done that, you can usually untangle the stems and make thinning cuts to remove unwanted growth at ground level. As a last resort, cut the entire vine to the ground in late winter or early spring and start training it all over again.

A Sampler of Vines

Bougainvillea　　　　**Deciduous clematis (*Clematis*)**　　　　**Carolina jessamine (*Gelsemium sempervirens*)**

Fiveleaf akebia (*Akebia quinata*)
Semievergreen or deciduous, zones 5–11. Regular water; full sun or partial shade. A lush yet delicate clinging vine. Foliage is fine textured, with each leaf consisting of five small leaflets radiating from the stem tip. The small, purplish spring flowers are a bonus (some say they smell like chocolate). The vine ascends rapidly to 15–30 feet, providing shade and hiding less-than-lovely structures from view.

Bougainvillea Evergreen, zones 10–11 and protected parts of zone 9. Regular to moderate water; full sun or partial shade. Gloriously colorful, shrubby vine. Summer blooms in bright shades of purple, red, orange, yellow, and white. Must be tied to a strong support. Vigorous varieties will grow to over 15 feet. Train to a warm, sunny wall or sturdy fence. Can also be used as sprawling ground cover.

Madame Galen trumpet creeper (*Campsis tagliabuana* 'Madame Galen') Deciduous, zones 5–11. Regular to moderate water; full sun to light shade. Vigorous climber attaches to almost anything with rootlets. Can reach 30 feet tall, so it's suitable for large areas. Large salmon red flowers are held in loose clusters. Prune to keep compact and within bounds.

Evergreen clematis (*Clematis armandii*) Evergreen, zones 8–11. Regular water; leaves in sun, roots in shade. Clusters of shiny white, fragrant flowers in spring. Attractive, deep green, divided foliage. Clings with tendrils, climbing to 20 feet. Perfect growing on eaves, trellis, fences, or a small arbor.

Deciduous clematis (*Clematis*)
Zones 4–10. Regular water; leaves in sun, roots in shade. Huge family of lovely, delicate vines. Large-flowered hybrids, most widely grown, bloom in every shade but green. Clings by

tendrils, climbing about 10 feet. Grow on trellis or allow to sprawl among other plants.

Creeping fig (*Ficus pumila*)
Evergreen, zones 8–11. Regular water; full sun, partial shade. Clean-looking, leathery foliage clings to anything it touches. Will damage any surface other than stone or masonry.

Carolina jessamine (*Gelsemium sempervirens*) Evergreen, zones 7–9 (7–11W). Regular water; full sun to partial shade. Cascading clusters of fragrant yellow flowers in late winter to early spring. Glossy green foliage on a shrubby, twining plant to 20 feet. Lovely trained to sunny trellis, arbor, fence, or wall.

Hardenbergia violacea 'Happy Wanderer' Evergreen, zones 9–11W. Moderate water; full sun to partial shade. Long clusters of sweet pea-shaped, small pinkish purple flowers late winter to early spring. Handsome divided leaves. Twines to 10

Hardenbergia violacea 'Happy Wanderer'   **Chinese jasmine (Jasminum polyanthum)**   **Honeysuckle (Lonicera sempervirens)**

feet. Ideal for trellis and in large containers. Cut back after bloom.

Chinese jasmine (*Jasminum polyanthum*) Evergreen (partially deciduous in cold areas), zones 8–11. Regular water; partial shade. Intensely fragrant white and pink flowers in spring. Bright green leaves on twining stems up to 20 feet high. Best in hot summer areas. Grow on a trellis, arbor, fence, or sprawling over a bank.

Honeysuckle (*Lonicera*) Evergreen and deciduous, zones vary by species. Regular water; full sun to partial shade. Tubular, white to yellow fragrant flowers mostly in summer. Rampant twining plants that can grow over 40 feet, depending on species. Two popular ones are goldflame honeysuckle (*L. heckrottii*) and trumpet honeysuckle (*L. sempervirens*). Avoid the seriously invasive *L. japonica.* All need sturdy supports, lots of room, and heavy pruning. Can be used as ground covers.

Boston ivy (*Parthenocissus tricuspidata*) Deciduous, zones 4–9 (4–11W). Regular water; full sun, partial shade, or full shade. Glossy, green, lobed leaves up to 8 inches wide turn to red, yellow, or orange in autumn. Stems cling tightly with rootlike disks called holdfasts, quickly climbing as high as 30 to 50 feet. For a finer-textured, smaller-leafed vine than the species, look for *P. t.* 'Veitchii'. Its foliage is burgundy red when new, and many believe it has the finest fall color. Virginia creeper (*P. quinquefolia*) is similar but has more open growth.

Silver lace vine (*Polygonum aubertii*) Deciduous to partially evergreen, zones 5–9 (5–11W). Regular water; full sun to partial shade. Silver white, frothy flower clusters spring to fall. Attractive glossy foliage on twining stems. Incredibly vigorous; can grow 100 feet in a year. Grow only on sturdy fences or a large arbor. Prune heavily to maintain size.

Climbing roses (*Rosa*) The diverse rose family includes many climbing roses. For more information, see page 354 in this chapter.

Star jasmine (*Trachelospermum jasminoides*) Evergreen, zones 8–10 (8–11W). Regular water; full sun to partial shade. White, sweetly scented summer flowers born in showy clusters. Lustrous dark green leaves. Twines to 20 feet high. Excellent on fences, trellises, and posts. Widely used ground cover.

Chinese wisteria (*Wisteria sinensis*) Deciduous, zones 5–10 (5–11W). Regular water; full sun. Grape-like clusters of fragrant violet-blue flowers in spring. Twining branches eventually become woody and classically gnarled. Can climb over 50 feet. Needs annual pruning for best flowering. Delicate divided leaves cast wonderful shade when grown on an arbor. Also beautiful when trained to eaves. Japanese wisteria (*W. floribunda*) is more cold hardy but less showy.

Combining ground covers that bloom at the same time produces a tapestry of color. Here red sunrose (*Helianthemum*) is accented by purple salvia, pink phlox, and yellow yarrow.

Ground Covers
THE GARDEN'S CARPET

You can count on these dependable plants to blanket the soil with dense foliage, adding beauty and variety to the landscape and suppressing weeds at the same time. Lawn is the best-known ground cover, unsurpassed as a surface to walk or play on. But in areas where foot traffic is infrequent and in sites inhospitable to lawn grasses—in the shade under large trees or on hot, steep banks, for example—ground covers offer the neatness and uniformity of a lawn for considerably less maintenance and water. These plants run the gamut of foliage textures and colors, and many are noted for their bright flowers. Height varies, too. Some are low mats, while others are knee-high or even taller. Some spread by underground runners or root on top of the ground as they grow. Others form clumps and should be planted close together to produce a tight cover. For a sampler of ground cover choices, see pages 334 to 337.

PLANTING GROUND COVERS

Where winters are cold, plant in spring to give the ground cover an entire season to become established before it must face the rigors of winter. In areas with hot, dry summers and mild winters, plant in fall; winter rains will help get the plants off to a good start.

Although ground covers are tough, they'll grow and spread more quickly if you prepare the planting area carefully. Dig out weeds, amend the soil with compost or well-rotted manure, and broadcast a complete fertilizer over the area (follow package directions for amounts). Work in amendments and fertilizer with a shovel or tiller, and then rake to level the soil. (Shrubby plants from gallon containers are an exception to this advice; these are often planted in the native soil, without amendments.)

Plant ground covers in a diamond pattern. This spreads the plants efficiently and gives any size of bed a neat, natural look as plants fill in.

SPACING GROUND COVER PLANTS

How much spacing to allow between ground cover plants depends on the particular plant and, to some extent, on how quickly you want the growth to cover the area.

When planting ground covers from smaller pots or flats, set them in holes just deep enough for and slightly wider than the rootball. To plant from gallon containers, dig a hole that tapers outward at the bottom to accommodate the loosened roots, leaving a plateau of undisturbed soil in the middle. The rootball rests on the plateau; the crown of each plant should remain slightly above the soil surface to prevent rot. (See page 306).

Set plants in staggered rows when planting a slope where erosion is likely. Make an individual terrace for each plant and create a basin or low spot behind each one to catch water.

After planting, water the plants thoroughly. As they become established over the next several weeks, water every few days, keeping the soil moist but not soggy. To help maintain soil moisture and prevent weed seeds from growing, spread a 2- to 4-inch-thick layer of an organic mulch between the young plants, taking care not to cover the plants' crowns.

Rejuvenate perennial ground covers by digging them up, dividing each clump, and then replanting strongest divisions.

CARING FOR GROUND COVERS

Most ground covers require little attention beyond routine watering, mulching, fertilizing, and grooming. In many cases, maintenance takes very little time—especially when compared to the hours typically invested in lawn care. However, in a few cases, some special attention pays dividends.

Weeding One of the primary reasons for planting a ground cover is to eliminate weeding. However, don't expect to be freed from the job starting from the moment the plants are in the ground; until they fill in, some weeding is usually necessary. Getting rid of weeds before they set seed is important to prevent ongoing problems. Replenishing the mulch as it decomposes also aids in weed control. For serious weed problems, you may be able to use a selective herbicide—one that will kill weeds but not your ground cover. For more on herbicides, see page 423.

Edging If not restricted, many ground covers will advance beyond the area you've allotted for them. If the plant spreads by underground stems or by rooting along stems that touch the soil, you may be able to control it by trimming the planting's edges with pruning or hedge shears or with a mower.

Pruning Some shrubby ground covers that are normally low-growing may occasionally send out upright stems that spoil the evenness of the planting; cotoneaster is one example. When you see such stems, cut them back to their point of origin or to a horizontally growing stem within the foliage mass.

Ground Cover Maintenance

Shearing

Use hedge shears to cut back vigorous ground covers. This removes old growth and keeps plants from spreading out of bounds. Rake up the clippings and compost them.

Mowing

A mower set to cut 3 to 4 inches high makes fast work of trimming large expanses of spreading ground covers, such as English ivy, creeping St. Johnswort, and periwinkle.

A Sampler of Ground Covers

Carpet bugle (*Ajuga reptans* 'Variegata')   Bearberry (*Arctostaphylos uva-ursi*)   Heather (*Calluna vulgaris*)

Bishop's weed (*Aegopodium podagraria*) Zones 4–9 (4–11W), 12 inches. Moderate water; sun or shade. Divided leaves are light green or variegated with white edges. Spreads vigorously—often too vigorously—by underground stems, forming dense colonies. Contain with underground barriers of wood or concrete.

Carpet bugle (*Ajuga reptans*) Evergreen perennial, zones 3–9 (3–11W), 4–5 inches. Regular water; full sun or partial shade. Spreads quickly by runners covered in dark green leaves and 4- to 5-inch blue-flower spikes in spring to early summer. Will invade lawns unless contained. Some varieties have purplish or yellow variegated leaves or white flowers.

Bearberry (*Arctostaphylos uva-ursi*) Evergreen shrub, zones 2–6 (2–11W), 6–12 inches. Moderate water; sun or light shade. Small, glossy oval leaves on spreading stems that root as they grow. Leaves turn red or purplish in

winter. White flowers followed by attractive red or pink fruits. Use on banks and near seashore, especially in sandy to gravelly soil.

Cape weed (*Arctotheca calendula*) Zones 10–11W, 20 inches. Moderate water; full sun. Spreads by underground runners. Six-inch leaves with woolly undersides form rosettes. Yellow flowers in spring to early summer. Use on banks or for edging.

Heather (*Calluna vulgaris*) Evergreen shrub, zones 5–7 (5–8W), 4–24 inches. Moderate water; full sun. Neat clump-forming shrubs with tiny scalelike leaves and very showy spikes of bell-shaped flowers in summer to fall. Many varieties with differing flower and foliage colors, hardiness, and growth habits. Best in cool, moist climates.

Carmel creeper (*Ceanothus griseus horizontalis*) Evergreen shrub, zones 9–11W, 18–30 inches. Little water, full sun or light shade. Handsome,

glossy leaves on stems that spread 5–15 feet wide. Light blue flowers. Best on West Coast. Point Reyes ceanothus (*C. gloriosus*) has similar habit with spiny, dark green leaves.

Dwarf plumbago (*Ceratostigma plumbaginoides*) Deciduous, zones 5–10 (6–11W), 6–12 inches. Moderate water; sun to partial shade. Dwarf plumbago provides a spot of vivid blue from midsummer to mid-autumn, when cool tones are most welcome in the garden. Loose clusters of intense blue flowers top wiry stems. Leaves turn bronzy red with frost. Shear after bloom.

Chamomile (*Chamaemelum nobile*) Evergreen, zones 3–10 (3–11W), 3–10 inches. Moderate water; full sun to partial shade. Soft-textured, spreading mat of bright, light green, aromatic foliage. Buttonlike yellow flowers in summer used to make herb tea. Useful as a lawn substitute or between stepping-stones. Mow or shear to keep compact.

Bearberry cotoneaster (*Cotoneaster dammeri*)　　**Ice plant (*Delosperma floribundum*)**　　**Epimedium (*Epimedium rubrum*)**

Bearberry cotoneaster (*Cotoneaster dammeri*) Evergreen shrub, zones 5–7 (5–11W), 3–6 inches. Moderate water; full sun. Bright glossy green leaves with bright red fruit. Prostrate branches spread 10 feet wide, rooting as they grow. Creeping cotoneaster (*C. adpressus*) is deciduous and spreads to 6 feet. Rockspray cotoneaster (*C. horizontalis*) grows quickly to 2–3 feet tall and 15 feet wide. Its stiff, horizontal branches form a flat herringbone pattern. Use on banks and retaining walls.

Ice plant (*Delosperma*) Succulent perennial, zones 6–10 (6–11W), 1–5 inches, depending on species. Little water; full sun. Fleshy, bright green leaves. Brightly colored golden yellow or purple flowers in spring or summer. Plant in rock gardens and areas with excellent drainage.

Indian mock strawberry (*Duchesnea indica*) Evergreen to semievergreen perennial, zones 4–9, 6 inches. Moderate water; sun or shade.

Looks and grows like strawberry, with trailing, rooting stems. Produces yellow flowers and ornamental red fruit carried above the leaves and enjoyed by birds. Useful under trees and open shrubs. Alpine strawberry (*Fragaria chiloensis*) is similar with white flowers.

Epimedium (*Epimedium*) Perennials, zones 4–9, 6–12 inches. Moderate water; partial shade. Creeping underground roots support thin, wiry stems holding leathery, divided heart-shaped leaves. Foliage is pinkish in spring, turning green, then bronze in autumn. Airy spikes of white to yellow or pink to red flowers in spring. Excellent under trees and open shrubs.

Wintercreeper (*Euonymus fortunei*) Evergreen shrub or vine, zones 4–9, 1–3 feet. Regular to moderate water; sun or shade. Spreads up to 20 feet and climbs by rooting, clinging stems. Dark green, oval 1- to 2-inch leaves with scalloped edges attractive in all

seasons. Many varieties with white or yellow variegated foliage, including 'Coloratus', 'Emerald Gaiety', and 'Emerald 'n' Gold'. Use to cover banks, control erosion, spacing 3 feet apart.

Blue fescue (*Festuca glauca*) Zones 4–8 (4–11W), 10 inches. Moderate to little water; full sun. Fine, threadlike blue green leaves form mounds. Pale gold flowers come in summer. 'Elija Blue' is an improved variety.

Sweet woodruff (*Galium odoratum*) Zones 4–8, 6–12 inches. Partial to full shade; regular water. Quickly forms a mat of stems bearing whorls of dark green leaves. Clusters of tiny white flowers appear from spring into summer. Use under trees and tall shrubs. Space plants 1 foot apart.

Trailing gazania (*Gazania rigens leucolaena*) Evergreen perennial, zones 8–10 (8–11W), 6–10 inches. Regular to moderate water; full sun. Spreads rapidly by trailing stems, and has

A Sampler of Ground Covers

English ivy (*Hedera helix* 'Buttercup')   **Dead nettle (*Lamium maculatum*)**   **Lantana (*Lantana montevidensis*)**

clean silvery gray leaves; flowers in yellow, white, orange, bronze. Varieties have larger flowers, greener leaves, more clumping habit. Use on banks and cascading over walls.

Bigroot cranesbill (*Geranium macrorrhizum*) Zones 4–8 (–11W), 8–10 inches. Regular to moderate water; full sun, afternoon shade in hot regions. Large, fragrant lobed leaves smother weeds. Spreads by underground stems, forming tidy clumps. One-inch-wide magenta, pink, or white flowers come in spring, depending on variety. Deer resistant.

English ivy (*Hedera helix*) Evergreen vine, zones 5–8 (4–11W), 4–6 inches. Regular to moderate water; partial to full shade. Lobed leaves on long, trailing stems that root deeply as they grow. May climb trees and buildings, clinging with aerial rootlets. Trim to control spread and density. Many varieties, some with variegated leaves and

differing foliage shapes and sizes. Good on banks to control erosion.

Creeping St. Johnswort (*Hypericum calycinum*) Evergreen shrublet, zones 5–9 (5–11W), 12 inches. Regular to moderate water; sun to partial shade in hot areas. Spreads vigorously by underground stems to form large colonies of medium yellow green leaves. Bright yellow blooms throughout summer. Use to control erosion or compete with tree roots. Mow every two to three years to renew.

Junipers (*Juniperus*) Needled evergreen shrub, zones 4–9 (4–11W), 6–24 inches. Regular to moderate water; sun to light shade. Widely used for mass plantings on banks and level ground. Many species and varieties: Creeping types grow very low, rooting along their stems and include varieties of blue carpet juniper (*J. chinensis* 'Wiltonii'), shore juniper (*J. conferta*), such as 'Blue Pacific'; and Bar Harbor juniper (*J. horizontalis*), like 'Blue Rug', 'Plumosa', and

'Prince of Wales'. Spreading types grow low, horizontal branches and include varieties of sargent (*J. c. sargentii*), tamarix (*J. sabina* 'Tamariscifolia'), and Virginia juniper (*J. virginiana* 'Silver Spreader').

Dead nettle (*Lamium maculatum*) Zones 4–8 (4–11W), 6–12 inches. Regular water; partial to full shade. Gray green to white or silvery variegated leaves light up shady areas. Short spikes of small pink or white flowers in early summer. Popular varieties include 'Beacon Silver', 'Pewter Pink', and 'White Nancy'.

Lantana (*Lantana montevidensis*) Evergreen shrub, zones 10–11, 2–3 feet. Moderate water; full sun. Branches trail to 3–6 feet. Dark green toothed leaves, often red-tinged in cold weather. One-inch clusters of white, pink, lavender, purple, or orange flowers. Many varieties.

Lily turf (*Liriope* and *Ophiopogon*) Evergreen perennials, zones 5–10

Lily turf (*Liriope* and *Ophiopogon*)

Trailing African daisy (*Osteospermum fruticosum*)

Japanese spurge (*Pachysandra terminalis*)

(5–11W), 6–12 inches. Regular to moderate water; partial sun or shade. Clump-forming perennials with grasslike leaves and spikes of white or lavender flowers in summer. Especially useful in borders and around pools and trees. Mow or cut back old foliage in winter to rejuvenate ragged plantings. Many varieties with differing leaf and flower colors.

Trailing African daisy (*Osteospermum fruticosum*) Zones 10–11, 6–12 inches. Regular to moderate water; full sun. Spreads rapidly by rooting branches, covering 2–4 feet per year. Lilac to purple daisylike flowers appear throughout the year, most heavily in fall and winter. Good in mass plantings and on slopes.

Japanese spurge (*Pachysandra terminalis*) Evergreen perennial, zones 4–8 (4–9W), 8–12 inches. Regular water; partial to full shade. Shiny, toothed dark green leaves in

neat whorls form large colonies under trees and near buildings. Spreads by underground runners. 'Silver Edge' has variegated leaves.

Cinquefoil (*Potentilla*) Evergreen perennial, zones 3–8 (3–11W), 4–12 inches. Moderate water; sun, shade in hot climates. Bright green to gray green divided leaves form low-growing carpets. Roselike 1-inch flowers in white, yellow, or pink to red bloom in spring and summer. Many species and varieties thrive, especially in cool climates.

Roses (*Rosa*) Among the many rose varieties are several that make useful ground cover. For a listing of them, see page 356.

Baby's tears (*Soleirolia soleirolii*) Zones 9–11, 1–4 inches. Regular water; partial to full shade. Creeping plant with tiny round leaves spreads aggressively to form large mats. Use under ferns and other shade-loving plants.

Star jasmine (*Trachelospermum jasminoides*) Evergreen vine, zones 9–10 (9–11W), 18–24 inches (as ground cover). Regular water; sun to shade in hot areas. Glossy green foliage on spreading, twining branches. Will climb supports. Profuse, 1-inch sweet-scented white flower clusters attract bees. Use as edging or under trees and shrubs, pruning frequently to control growth.

Periwinkle (*Vinca minor*) Evergreen perennial, zones 4–9 (4–11W), 6 inches. Moderate water; sun or partial shade. Trailing, arching stems with shiny 1-inch oval leaves and bright blue, lavender, or white flowers in spring to summer. Excellent under trees and for edging. Varieties have various flower and leaf colors, including white-flowering 'Alba' and variegated 'Ralph Shugert'. Greater periwinkle (*V. major*) has larger leaves to 3 inches long, spreads rapidly in zones 7–11, and is extremely invasive in sheltered, wooded areas.

A freshly mowed lawn of tall fescue makes a lush carpet and comfortable lounging spot. Brick mowing strip surrounding the lawn reduces maintenance by eliminating the need for edging.

Lawns
THE PERFECT GROUND COVER

Although the lawn is usually the most conspicuous feature of a home landscape, it need not be large to enhance the overall beauty of the property. A well-designed small lawn can be just as functional and handsome as a big expanse of grass, and because both must be regularly fertilized, irrigated, and mowed, a small lawn requires much less work.

New, lightweight push mowers make it easy to keep a small lawn trimmed. Hybrid grasses being developed for every climate grow more slowly than their predecessors—and thus require less frequent mowing.

Some water-conscious gardeners question the need for a grass lawn at all, but it does have advantages. Grass is one of the best planting materials to keep the ground attractively covered, and it provides a uniquely safe and inviting surface for children's play and for recreational activities.

THE LAWN IN YOUR LANDSCAPE
Lawns combine handsomely with flower borders, naturalistic plantings, and paved entertainment areas. Don't think of a lawn as a simple rectangle or square; a small circle of lawn ringed by trees and flowers, for example, can be the centerpiece of a formal garden, while a curved or kidney-shaped lawn can direct the eye to a focal point, such as a tree or sculpture. A grassy pathway can lure a visitor around a stand of shrubs to a secret garden waiting beyond. Squares of turf alternated with paving can create a cool and interesting space for patio tables and chaises.

When designing or redesigning a lawn area, give some thought to the amount of care the grass will need. A shady spot under a tree may be better planted with a ground cover, such as sweet woodruff. To eliminate tedious hand-trimming, install mowing strips along the perimeter of your lawn. A ribbon of concrete, brick, or flat pavers, just wide enough to accommodate the wheels of a mower, will allow you to cut right to the edge of the grass. Lawns with rounded or simple geometric shapes are quicker to mow than ones with irregular or rectangular shapes.

If you don't use mowing strips, use edgings (plastic, metal, or wood benderboard) to contain your lawn, as well as any plantings on the other side. If you plant a grass that spreads by runners, 8-inch-deep edging will keep it from invading nearby flower beds.

Especially in the arid West, make sure you have a plan for irrigating your lawn. Will a simple hose and hose-end sprinkler serve your purposes? Do you have an existing system that needs upgrading or repair? A built-in automatic sprinkler system is simplest to install before the turf is planted.

GRASS ZONES

A Climate Map for Lawns

Lawn grasses fall into two general categories: northern cool-season grasses, and southern warm-season grasses. Water and fertilizer needs differ between the two groups, and susceptibility to some pests and diseases varies, as well. Where you live usually dictates the type of grass you can grow.

The map at right is divided into seven regions, each characterized by particular climate conditions. Grasses that grow well in each zone are listed.

Keep in mind that the map is only a guide. Specific areas within a zone vary in rainfall, temperature, altitude, terrain, and soil. Areas near the dividing lines are transitional: Grasses that flourish in those areas may be different from those that do well throughout the rest of the region. For help, consult your Lowe's associate or nearest cooperative extension office.

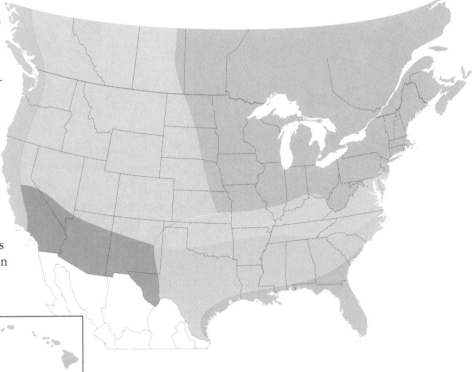

West, Pacific Northwest, and Western Canada
Climate is cool and humid along the coast, but hot and dry in inland valleys. Rain comes in winter; summers are dry. Lawns seeded from cool-season grasses—bent, fine and tall fescue, Kentucky blue, and perennial rye—do well throughout the region. Use tall fescue or bermuda in inland regions.

Southwest Summer high temperatures and little rain put pressure on lawns. Most grasses require supplemental irrigation. Bermuda is the primary lawn grass, with some zoysia and St. Augustine. Given adequate irrigation, tall fescue provides year-round green turf. Perennial rye is excellent for overseeding dormant bermuda in the fall.

Mountains, Great Plains, and Central Plains of Canada Climate is dry and semiarid, with wide temperature fluctuations. Drought-tolerant native grasses—buffalo, crested wheatgrass, and blue grama—do well. With irrigation, fine fescues and Kentucky and rough-stalk bluegrasses succeed in northern areas, and tall fescue, bermuda, and zoysia in southern areas.

Midwest, Northeast, and Eastern Canada
Summers are hot and humid, winters cold and snowy. Rainfall is abundant, and soils are often acidic. Colonial and creeping bent, Kentucky and rough-stalk bluegrasses, and perennial and annual ryegrasses are common; fine fescues are used throughout this region.

Upper South Summers are warm and humid, with abundant rainfall throughout the growing season. Winters are relatively mild but can be severe. Bermuda, tall fescue, and zoysia grasses perform well. Kentucky and rough-stalk bluegrass, and perennial and annual ryegrasses are also widely planted.

Central South Climate is warm and humid with abundant rainfall; winters are mild. Bermuda, centipede, tall fescue, and zoysia do well. Kentucky bluegrass is used in cooler areas, St. Augustine in southern areas.

Florida, Gulf Coast, and Hawaii Climate is subtropical to tropical with a year-round growing season. Rainfall is generally very high. Bahia, bermuda, centipede, St. Augustine, and zoysia grasses grow well throughout most of the region. Use cool-season grasses for winter overseeding of dormant warm-season lawns.

With a rotary tiller, work organic amendment deep into the soil. After tilling, remove any large stones, level, and rake smooth.

PLANTING A NEW LAWN

Establishing a new lawn takes advance planning and work. Sowing seed or laying sod is only the final step.

When preparing the area to be planted, make sure it has a gentle slope away from buildings and other areas that could be damaged by standing water. In general, allow a 3-inch of slope for every 10 feet, or about 2½ feet for every 100 feet (see page 208). As you measure for slope, you may find that some areas are higher or lower than others; grade these for an overall even appearance. If you need to bring in additional soil, buy the same type as your existing soil (to the extent this is possible) and mix it with the existing soil as you prepare for planting.

If you're installing an underground sprinkler system, allow enough time in your schedule to design it carefully for complete, even coverage. Otherwise have a licensed landscape contractor do the design, installation, or both.

Test the soil See page 303 for information on how to determine your soil's acidity or alkalinity. If tests indicate a highly acid soil (pH below 6.0), add ground limestone.

If the soil is highly alkaline (pH above 8.0), add iron sulfate or elemental sulfur. Iron sulfate is fast acting and will supply the iron that is lacking in alkaline soils. Your nursery advisor or cooperative extension office can recommend amounts and types of amendments that are best for adjusting soil pH in your area.

Add organic soil amendments Nitrogen-stabilized soil amendments derived from sawdust and ground bark are available at most garden supply stores. Although more costly, these materials are easier to use than raw sawdust or bark products, which require additional nitrogen to hasten breakdown.

Always sow hulled bermuda and buffalo grass seed because it will germinate much better than unhulled seeds. Grasses prone to seedling disease have a better chance of success if coated with fungicide.

UNHULLED BERMUDA

FESCUE COATED WITH FUNGICIDE

HULLED BERMUDA

UNCOATED TALL FESCUE

How to Sow Grass Seed

1 After the site is prepared, scatter seed and lawn fertilizer.

2 Lightly rake seed into soil.

3 Spread ¼ inch of mulch, then roll with an empty roller to press seed into soil.

Smooth the seed bed Usually you have to conform to surrounding paving, but if you have a choice, try to have a slight pitch away from the house. Because grass forms a thick mat about 1 inch high, the prepared planting area should finish out about an inch lower than surrounding areas. After raking and leveling, firm the seed bed with a full roller, making passes in two directions. If necessary, level again.

Starting from seed Seeding applies primarily to cool-season grasses; most warm-season kinds are started from sprigs or plugs. Lawns started from seed are best planted in fall, early enough in the season to give the grass time to establish before cold weather comes. The next best time is spring, as soon as soil can be worked (cool-season); after all danger of frost is past and before the weather turns hot (warm season).

When you prepare the soil, don't cultivate it too finely—it may crust, forming a hard surface that emerging seedlings cannot penetrate. Ideally, aim for pea-sized to marble-sized soil particles. Do the final leveling with a garden rake. Choose a windless day and sow the seeds

SEED OR SOD? WEIGH COST AND CHOICE AGAINST CONVENIENCE

The greatest advantage seeding has over sod is cost. Although improved growing, harvesting, and distribution have made sod less expensive than in the past, seeded lawns remain much cheaper to plant. Also, while sod offers a wider choice than it once did, seed still provides the most variety. You can easily find hybrid seed mixtures that thrive in shade, for example, but these are harder come by in sod. Sod also has occasional problems bonding to the soil beneath; if it fails do so, you'll get a shallow-rooted lawn at best—or, at worst, one that fails completely.

On the other hand, many gardeners can't stay at home to keep a newly seeded lawn constantly moist for weeks, and not everyone has an automatic sprinkler system that allows for watering several times per day. Sodded lawns must be kept moist, too, of course, but they don't dry out as fast as seeded lawns; watering just twice a day (before and after work, for example) is often enough to do the job. Sod also provides an instant reward for your labors—a morale booster if the entire garden is brand new, with only small trees and shrubs dotting the landscape.

evenly, using a drop or rotary spreader. Apply a complete dry granular fertilizer, also using a spreader. Several manufacturers offer fertilizers formulated especially for starting new lawns.

Water thoroughly, taking care not to wash away the seed. Keep the seeded area moist for about three weeks or until all grass is sprouted, watering briefly (in 5- to 10-minute spells) and frequently. During warm periods, you may need to water three, four, or more times a day.

Mow for the first time when the grass is one-third taller than its optimum height. Mow slowly to keep from disturbing the barely set roots. After the initial mowing, continue to water frequently; the top inch of soil should not be allowed to dry out until the lawn is well established (this usually takes about six weeks and four mowings).

If weeds emerge, don't attempt to control them until the young lawn

has been mowed four times. By this stage, many weeds will have been killed by mowing or crowded out by the growing lawn. If weeds are still a problem after four mowings, many gardeners prefer to treat the lawn with an herbicide; unlike hand pulling, it kills weeds without the risk of disturbing the root systems of the grass.

Try to avoid walking on the lawn too much during the initial four to six weeks.

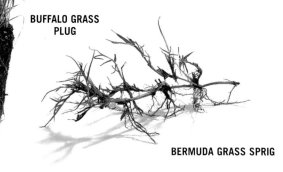

BUFFALO GRASS PLUG

BERMUDA GRASS SPRIG

How to Plant Sod

Sod lawns can be started almost any time of year, except when weather is very cold. It's also best to avoid installation during a summer heat wave. The following are the basic steps.

Water the planting area thoroughly the day before the sod is delivered. Time the delivery of sod so you can cover the whole area in a single day, beginning early in the morning. When you lay out strips, stagger them so the ends aren't adjacent; butt the sides tightly together.

With a sharp knife, cut the sod to fit it into odd-shaped areas. Roll the entire lawn with a roller half-filled with water to smooth out rough spots and press the roots of the sod firmly against the soil. Water once a day (more often if the weather is hot), keeping the area thoroughly moist for at least six weeks.

Mow for the first time when the grass is a third taller than its optimum height. When mowing during the initial six weeks, be very careful not to disturb the seams.

1 **To install sod,** moisten prepared soil, then unroll strips and lay in brick-bond fashion, pressing edges together firmly.

2 **Use a knife** to trim sod to fit snugly around paving and obstacles.

3 **Roll the lawn** with a roller half-filled with water to press roots firmly into the soil. Water every day (more often in hot weather) for six weeks.

LEFT: Circular lawn, just big enough for romping toddlers and perhaps a picnic basket, is a green island surrounded by shrubs, perennials, and herbs.
RIGHT: Antique millstones make stepping-stones in a turf-covered path.

How to Plant Plugs and Sprigs

Many warm-season grasses are sold as sprigs or plugs. A sprig is a piece of grass stem with roots and blades. A plug is a small square or circle cut from sod. Early spring is the best time to plant.

Plugs are usually 2 to 3 inches across and are often sold 18 to a tray—enough to plant 18 square feet on 1-foot centers. Plant in the prepared area, spacing them 8 to 12 inches apart. Sprigs are usually sold by the bushel; the supplier can tell you how much area a bushel will cover. The fastest way to plant them is to scatter them evenly by hand over the prepared area, and then roll them with a cleated roller.

Plugs Two-inch plugs of buffalo grass, planted at 8-inch intervals, will grow together in a year.

Sprigs Torn to pieces by a machine, sprigs of hybrid bermuda grass will root and spread quickly in well-prepared soil.

A Sampler of Lawn Grasses

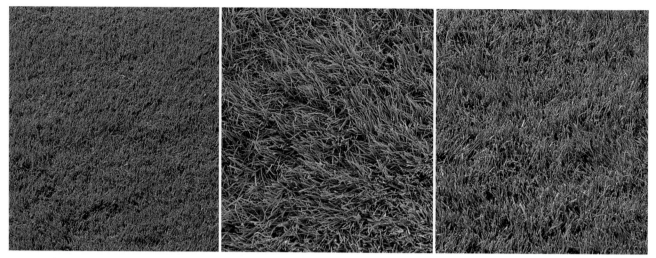

Creeping bent grass (*Agrostis stolonifera*)   **Buffalo grass (*Buchloe dactyloides*)**   **Tall fescue (*Festuca arundinacea*)**

Creeping bent grass (*Agrostis stolonifera*) Cool-season. Fine textured grass requires more water and care than other lawn grasses. Grow in acidic soil, in sun or light shade. Mow at ½ to ¾ inch. Sold as seed, sod. Varieties include 'Penneagle', 'Penncross', and 'Seaside'.

Blue grama grass (*Bouteloua gracilis*) Warm-season. Tolerates drought, extremes of temperature, and a wide range of soils. Does best in sun. Makes a better-quality turf when blended with buffalo grass. Mow at 2 to 3 inches, three or four times a year. Sold as seed.

Buffalo grass (*Buchloe dactyloides*) Warm-season. Very drought-tolerant lawn for sun; slow upright growth. Mow at 3 inches, four or five times a year. Sold as seed, sod, plugs. Several improved varieties are available. The best seed varieties are 'Cody', 'Tatanka', and 'Topgun'. Best sod varieties are '609', 'Prairie', and 'Stampede'.

Bermuda grass (*Cynodon dactylon*) Warm-season. Hybrid bermuda is similar to common bermuda, but it's finer textured and does not self-sow. Mow at ½ to ¾ inch. Sold as sod, sprigs, plugs. Varieties available as seed include 'Cheyenne', 'NuMex Sahara', and 'Sundevil'. The softest- and finest-blade bermudas are sterile hybrids that come as sod, plugs, or sprigs including 'Tifgreen', 'Tiflawn', and 'Tifway'. Use them for golf or putting greens in southern regions. Plant 'Santa Ana' sod for hardy, attractive play lawn.

Centipede grass (*Eremochloa ophiuroides*) Warm-season. Light green medium- to fine-textured grass spreads by underground stems. A chief virtue is its ability to thrive in acidic, poor soils. Very little maintenance is required; it's even resistant to chinch bugs. But cool temperatures push it into dormancy and below 5°F, it dies. Look for varieties 'Centennial', 'Centiseed', or 'Oklawn'.

Tall fescue (*Festuca arundinacea*) Cool-season. Tolerates heat and some drought, and flourishes in sun or shade. It freezes out in the coldest climates. Newer selections (dwarf tall fescue) are finer bladed, deeper green. Mow at 2 to 4 inches. Sold as seed, sod. A few varieties— such as 'Rebel III', 'Earth Save', 'Shenandoah', 'Titan II', and 'Tarheel'—have *endophytes*, a pest-repelling fungus bred into them. The many named varieties include: 'Aztec II', 'Bonsai 2000', 'Cochise', 'Crewcut', 'Falcon III', 'Guardian', 'Jaguar 3', 'Millennium', 'Mustang II', 'Ninja', 'Pixie', 'Plantation', 'Rebel 2000', 'Rembrandt', 'Shenandoah II,' and 'Tar Heel'.

Fine fescue (*Festuca rubra* and others) Cool-season. Fine-bladed grasses succeed in well-drained soil in shaded sites. Fairly drought tolerant. Sometimes blended with Kentucky bluegrass or perennial ryegrass or to overseed warm-season grasses. Mow at 1½ to 2 inches. Sold

Perennial ryegrass (*Lolium perenne*)   **Kentucky bluegrass (*Poa pratensis*)**   **St. Augustine (*Stenotaphrum secundatum*)**

as seed. Chewings fescues include 'Ambassador', 'Jamestown II', and 'Longfellow II'. Hard fescues include 'Bighorn', 'Defiant', and 'Scaldis.' Creeping red fescues include 'Boreal' and 'Shademaster'. All are often mixed with Kentucky bluegrass and perennial ryegrass, adding greater shade and drought tolerance.

Perennial ryegrass (*Lolium perenne*) Cool-season. Deep green grass does best in sun. Needs frequent watering. Used as year-round lawn in cooler regions or to overseed winter-dormant grasses. Mow at 2 to 3 inches. Sold as seed or sod. Look for 'Applaud', 'Charismatic', 'Exacta', 'Dimension', 'Manhattan II', 'Palmer', 'Pennant', 'Pick 715', 'Pizzazz', 'Riviera', and 'SR-4100'. 'Manhattan II' has pest-repelling endophytes (see tall fescues).

Bahia grass (*Paspalum notatum*) Warm-season. A tough, low-growing, coarse grass used in the Southeast for a low-maintenance lawn. It is drought and shade tolerant, but requires frequent mowing. Improved varieties include 'Argentine', 'Paraguay', and 'Pensacola'.

Seashore paspalum (*Paspalum vaginatum*) Warm-season. A glossy, deep green, medium-textured grass, and an alternative to Bermuda in coastal areas where soil is too salty. It takes heat, drought, and salty soil in stride, and shrugs off pests. Plant it by sprigs, plugs, or sod. Look for the varieties 'Adalayd' (same as Excalibre), or 'Sea Isle 2000'.

Kentucky bluegrass (*Poa pratensis*). Cool-season. Classic blue-green grass for cooler, northern regions. Needs regular water. Takes sun, light shade. Mow at 1 to 3 inches. Widely available as seed or sod. Usually mixed with other cool-season grasses. Top varieties include 'A-34', 'America', 'Award', 'Blacksburg', 'Chateau', 'Eclipse', 'Glade', 'Liberator', 'Midnight', 'Princeton 104', 'Rugby II', and 'Showcase.'

St. Augustine grass (*Stenotaphrum secundatum*) Warm-season. Coarse-textured grass adapted to wide range of soils but does best along coast. Dark green blades have rounded tip. Grows best in sun but tolerates shade. Needs regular water. Spreads fast by surface runners that root at joints, and can invade other parts of the garden (but shallow roots pull up easily). Mow at 1½ to 3 inches. Sold as sod, sprigs, plugs. Top varieties are 'Bitterblue', 'Floratine', 'Floralawn', 'Jade', 'Palmetto', 'Raleigh', and 'Seville'.

Zoysia (*Zoysia matrella*) Warm-season. Tolerates drought and heat; takes sun or shade. Mow at 1 to 2 inches. Sold as sod, sprigs, plugs. Fine textured with stiff, wiry blades. It's deep rooted and slow to spread. A tough grass, a downside is its long winter dormant season. Varieties such as 'Cashmere', 'De Anza', 'Emerald', and 'Victoria', minimize dormancy. Plant 'Zen 300' and 'Zenith' from seed.

Perennial Flowers
GLORIOUS COLOR YEAR AFTER YEAR

Long-lived bloomers, perennial flowers are prized because they come back year after year. Most are easy to grow, although it may take a few years to get them established, and they vary in the length of time they can grow in one spot without revitalization.

You can find perennials suitable for every location and condition. Some are hardy in the snowiest mountain areas; others live in the driest deserts. Some die down to the ground after blooming, only to reappear the following year. Others are evergreen in mild-winter climates, including lily-of-the-Nile and some daylilies. A few, such as coral bells, live most of the year as low-key foliage plants, and then explode in brilliant color. With deadheading (removing old flowers), many perennials offer repeat shows throughout the season. Becoming familiar with the various characteristics of perennials will help guide your selections.

Many gardeners like to create a mixed border, which can include small trees and shrubs, bulbs, roses, ornamental grasses, and annual flowers in addition to perennials. The perennials supply successive color throughout the year, lengthening the border's period of attraction and lending it enormous variety in color and form.

Before buying, always consider how wide and high a perennial will ultimately grow. Some reach 7 to 8 feet tall, while others are quite low. Plants only a few inches across when brought home from the nursery may eventually form mounds 3 to 4 feet wide. To avoid crowding problems, space plants and choose planting locations with an eye toward each plant's mature size.

Perennials including lavender Russian sage, purple coneflower, black-eyed Susan, light purple Joe Pye weed, light pink sedum 'Autumn Joy' and ornamental grasses combine to create colorful late-summer display.

How to Divide Clumping Perennials

1 **Lift overgrown plant** from the ground after loosening soil around and under the clump with a spading fork.

2 **Slice through clump** with a trowel, dividing it into four sections. Break each section by hand into 4- by 4-inch pieces.

3 **Immediately plant** divisions in prepared bed. Water new divisions regularly until established.

PLANTING AND CARING FOR PERENNIALS

Most perennials are purchased in 4-inch to 1-gallon containers; mail-order sources often also ship them bare-root. Plant them as directed on pages 307.

Soil, water, and fertilizer In general, perennials prefer soil that is well amended with organic matter, but a surprising number do well in ordinary or even poor garden soil. Some thrive in full sun; others need some shade, especially in hot-summer climates. Water needs differ, too: Some perennials are thirsty, while others succeed with little water. Most perennials appreciate an annual feeding, either in the form of organic amendments worked into the soil in spring or fall or with a complete fertilizer applied in spring. Some, however, need regular fertilizing throughout the growing season.

GROWING SEASON CARE

Perennials look their best with regular maintenance during the growing season.

Deadheading keeps the landscape looking neat and can prolong blooms for several weeks. For many flowering perennials, trimming and pinching also improve appearance. After a spring-flowering plant's blooming period ends, cut back all stems and foliage by a third; a healthy mound of new growth soon fills in and remains throughout the growing season. To prevent lanky, floppy growth on some summer- and fall-blooming perennials, control growth early in the season. Pinch individual terminal buds (see illustration below) to encourage bushier growth; to make plants bushier still, cut back entire branches by a few inches rather than just pinching the top bud.

Dividing Gardeners divide perennials for at least two reasons: to improve the health and flower production of overgrown, crowded plantings and to gain new divisions to increase a planting. Note that division is usually feasible only for perennials that grow in clumps with an expanding root mass. It is not practical to divide those that grow from a taproot; if you try to divide the taproot, you'll probably kill the plant.

Pruning techniques

Pinch growing tips to make plants more compact and bushy.

Cut back to improve appearance and promote continued flowering.

A Sampler of Perennials

Lady's mantle (*Alchemilla mollis*)

Columbine (*Aquilegia*)

New England aster (*Aster novae-angliae*)

Common yarrow (*Achillea mille-folium*) Zones 3–9 (3–11W), 24 inches. Moderate water, full sun. Large, flat-topped flower clusters on 1- to 3-foot stalks from clumps of lower-growing fernlike foliage. White, yellow, pink to red flowers throughout summer. Choices include Summer Pastels and Debutante strains. Other yarrows include fern-leaf yarrow (*A. filipendulina*), *A.* 'Moonshine', *A.* 'Taygetea'.

Lady's mantle (*Alchemilla mollis*) Zones 4–7 (4–11W), 12 inches. Regular water; sun to deep shade. Neat mounds of rounded, scallop-edged pale green leaves appear silvery, especially after rain or dew. Airy clusters of tiny yellow-green flowers above the foliage in summer. Excellent for edging, front of borders, lightly shaded landscapes.

Columbine (*Aquilegia*) Zones 3–9 (3–11W), 6–30 inches. Moderate water; full sun to filtered shade. Lacy, divided gray-green leaves and colorful spurred flowers in nodding or upright clusters. Single and double yellow, red, white, purple, blue, pink flowers often bicolored. Self-sows readily. McKana Giants are a popular hybrid strain.

Wormwood (*Artemisia*) Zones 4–9 (4–11W), 6–60 inches. Moderate water; full sun. Many species and varieties, all prized for silvery gray to white aromatic foliage. Feathery 'Silver Mound' and deeply lobed, white-leafed 'Silver Brocade' are good for edging. 'Silver Queen' and 'Powis Castle' grow to 3 feet.

Butterfly weed (*Asclepias tuberosa*) Zones 4–9 (4–11W), 3 feet. Moderate water; full sun. Clusters of bright orange to yellow flowers in summer. Narrow lance-shaped leaves on straight, unbranched stems. Monarch butterflies lay eggs on the leaves.

New England aster (*Aster novae-angliae*) Zones 4–8 (4–11W), 1–5 feet. Regular water; full sun. Forms clumps of strong, hairy stems topped by brightly colored clusters or plumes of flowers in late summer to autumn. Hundreds of varieties of varying growth habits and with flower colors ranging from white to blue to deep purple, most with yellow centers.

Astilbe (*Astilbe arendsii*) Zones 4–8 (4–11W), 1–4 feet. Regular water; full sun to partial shade. Deeply divided, fernlike leaves are attractive in all seasons. White, pink, red, purple flower plumes grow above the foliage in summer. Mainstay of shady borders. Varieties include white 'Deutschland', dark red 'Fanal', and pink 'Glow' and *A. simplicifolia* 'Sprite'.

Bergenia (*Bergenia*) Zones 3–8 (3–11W), 12–18 inches. Regular water; full sun in cool climates or partial shade. Large, glossy evergreen leaves form attractive colonies in borders, edges, under trees. White, pink, or rose flowers in spring.

Painted daisy (*Chrysanthemum coccineum*) Lanceleaf coreopsis (*Coreopsis lanceolata*) Bleeding heart (*Dicentra spectabilis*)

Carpathian bellflower (*Campanula carpatica*) Zones 3–7 (3–11W), 4–12 inches. Regular to moderate water; full sun to partial shade. Small heart-shaped, toothed leaves form neat mounds. Covered with white or blue to violet bell-shaped flowers in summer. Varieties include 'Blue Clips' and 'White Clips'. Over 300 other campanula species and many varieties vary widely in height, form, and flower habit. Other popular bellflowers include spreading clustered bellflower (*C. glomerata*), trailing Italian bellflower (*C. isophylla*), and upright peach-leaf bellflower (*C. persicifolia*).

Painted daisy (*Chrysanthemum coccineum*) Zones 4–9 (4–11W), 18–30 inches. Regular to moderate water; full sun. Upright clumps of stems with finely divided leaves, topped by brightly colored pink, crimson, or white daisy flowers with yellow centers. Varieties include 'James Kelway', 'Snow Cloud'. Shasta daisy (*C. superbum*) is

similar with large white flowers. Use in mixed borders.

Lanceleaf coreopsis (*Coreopsis lanceolata*) Zones 4–9 (4–11W), 12–24 inches. Moderate water; full sun. Profuse 1½- to 2-inch yellow daisylike blooms all summer. Narrow, often lobed leaves form a loose clump. Thread-leaf coreopsis (*C. verticillata*) has finely divided leaves on clumps of erect 18- to 30-inch stems topped by bright yellow flowers summer through fall.

Delphinium (*Delphinium elatum*) Zones 3–6 (3–11W), 3–7 feet. Regular water; full sun to part shade. Tall spires of showy white, pink, blue to purple flowers for the back of the border. Divided to lobed foliage clumps at base and partway up flower spikes. Give support in wind-prone areas. Popular hybrids include Belladonna, Magic Fountain Mix, and Pacific Giants. Easiest in cool climates.

Cottage pink (*Dianthus plumarius*) Zones 3–9 (3–11W), 12–16 inches. Regular water; full sun to light shade. Flowering stems hold fragrant single or double fringed blooms in shades of white, red, or pink above narrow gray-green foliage. Hundreds of species and varieties, including maiden pinks (*D. deltoides*), cheddar pinks (*D. gratianopolitanus*), and biennial sweet William (*D. barbatus*). Plant under open shrubs, in rock gardens, and along edges.

Bleeding heart (*Dicentra spectabilis*) Zones 3–9 (3–11W), 2–3 feet. Regular water; partial shade. Stems bearing pendulous pink and white, heart-shaped flowers in spring. Soft green, fernlike foliage dies down by mid to late summer. Long-time favorite. 'Alba' has white flowers. Other popular species and varieties include 'Adrian Bloom', 'Luxuriant', eastern bleeding heart (*D. eximia*), and western bleeding heart (*D. formosa*).

A Sampler of Perennials

Purple coneflower (*Echinacea purpurea*)   Blanket flower (*Gaillardia grandiflora*)   Daylily (*Hemerocallis* 'Tahitian Sunrise')

Purple coneflower (*Echinacea purpurea*) Zones 3–9 (3–11W), 3–5 feet. Moderate water; full sun. Very showy daisylike flowers with drooping purple petals and bristly cone-shaped centers from mid- to late summer. Large, stiff, coarse-textured plant with hairy leaves and stems. 'Bright Star' has rosy pink flowers, 'Magnus' grows to 3 feet, and 'White Swan' has white flowers.

Blanket flower (*Gaillardia grandiflora*) Zones 3–8 (3–11W), 8–18 inches. Moderate water; full sun. Flowers in warm shades of red and yellow with maroon or orange markings bloom from early spring to autumn frost. Rough gray-green foliage. Often short-lived, but self-sows. Many varieties with differing flowers, habits.

Cranesbill (*Geranium*) Zones 3–9 (4–11W), 6–36 inches. Regular water; sun to afternoon shade. Over 300 species and many varieties. Rounded, lobed, or divided leaves form neat mounds to sprawling carpets, depending on species. Five-petaled flowers in white, blue, pink to purple in spring to fall. Popular cranesbills include 'Claridge Druce', 'Johnson's Blue', and 'Wargrave Pink'.

Baby's breath (*Gypsophila paniculata*) Zones 4–9, 2–4 feet. Moderate water; full sun. Many-branched sprays of small white flowers used in bouquets. Slender, pointed leaves. Varieties include 'Bristol Fairy' and 'Pink Star'. Creeping baby's breath (*G. repens*) forms a 6- to 10-inch-tall mat of white to pink flowers.

Hellebore (*Helleborus*) Zones 4–9 (4–11W), 12–30 inches. Regular to moderate water; partial to full shade. Many species and varieties form clumps of thick, long-stalked divided leaves. Large green to pink or purple flowers bloom over a long period from winter through spring. Elegant woodland plant.

Daylily (*Hemerocallis*) Zones 3–10 (3–11W), 1–4 feet. Regular to moderate water; full sun to light shade. Long, arching, straplike leaves form spreading clumps. Branched stalks in summer hold trumpet-shaped blooms in shades of yellow, orange, red, pink, and cream. Use for borders and edges. Thousands of varieties, including 'Eenie Weenie', 'Mary Todd', 'Pardon Me' 'Stella de Oro', and 'Tahitian Sunrise'. Lemon daylily (*H. lilioasphodetus*) has fragrant yellow flowers in early summer.

Coral bells (*Heuchera*) Zones 4–8 (4–11W), 12–24 inches. Regular water; sun to light shade in hot areas. Prized for low mounds of ornamental foliage and tall stalks of airy white, pink, or red flowers. Leaves vary from round with scalloped edges to mapleleaf-shaped; colors from glossy green to purple to silvery gray. Many varieties, including 'Palace Purple', 'Persian Carpet', and 'Pewter Moon'.

Hosta

Beebalm (_Monarda didyma_ 'Cambridge Scarlet') **Peony (_Paeonia_)**

Hosta (_Hosta_) Zones 3–8 (3–11W), 3–36 inches. Regular water; partial to full shade. Hundreds of varieties with wide range of foliage colors, shapes, and sizes. Heart-shaped to rounded to lance-shaped leaves form neat, spreading clumps. Colors vary from yellow to all shades of green to blue gray, many variegated white or yellow. Often-showy stalks of white to purple flowers in summer. Popular varieties include 'August Moon', 'Aureo-marginata', 'Frances Williams', 'Golden Tiara', 'Gold Standard', 'Halcyon', 'Honeybells', 'On Stage', 'Sum and Substance', and 'Wide Brim'.

Lavender (_Lavandula_) Zones 5–9 (5–11W), 12–36 inches. Moderate water; full sun. Prized for fragrant lavender or purple flowers used for soaps and perfumes, and aromatic gray to gray-green needlelike foliage that forms spiky clumps. Use for edging, massing, mixed borders. Many varieties and species.

Gayfeather (_Liatris spicata_) Zones 4–9 (4–11W), 3–5 feet. Regular to moderate water; full sun. Tall stalks of fluffy purple flowers emerge from tufts of narrow, grasslike leaves in late summer. Very showy in mixed borders, good for bouquets. 'Kobold' has magenta flowers, 'Alba' white flowers.

Virginia bluebells (_Mertensia virginica_) Zones 3–7 (3–9W), 18–24 inches. Regular water; partial to full shade. Loose clusters of nodding 1-inch pink to blue flowers in early spring. Blue-green leaves die back by midsummer. Plant with spring bulbs and ferns in woodland landscapes.

Beebalm (_Monarda didyma_) Zones 3–9, 2–4 feet. Regular to ample water; full sun to light shade in hot areas. Fragrant, dark green leaves in vigorously spreading clumps. Tubular flowers of red, pink, white, or purple attract hummingbirds in summer. Many varieties, including 'Cambridge Scarlet' and 'Marshall's Delight'.

Catmint (_Nepeta faassenii_) Zones 3–9 (3–11W), 12–36 inches. Moderate water; sun to light shade in hot areas. Clump-forming to spreading, aromatic-leaved plants with blue to purple, pink, or white flower spikes. Downy foliage, often gray-green. Use in mixed borders and along edges. Popular catmints include 'Six Hills Giant' and 'Dropmore Hybrid'.

Peony (_Paeonia_) Zones 3–8 (4–10W), 20–40 inches. Regular water; full sun to light shade in hot areas. Large, showy, often fragrant blossoms, white to pink to deep red, in early summer. Several flower forms, from single with prominent yellow centers, to double with many crowded petals. Divided leaves on long stalks form attractive, shrublike clumps that die to the ground in autumn. Hundreds of varieties. Tree peonies have woody stems and flower colors that include yellow and apricot. Plants need at least 2 to 3 years in the garden to reach flowering size.

A Sampler of Perennials

Russian sage (*Perovskia atriplicifolia*) **Garden phlox (*Phlox paniculata*)** **Black-eyed Susan (*Rudbeckia* 'Goldsturm')**

Oriental poppy (*Papaver orientale*) Zones 3–9, 2–4 feet. Regular to moderate water; full sun. Bowl-shaped flowers with silky petals on leafy stalks above a low mound of long, narrow, notched foliage. Red, orange, white, or pink flowers with black centers bloom in early summer followed by attractive seedpods.

Beard tongue (*Penstemon*) Zones 3–10 (3–11W), 12–30 inches. Regular to moderate water; sun to afternoon shade. Spikes of tube-shaped flowers in white, pink to red in summer above sprawling clumps of narrow, pointed foliage. Many varieties, including 'Elfin Pink' and 'Husker Red'. Useful in mixed borders and hummingbird gardens.

Russian sage (*Perovskia atriplicifolia*) Zones 4–10 (4–11W), 3–4 feet. Drought resistant; full sun. Woody-based clump with many grayish white, upright-growing stems clothed in gray-green foliage. Lavender-blue flowers come late

spring and summer in sprays atop branched stems creating a soft purple haze above foliage. Varieties include 'Blue Spire' (also sold as 'Superba' and 'Longin'), lighter blue 'Blue Mist' and 'Blue Haze', and silver leaved 'Filagran'.

Garden phlox (*Phlox paniculata*) Zones 3–8 (4–9W), 3–4 feet. Regular water; full sun. Showy dome-shaped clusters of fragrant flowers atop tall, leafy stems in mid- to late summer. Colors from white to deep pink to blue to orange, often with contrasting centers. Other phlox include spring-blooming creeping phlox (*P. subulata*) with needlelike leaves, and thick-leaf phlox (*P. maculata*), which blooms in early summer.

Primrose (*Primula*) Zones 2–8 (2–11W), 4–18 inches. Regular to ample water; full sun to shade in hot climates. Rosettes of rounded to tongue-shaped foliage, often toothed or puckered. Leafless stalks carry clusters of rounded five-petaled

flowers in many differing colors, usually in spring. Use at front of borders, in woodland landscapes, near water, or in rock gardens. Hundreds of species and hybrids.

Lungwort (*Pulmonaria*) Zones 4–8 (4–11W), 12–18 inches. Regular water; partial to full shade. Hairy, ornamental foliage, often spotted with silver, forms neat, spreading clumps. Drooping clusters of funnel-shaped blue or pink flowers in spring. Excellent with spring bulbs, in shady borders, and under trees. Varieties include 'Mrs. Moon' with blooms that turn from pink to blue.

Black-eyed Susan (*Rudbeckia*) Zones 3–9 (3–11W), 1–4 feet. Regular to moderate water; full sun. Masses of large bright yellow to orange or rust daisylike flowers with brown, black, or green centers in summer to fall. Useful in mixed borders and bouquets. Many popular strains and varieties including 'Goldsturm', and 'Rustic Dwarfs'.

Spiderwort (*Tradescantia*) **Speedwell (*Veronica* 'Crater Lake Blue')** Violet (*Viola*)

Sage (*Salvia*) Zones 4–10 (4–11W), 1–8 feet. Regular water; full sun. Over 60 species and many varieties of prized landscape perennials, annuals, and shrubs. Very showy spikes of white, blue, scarlet, or pink flowers in summer. Foliage varies widely, from smooth to hairy, lance-shaped to rounded, green to purple to silvery. Excellent for borders, edges, and massing. Most need full sun, good drainage, and little pruning. Popular perennials include pineapple sage (*S. elegans*), *S. nemorosa* 'East Friesland', common sage (*S. officinalis* 'Tricolor'), and clary sage (*S. sclarea*).

Stonecrop (*Sedum*) Zones 3–11, 2–24 inches. Moderate to little water; full sun to light shade. Growth habits vary from creeping or spreading to upright. Fleshy leaves from bright green to blue green or gray green to red or plum. Many species and varieties have brightly colored, showy flower clusters. Favorites include trailing gold-

moss sedum (*S. acre*), *S. spectabile* 'Autumn Joy', two-row stonecrop (*S. spurium* 'Tricolor'), and spreading *S.* 'Vera Jameson'.

Lamb's ears (*Stachys byzantina*) Zones 4–8 (4–11W), 12–18 inches. Moderate water; sun to light shade in hot areas. Popular for its tongue-shaped, silvery-green to white, wooly leaves that form clumps of rosettes. Flower stalks bear small purple flowers in early summer. Foliage contrasts nicely with more brightly colored perennials. Use in borders, as edging, and for ground cover.

Spiderwort (*Tradescantia*) Zones 4–9 (4–11W), 18–36 inches. Tough plants with long stems. Ample water; sun or shade. Long, deep-green, arching, grasslike foliage; three-petaled flowers in clusters. Bloom varies from white to pink to purple in spring through summer. Many varieties and other species. Use for edging and ground cover.

Speedwell (*Veronica*) Zones 3–8 (3–9W), 6–18 inches. Regular to moderate water; full sun. Spikes of small bright blue, white, or purple to pink flowers bloom over a long period in summer. Shapes range from upright clumps to creeping mats. Narrow to rounded, toothed foliage varies from bright, glossy green to silvery gray. Varieties include 'Crater Lake Blue', 'Goodness Grows', and creeping *V. prostrata* 'Heavenly Blue'.

Violet (*Viola*) Zones 4–9 (4–11W), 2–12 inches. Regular water; sun to shade. Scalloped round to heart-shaped or narrow leaves. Smooth stalks hold colorful, often fragrant flowers in spring through fall, depending on species. Blooms in all colors, including bicolors. Popular kinds include Australian violet (*V. hederacea*) and sweet violet (*V. odorata*). Some violas, such as the Sorbet series (*V. cornuta*), are perennial two zone 8. Use in borders, containers, and edges.

Roses

QUEEN OF FLOWERS

'Dortmund', a large, vigorous climbing rose, covers a chain-link fence. It is repeat-blooming and virtually disease-free.

Long a gardener's favorite and America's national flower, roses still suffer from a reputation of being difficult to grow. In reality, roses are tough and long-lived. No plant is more flexible or more versatile than this flowering shrub.

ROSES IN THE LANDSCAPE

Roses offer much more than simple beauty. For example, climbing roses on trellises can form the walls of outdoor rooms or create a passageway underneath a series of arched arbors. Thorny shrub roses can function as protective hedges. Roses clambering atop an arbor can supply needed summer shade. And roses that form colorful hips can attract birds and other wildlife.

There's a rose for every garden situation. Miniature roses can be used to edge beds and pathways, climbing roses can take the place of vines, standard roses can work as accents or focal points in place of flowering shrubs or ornamental grasses, and many shrub roses can be mixed in with other plants to form spectacular borders or foundation plantings. Use drifts of roses in place of annuals and long-flowering perennials or mix them with a single plant, such as lavender or clematis, for dramatic contrasts. Roses can even bring color into a vegetable or herb garden.

PLANTING AND CARING FOR ROSES

The best time to buy roses is in late winter, when they're available as dormant bare-root plants, or during the first bloom flush of spring, when they're sold as flowering container plants. Shop early for the widest selection.

Roses need well-amended soil. If you know you'll be planting bare-root roses in winter, clean up the area and amend the soil in fall or early spring. That will leave you with less work to do come planting time, when the weather is often cold and unpredictable, and planting may have to be rushed in between storms.

Because most modern roses put out new growth and flowers throughout the growing season, they need regular water and consistent fertilizing during that time. In general, keep soil moist (but not soggy) to the full depth of the roots. This can take up to 5 gallons of water per rose in sandy soil, almost 8 gallons in loam, and up to 13 gallons in clay. Water again when the top few inches of soil are dry—usually within a week for sandy soil, 10 days for loam, and up to two weeks for clay. To enhance moisture retention, mulch around plants.

Roses are heavy feeders. Many gardeners prefer to work a controlled-release complete fertilizer into the top few inches of soil at the start of the growing season, before applying a mulch. If you don't use a controlled-release kind, feed repeat-flowering roses every six weeks with a dry granular fertilizer or every month with a liquid fertilizer. Stop fertilizing about six weeks before the first frost date or in September if you live in a mild-winter climate.

With repeat-flowering roses, remove old flowers

from spent blooms regularly, cutting back several inches to a five-leaflet leaf. If the rose bears attractive hips, stop deadheading in September. You'll be able to enjoy the brightly colored hips during autumn, and you'll also be sending a signal to the plant that it's time to slow down and prepare for dormancy. There's no need to deadhead roses that flower just once a year.

PRUNING

Prune repeat-blooming roses just before dormancy ends in late winter or early spring. But prune roses that bloom only once a season, such as many old-fashioned types, just after the bloom period ends. Strong new growth produced after bloom will bear flowers the following spring.

The amount of pruning you'll do depends on the rose. Most old garden and modern shrub roses need little pruning; prune simply to remove dead or damaged limbs or to lightly control growth. Other roses, such as hybrid teas and grandifloras, usually get more extensive pruning; they tend to produce larger blooms on longer, stronger stems if a portion of the previous year's growth is shortened, and weak and old wood is removed. When you prune, first remove any weakened or winter-damaged stems, then cut out stems growing at odd angles (see the illustrations below).

After you have removed all unwanted growth, reduce the length of the remaining stems. In mild-winter regions, cut them back by about a third to a half. In cold-winter regions, cut out dead and damaged stems after you remove protection; the final size of the bush depends on the severity of the past winter.

PLANTING BARE-ROOT ROSES

Dig a planting hole broad and deep enough to accommodate the roots easily without cramping or bending them to fit. Make a firm cone of soil in the hole and position the plant at the same depth it grew in the field (or slightly higher) with the bud union above the surrounding soil; use a stick to check the level. Fill in with backfill nearly to the hole's top, firming it with your fingers. Then add water. If the plant settles, raise it to the proper level. Fill the hole with remaining soil.

Pruning Roses

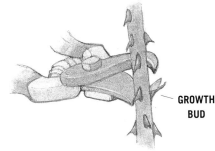

GROWTH BUD

1 Pruning shears with bypass (scissor-action) blades make the cleanest cuts. Hold them with the cutting blade lower-most and the hook above.

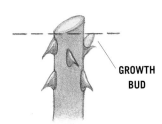

GROWTH BUD

2 A good pruning cut slants at about a 45° angle. Its lowest point is opposite to and slightly higher than the growth bud on the stem.

BUD UNION

3 When removing an entire cane, cut it flush with the bud union or growth from which is sprang. If you leave a stub, it will die back into the union, allowing entry for disease.

A Sampler of Roses

'Margo Koster'   'Ballerina'   'Double Delight'

Small hedges, borders, and containers Little roses that bloom constantly will never go out of fashion; they're just too effective in too many settings. Use them in drifts like perennials, as color accents in containers, and as low hedges or borders along a bed, path, or driveway. Expect these roses to form bushy plants 1½ to 3 feet high. Superb choices include miniatures, polyanthas, and floribundas, such as 'Magic Carrousel' or 'Sweet Vivien' (pink and white), 'Green Ice' (green and white), 'Fairhope' or 'Rise 'n' Shine' (yellow), 'Sweet Chariot' (mauve), 'Katharina Zeimet' or 'White Pet' (white), 'Margo Koster' or 'Millie Walters' (coral), 'China Doll' or 'Pinkie' (pink), or 'Jean Kenneally' (pale apricot), 'Impatient' or 'Pride 'n' Joy' (orange), 'Beauty Secret' or 'Martha Gonzales' (red), 'Show Biz' (scarlet).

Medium hedges, borders, and specimens These grow 4–5 feet tall and wide: 'Iceberg' (white),

'Europeana' (red), 'La Marne' (pink and white), 'Perle d'Or' (apricot), 'Valentine' (red), 'Carefree Wonder' (pink), 'Ballerina' (pink and white), 'Belinda's Dream' (pink), 'Archduke Charles' (red and pink), and 'Bonica' (pale pink).

Tall hedges and borders Big bushes that grow 6 feet tall and wide include 'Sally Holmes' (pale peach), 'Sparrieshoop' (light salmon pink), 'Mutabilis' (multicolored), 'Hansa' (mauve), 'Westerland' (orange), 'Graham Thomas' (gold yellow), 'Heritage' (pale pink), 'Queen Elizabeth' (salmon pink), 'Mrs. B.R. Cant' (soft crimson), and 'Linda Campbell' (red).

Ground covers Some roses sprawl on the ground or form low, graceful mounds. They cover banks, cascade over walls, or fill large containers: 'Ralph's Creeper' (red and white), 'Magic Carpet' (mauve), 'Alba Meidiland' (white), 'Pearl Drift' (pale pink), 'The Fairy' (pink),

'Memorial Rose' (white), 'Red Cascade' (red), and 'Flower Carpet' (pink, white, and red).

Super fragrant Distinctively scented roses are a double delight. Place them where you can enjoy the beauty and perfume close up. Good choices include 'Hermosa' (blue-pink), 'Mrs. Oakley Fisher' (apricot), 'Souvenir de la Malmaison' (pale pink), 'Sun Flare' (yellow), 'Fair Bianca' (white), 'Ambridge Rose' (pale peach), 'Bayse's Blueberry' (dark pink), 'Kronprincessin Viktoria' (white), 'Clotilde Soupert' (creamy pink), 'Belle Story' (creamy peach), 'La France' (silvery pink), 'Rose de Rescht' (dark pink), 'Angel Face' (lavender), 'Fragrant Cloud' (orange), 'Madame Isaac Pereire' (dark pink), 'Oklahoma' (dark red), and 'Double Delight' (red and white).

Short climbers for pillars These are tall roses that produce long, 8–10 foot stems that are perfect for train-

'Abraham Darby'　　　　**'Heritage'**　　　　**'Graham Thomas'**

ing around posts and columns. 'Don Juan' (dark red), 'Abraham Darby' (apricot pink), 'Golden Showers' (yellow), 'Prosperity' (white), 'Aloha' (pink), 'Maggie' (soft crimson), and 'Madame Isaac Pereire' (dark pink).

Medium-sized flexible climbers for fences and trellises Limber-limbed roses have stems 10–12 feet long: 'Red Fountain' (red), 'Sombreuil' (white), 'Compassion' (peach), 'Buff Beauty' (apricot), 'Climbing Angel Face' (lavender), 'Parade' (pink), and 'Yellow Blaze' (yellow).

Large, vigorous climbers for arbors and walls These are the biggest, to 20 feet, for situations where you have a lot of space to cover: 'Climbing Queen Elizabeth' (salmon pink), 'Climbing Iceberg' (white), 'Madame Alfred Carrière' (cream), 'Climbing Crimson Glory' (red), 'Dortmund' (red), 'New Dawn' (pale pink), and 'Mermaid' (yellow).

Thornless roses These include Lady Banks (white or yellow climber), 'Aimée Vibert' (white climber), 'Crépuscule' (apricot climber), 'Zépherine Drouhin' (deep pink climber), 'Climbing Pinkie' (pink climber), 'Heritage' (light pink bush), 'Paul Neyron' (cerise pink bush), 'Reine des Violettes' (purple bush), 'Mrs. Dudley Cross' (yellow and pink bush), 'Marie Pavié' (white bush), 'Smooth Prince' (red bush), and 'Veilchenblau' (purple rambler).

Roses that bloom in light shade Look for 'Lavender Lassie' (lavender pink climber), 'Climbing Cécile Brunner' (pale pink), 'Old Blush' (pink bush or climber), 'Marie Pavié' (white bush), 'Penelope' (pale apricot bush), and 'Eutin' (red bush).

Hardy roses If you live in zones 3–5 you need roses that are cold-tolerant. These are some of the best, grouped by color with the type rose noted in parentheses.

Pink: 'Belle Poitevine' (hybrid rugosa), 'Celestial' (alba), 'Delicata' (hybrid rugosa), 'Frau Dagmar Hartopp' (hybrid rugosa), 'Great Maiden's Blush' (alba), 'Jens Munk' (hybrid rugosa), 'John Cabot' (shrub), 'The Fairy' (polyantha), 'Thérèse Bugnet' (hybrid rugosa), 'William Baffin' (shrub).

White: 'Blanc Double de Coubert' (hybrid rugosa), 'Henry Hudson' (hybrid rugosa), 'Madame Plantier' (alba), *Rosa rugosa alba* (species).

Red: 'Champlain' (shrub), 'Dortmund' (shrub), 'F. J. Grootendorst' (hybrid rugosa), 'Hansa' (hybrid rugosa), 'Roseraie de l'Hay' (hybrid rugosa), 'Rugosa Magnifica' (hybrid rugosa).

Yellow: 'Golden Wings' (shrub), 'Graham Thomas' (shrub), 'Sun Flare' (floribunda).

Annual and Biennial Flowers
FAST AND FURIOUS BLOOMS

Rosy 'Dreamland' zinnias and white and blue types of annual sage produce a carpet of color from midsummer to fall.

USING ANNUALS

Flowering annuals provide quick and showy color that can bring instant drama to an otherwise quiet corner of the landscape. Use annuals to fill spaces between shrubs in mixed borders, set them out for temporary color in a newly planted rose garden or perennial flower border, and put them in pots or window boxes where you want continuous color.

For the best effect in beds and borders, group at least three plants (six are better) of a single color. Certain annuals, however, seem to look most natural in a confetti mix of colors—pastel cosmos and the State Fair strain zinnias for example.

Where you would like broad sheets of color, limit annuals to a single shade and species. A long, sweeping bed of pink petunias or bright red salvias can be an attention-getter in front of an evergreen hedge or along a brick patio.

Consider seeding annuals in a kitchen garden; they will add color and fragrance. And many annuals provide a supply of cut flowers for indoor arrangements. Those that keep their color when dried—sea lavender (*Limonium*) is an example—are ideal for floral crafts.

PLANTING ANNUALS

The best time to plant annuals depends on the specific plant and your climate. Annuals are designated as cool-season or warm-season, based on their hardiness and ability to grow in cool soils.

Cool-season annuals, such as pansy (*Viola*), primrose (*Primula*), and calendula, grow best in the cool soils and

Annuals fill the landscape with quick, dependable color in every imaginable hue. These are plants that germinate, flower profusely, set seed, and die, all in a single growing season. In contrast, biennials take two seasons to complete their life cycle, while perennials (pages 346 through 353) can live and bloom for many years. Although the annual-biennial-perennial distinction seems clear on paper, it's somewhat blurred in the garden. For example, some tender perennials—such as geranium (*Pelargonium*), some kinds of salvia, and verbena—flower year after year in mild-winter climates but are grown as annuals where winters are cold.

RECOMMENDED SPACING BETWEEN PLANTS	AREA PLANTS WILL COVER	
	48 PLANTS*	64 PLANTS*
4 in.	4½ sq. ft.	6 sq. ft.
6 in.	10 sq. ft.	13½ sq. ft.
8 in.	18 sq. ft.	24½ sq. ft.
10 in.	28½ sq. ft.	38½ sq. ft.
12 in.	41½ sq. ft.	55½ sq. ft.

*Typical number of plants in a nursery flat

mild temperatures of spring and fall. Most withstand fairly heavy frosts. When the weather turns hot, they set seed and deteriorate. If you live in a cold-winter area (zones 3 through 7), plant these annuals in very early spring, as soon as the soil can be worked. To bloom vigorously, they must develop roots and foliage during cool weather. In mild-winter regions (zones 8 through 11), plant cool-season annuals in fall for bloom in winter and early spring.

Warm-season annuals include marigold (*Tagetes*), zinnia, and impatiens. These plants grow and flower best in the warm months of late spring, summer, and early fall; they're cold-tender and may perish in a late frost if planted too early in spring. In cold-winter climates, set out warm-season annuals after the danger of frost has passed. In warm-winter areas, plant them in midspring.

Careful soil preparation helps get annuals off to a good start and keep them growing well all season. Dig out any weeds on the site and add a 3-inch layer of compost, well-rotted manure, or other organic amendment. It's also a good idea to add a complete fertilizer; follow the package directions for amounts. Dig or till amendments and fertilizer into the soil, and then rake the bed smooth.

Start annuals from seed sown in pots or directly in the garden (the steps for this are outlined at right), or buy started plants at a nursery. For best results, choose relatively small plants with healthy foliage. Plants with yellowing leaves and those that are leggy, rootbound, or too big for their pots will establish slowly in your garden, and they'll usually bloom poorly.

For even spacing, measure the distance between plants with a piece of wood of the desired length. The table of recommended spacing on the bottom of the facing page shows the area that will be covered by a particular number of plants set out at various spacings. Plant in a diamond pattern as shown for ground covers on page 332.

After planting, water thoroughly. Apply a 2- to 4-inch layer of mulch (such as compost, ground bark, or pine needles) to conserve moisture and help prevent weeds from becoming established.

TIPS

- Wait until late spring or early summer to sow seeds of zinnias and marigolds. They'll languish or fail in cool soil.
- Where winters dip rarely or briefly below freezing, plant cool-season annuals in fall.
- When you have a choice, choose bedding plants that are not yet flowering rather than ones that are.

Broadcasting Seeds in a Prepared Bed

1 Outline the areas for each kind of seed with gypsum, flour, or stakes and string.

2 For more even cover, shake each kind of seed in a covered can with several times its bulk of sand.

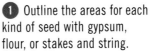

3 Scatter the seed-sand mixture evenly over planting areas. Rake lightly, barely covering the seeds with soil.

4 Spread a very thin layer of mulch over the bed to retain moisture, keep surface from crusting, and hide the seeds from birds.

5 Water with a fine spray to keep the soil surface barely damp until the seeds sprout. Gradually decrease watering frequency after they sprout.

6 After seedlings have two sets of true leaves, thin those that are too closely spaced. Transplant thinned seedlings to fill empty spaces in bed.

A Sampler of Annuals

Floss flower (*Ageratum houstonianum*)   Madagascar periwinkle (*Catharanthus roseus*) Yellow cosmos (*Cosmos sulphureus*)

WARM-SEASON ANNUALS

Floss flower (*Ageratum houstonianum*) Full sun or partial shade. Fluffy flower tassels come in azure blue, lavender, pink, or white on plants 1 to 2½ feet tall. Blooms early summer to fall. Space dwarf varieties 6 inches apart, tall ones, 1 to 1½ feet apart.

Amethyst flower (*Browallia*) Partial shade. Choice plants for connoisseurs of blue flowers. Bears one-sided clusters of lobelialike blooms in brilliant blue, violet, or white; blue and violet flowers are accented by contrasting white center. Grows 1–2 feet tall. Easy from seed. Plant 9–12 inches apart.

Madagascar periwinkle (*Catharanthus roseus*) Full sun or partial shade. Phloxlike flowers bloom in shades of pink, rose, lavender, and white on plants 4 to 24 inches tall, depending on the variety. Thrives in hot conditions, whether dry or humid. Space 8–12 inches apart.

Celosia (*Celosia argentea*) Full sun. Unusual blooms in electric shades of yellow, orange, pink, red, and purple. Flowers come in two forms: *C. a. plumosa* has blossoms resembling ostrich plumes, while *C. a. cristata* has velvety crested flowers that resemble the vivid combs of a rooster. Both types make excellent dried flowers. Plants range in height from 1–3 feet, depending on variety. Space plants 9–12 inches apart.

Coreopsis (*Coreopsis tinctoria*) Full sun. Daisylike flowers in yellow, orange, and reddish; some forms are banded with contrasting colors. Grows 1½–3 feet tall. May need staking. Easy to grow from seed. Thin seedlings to 6–8 inches apart. Thrives in heat. Can take some dryness. (Don't confuse it with perennial lanceleaf coreopsis; see page 349.)

Cosmos Full sun or partial shade. Showy daisylike flowers nod above lacy foliage from summer through fall. Fast growing plants range from 2–7 feet; tall kinds are good for background planting. *C. bipinnatus* has flowers in white, bicolors, and shades of pink, lavender, purple, and crimson. Yellow cosmos (*C. sulphureus*), has bold yellow to deep orange blossoms. Both grow best in soil that is dry and not very fertile. Space 1 foot apart.

Globe amaranth (*Gomphrena*) Full sun. Cloverlike blossoms in red, pink, orange, purple, and white are borne on plants 9 inches to 2 feet tall. Easy to dry for winter bouquets. Space plants 8–12 inches apart.

Sunflower (*Helianthus annuus*) Full sun. Huge radiant blooms in yellow, orange, maroon, creamy white, and bicolors. Depending on variety, plants grow 2–12 feet tall, with flower heads 4–12 inches across. The flowers are followed by edible seeds that are relished by birds. Stake the tallest varieties. Plant 1½ feet apart.

Impatiens (*Impatiens walleriana*) **Monkey flower (*Mimulus hybridus*)** **Petunia (*Petunia hybrida*)**

Strawflower (*Helichrysum bracteatum*) Full sun. Flowers have straw-like petals with velvety centers in shades of yellow, orange, red, pink, and white. They hold their color indefinitely when dried. Grows 12–36 inches tall, depending on variety. Easy from seed or transplants. Space 12 inches apart.

Impatiens (*Impatiens walleriana*) Partial to full shade. Invaluable for providing months of color in sites too shady for most other annuals. Single or double flowers come in every color but blue. Dwarf varieties grow 4–12 inches tall; space these 6 inches apart. Tall kinds reach 2 feet; space 1 foot apart.

Morning glory (*Ipomoea tricolor*) Full sun. Large trumpet-shaped flowers, mostly in shades of blue, pink, and white, are borne on a fast-growing, climbing vine. Individual flowers last only one day. Needs a trellis or fence to climb on. Can also be grown among corn or sunflower

stalks. Grow from seed, which should be nicked and soaked overnight before sowing. Reseeds easily and can become weedy. Space plants 12 inches apart.

Sweet alyssum (*Lobularia maritima*) Full sun to partial shade. Masses of tiny flowers in white, pink, or violet. Low-growing, spreading plants reach 6–12 inches tall. Use as a quick ground cover in bulb bed or as a low border. Space 6–8 inches apart. Easy to grow from seed.

Monkey flower (*Mimulus hybridus*) Partial to full shade. Showy, velvety blooms in bright shades of red, yellow, and orange. The two-lipped flowers are often spotted and give the impression of a smiling monkey's face. Neatly mounded plants grow 12–18 inches high. Space plants 6–8 inches apart.

Flowering tobacco (*Nicotiana alata*) Full sun to light shade. Upright, open plants topped with tubular

flowers in shades of white, pink, red, purple, and green. Some are fragrant at night. Grow 12–48 inches tall. Space seedlings 12–24 inches apart, depending on the ultimate height of variety.

Petunia (*Petunia hybrida*) Full sun. Richly colored flowers come in red, pink, blue, purple, yellow, cream, white, and bicolors. There are two main flower types, single and double; single blossoms are simple trumpets, while double ones are ruffled blooms resembling carnations. Plants range from 8–27 inches tall. Space 7–10 inches apart.

Phlox (*Phlox drummondii*) Full sun. Clusters of colorful, slightly fragrant 1-inch flowers in shades of lavender, pink, red, white, and yellow. Profuse bloom is best used in masses and is great in containers. Flowes are also ideal for cutting. Grows 6–20 inches tall. Space transplants 10 inches apart.

A Sampler of Annuals

Scarlet sage (*Salvia splendens*)   Marigold (*Tagetes*)   Black-eyed Susan vine (*Thunbergia alata*)

Moss rose (*Portulaca grandiflora*)
Full sun. An old-fashioned favorite that flourishes in sunny, dry areas where few other annuals will thrive. Silky-petaled roselike blossoms in shades of white, yellow, orange, red, and pink cover the sprawling, succulent plants. Flowers open in sun and close in late afternoon. Excellent in pots and hanging baskets. Start from seed or transplants, spacing plants 9–12 inches apart.

Scarlet sage (*Salvia splendens*)
Full sun or partial shade. Red, salmon, purple, lavender, or white flowers on gray-green plants 8–30 inches tall. Use as a tall border or background plant. Space transplants 8–12 inches apart. Perennial mealy-cup sage (*S. farinacea*) is usually grown as an annual. Tall spikes of deep blue or silvery white flowers bloom spring until fall.

Painted tongue (*Salpiglossis sinuata*) Full sun. Brilliant display of trumpet-shaped flowers in an

unusual combination of velvety texture, delicate veining, and muted, rich colors. Blooms in shades of white, yellow, pink, red, purple, and brown are held in loose clusters on wiry stems. Grows 12–36 inches tall, depending on variety. Does best in cool-summer climates. Space transplants 12 inches apart.

Creeping zinnia (*Sanvitalia procumbens*) Full sun. Tiny, bright, zinnia-like flowers and creeping habit make an attractive edging for a border, clumped in a rock garden, or cascading from a window box or hanging basket. Produces masses of single or double blooms in warm shades of orange, yellow, and white with purplish brown centers. Easy to grow from seed. Space plants 3–6 inches apart.

Marigold (*Tagetes*) Full sun. Robust, fast growing, and virtually trouble-free, with flowers in vibrant shades of yellow, orange, and orange red, as well as white and bicolors. Foliage

has a pungent scent. *T. erecta*, called African marigold (although all garden marigolds are descended from species native to Mexico), has large blossoms—fully double in most varieties—on plants 20–36 inches tall. *T. patula*, the French marigold, bears single or double flowers and grows 6–18 inches tall. Space dwarf varieties about 6 inches apart, taller kinds 1–2 feet apart. Stake tall marigolds early in the season to keep them from toppling.

Black–eyed Susan vine (*Thunbergia alata*) Full sun to light shade. This twining vine is studded with flaring 1-inch flowers in shades of white, yellow, and orange with the name-sake dark center. A perennial in mild winter climates, it is usually grown as an annual. Looks great on fences and trellises, and dwarf types are attractive when trailing from hanging baskets and window boxes. Can climb up to 10 feet high. Space transplants 12 inches apart.

Zinnia (*Zinnia elegans*)

Snapdragon (*Antirrhinum majus*)

Calendula (*Calendula officinalis*)

Garden verbena (*Verbena hybrida*)
Full sun. Small, richly colored flowers in shades of white, pink, red, purple, blue, and bicolor are borne in flat clusters 2–3 inches wide. Plants, available in mounded, trailing, and dwarf forms, cover themselves with bloom. Leaves are bright green and serrated. Can be used as a small-scale ground cover. Perennial in mild winter climates. Space transplants 12–18 inches apart.

Zinnia (*Zinnia elegans*) Full sun. On plants 1–3 feet tall, colorful daisylike flowers bloom in shades of yellow, orange, red, pink, and purple, as well as white and bicolors. Excellent cut flowers. These are hot weather plants that don't benefit from early planting. Easy from seeds sown where you want plants to grow. Space 6–12 inches apart. Favorite cutting variety is 4-foot-tall Blue Point strain. Zinnias are susceptible to mildew; to prevent it, water at ground level rather than sprinkling.

COOL-SEASON ANNUALS
Snapdragon (*Antirrhinum majus*)
Full sun. Bright colors, pastel shades, and white flowers bloom on plants that range from 6- to 8-inch dwarfs to 3-foot-tall giants. Several flower forms including double, bell-shaped, and azalea-shaped flowers. Space dwarf plants 9 inches apart, taller kinds 15 inches apart. Choose rust-resistant varieties.

Calendula (*Calendula officinalis*)
Full sun. Bushy, upright plants with pungently scented foliage reach 1 to 1½ feet tall and bear abundant blossoms reminiscent of double daisies. Colors include orange and bright yellow as well as white and more subtle shades of cream, apricot, and soft yellow. The edible petals have a slightly tangy flavor. Space plants 12–14 inches apart.

Bachelor's button (*Centaurea cyanus*) Full sun. Lovely blue, red, or white flowers atop wiry stems 1–2 feet tall. Great fresh or dried cut flower; blue is the classic boutonniere. Easy from seed, and self sows. Thin seedlings to 12 inches apart.

Miniature marguerite (*Chrysanthemum paludosum*) Full sun. Perfect miniature daisylike flowers on compact, mounded plants 6–12 inches high. Ideal edging or pot plant. Grow from seed or transplants, spacing 12 inches apart.

Larkspur (*Consolida ambigua*)
Partial shade. Delicate flowers in blues, lilac, rose, and white on 4-foot-tall stalks. May need staking. Chill seeds in refrigerator for a week before sowing. Thin seedlings 1–2 feet apart.

California poppy (*Eschscholzia californica*) Full sun. California state flower. Brilliant-colored silky flowers in shades of gold, orange, pink, red, and white dance above ferny foliage. Easy from seed. Grows 8–24 inches tall. Thin seedlings to 6–8 inches.

A Sampler of Annuals

Sweet pea (*Lathyrus odoratus*)

Stock (*Matthiola incana*)

Forget-me-not (*Myosotis sylvatica*)

Globe candytuft (*Iberis umbellata*)
Full sun to partial shade in hot areas. Clusters of white and pastel blooms on compact plants reaching 6–15 inches tall. Edging or cover for spring blooming bulbs. Easy from seed. Thin to 6–9 inches apart.

Sweet pea (*Lathyrus odoratus*) Full sun. Fragrant blooms in shades of pink, purple, blue, salmon, red, white, cream, and bicolors. Bush types grow 1–3 feet high; vines can reach 5 feet or taller. Space seeds or plants 6–12 inches apart. Provide a trellis for climbing types at planting time.

Lobelia (*Lobelia erinus*) Full sun to partial shade. Tiny white or blue flowers on low-growing to trailing plants. Reach 6–8 inches tall. Excellent low border. Space plants 6–8 inches apart.

Stock (*Matthiola incana*) Full sun or partial shade. These old-fashioned favorites bear 1- to 3-foot spikes of clustered single or double flowers with a wonderful spicy-sweet scent. Colors include white, cream, pink, lavender, purple, and red. Long, narrow leaves are soft gray-green. Space plants 9–12 inches apart.

Forget-me-not (*Myosotis sylvatica*)
Partial shade. Sprays of tiny blue or white flowers on plants to 2 feet tall. Good planted under shrubs or as a bulb cover. Best sown directly where you want plants to bloom. Comes back year after year.

Nemesia Full sun. Wide range of brightly colored flowers on sprawling 10–18 inch tall plants. Great in pots or hanging baskets. Start from seed or transplants. Space 6–8 inches apart.

Iceland poppy (*Papaver nudicaule*)
Full sun. Cupped, slightly fragrant flowers up to 4 inches wide come in shades of white, cream, yellow, and pink. Borne on hairy stalks 1–2 feet tall. Space transplants 12 inches apart.

Nasturtium (*Tropaeolum majus*)
Full sun to partial shade. Broad, 2½-inch-wide spurred flowers in shades of red, orange, maroon, and white are lightly fragrant. Roundish dark green leaves are edible (as are flowers). Climbing varieties reach about 6 feet high; there are also smaller bush varieties. Climbs on string or wire. Can also be used as a sprawling ground cover in full sun or partial shade. Sow seeds where you want plants to grow.

Pansy and viola (*Viola*) Full sun or partial shade. Pansies (*V. wittrockiana*) are much hybridized, and numerous strains are available. Most have 2- to 4-inch flowers in white, blue, mahogany, rose, yellow, apricot, and purple; the petals are often striped or blotched. Viola (*V. cornuta*) has blossoms about 1½ inches across, in bicolors as well as in many clear solid colors. Both pansy and viola grow 8–10 inches tall; space both 6–8 inches apart.

A Sampler of Biennials

Hollyhock (*Alcea rosea*)   **Canterbury Bells (*Campanula medium)*****   **Foxglove (*Digitalis purpurea*)**

Hollyhock (*Alcea rosea*) Full sun. Old-fashioned favorite has 3- to 6-inch-wide single to double flowers on stems that range from 2½ feet to a towering 9 feet tall. Blossoms appear in summer; colors include yellow, cream, white, pink, red, and purple. Rust can be a serious problem; choose rust-resistant varieties, remove any infected leaves you see, and avoid overhead watering (it can spread rust spores). Plants self-sow freely. Space 1½ feet apart.

Canterbury bells (*Campanula medium*) Full sun or partial shade. Another choice for an old-fashioned garden, plants send up leafy 2½- to 4-foot stems bearing loose clusters of bell-shaped flowers 1–2 inches across. Blossoms come in late spring or early summer. Besides the traditional blue, colors include purple, violet, lavender, pink, and white. Space 15–18 inches apart.

Sweet William (*Dianthus barbatus*) Full sun. With clumps of narrow leaves and fringed flowers, sweet William bears an obvious resemblance to its perennial relative, cottage pinks (*D. plumarius*). But its leaves are green rather than blue gray, and ½-inch flowers come in large, dense clusters rather than singly. A number of named strains are available, including some with double flowers; heights range from 6–18 inches. Flowers come in white, pink shades, red, and purple, and in striking bicolor combinations, usually with concentric bands of color. Space transplants 12–18 inches apart.

Foxglove (*Digitalis purpurea*) Light shade. This cottage garden staple forms clumps of large, furry leaves from which tall flowering spikes (to 4 feet or taller) emerge in spring to early summer. Pendulous, tubular, 2- to 3-inch-long flowers bloom in white, lavender, pink, or purple. Volunteer seedlings often have white or light-colored blossoms. The leaves are a source of digitalis, a valuable medicinal drug (but all parts are poisonous if ingested). Space plants 1½ feet apart.

Money plant (*Lunaria annua*) Full sun to partial shade in hottest areas. Old-fashioned plant grown for coinlike, translucent seed pods that hang on flower stalks. Small white to purple flowers appear in spring on 1½ to 3 foot stalks. Best used in an out-of-the-way area; reseeds and can become weedy. Space plants about 12 inches apart.

Silver sage (*Salvia argentea*) Full sun. Silver sage provides highly ornamental foliage to admire even when it's out of bloom. Each plant is a 2-foot-wide rosette of 6- to 8-inch-long, gray-white leaves covered with silvery, woolly hairs. In the summer of the plant's second year, branched, white, woolly flowers rise to 3 feet, bearing pink- or yellow-tinted white flowers that are 1½ inches long. Space plants 12–24 inches apart.

Flowering Bulbs

BIG COLOR FROM SMALL PACKAGES

Spring-blooming bulbs in full display include various tulips, pale blue anemones, a wash of dark blue grape hyacinths, and lofty red-and-orange crown imperial (*Fritillaria*).

Some of the best-loved garden flowers, such as tulips and daffodils, arise from bulbs—or from corms, tubers, rhizomes, or tuberous roots. Although traditionally associated with spring, some bloom in late winter, summer, or fall, making bulbs ideal for single displays and for mixed borders.

Bulbs are inexpensive, and to get a good splash of color, you should plant them by the dozens. Bulbs that multiply and spread from year to year, such as grape hyacinths, can be naturalized under trees or in meadows.

In naturalized settings, grassy cover disguises bulb foliage, which must be left until it has yellowed and can easily be pulled away. In formal landscapes, plant annuals over newly planted bulbs. The flowers will bloom simultaneously, but the long-blooming annuals will camouflage the wilting bulb foliage.

In fall, plant bulbs in containers, in flower boxes, or along a walkway or path for spring color. Spring-planted bulbs, such as gladiolus, can be set out at four-week intervals to provide an ongoing source of cut flowers. Autumn-blooming bulbs, such as autumn crocus, saffron crocus, and spider lily, offer special bursts of late-season color.

HOW BULBS GROW

All these plants grow from underground structures that serve as storage organs, accumulating a reserve of nutrients to supply energy for growth and bloom in the year to come. Although gardeners typically call all such structures "bulbs," botanists divide them into five types: true bulb, corm, tuber, rhizome, and tuberous root.

Five Types of Bulbs

TRUE BULB
(*LEUCOJUM*)

CORM
(*WATSONIA*)

TUBER
(TUBEROUS BEGONIA)

RHIZOME
(CALLA LILY)

TUBEROUS ROOT
(DAHLIA)

BUYING BULBS

When you shop, look for plump, firm bulbs that feel heavy for their size. Avoid soft or squashy bulbs; they may have some sort of rot. Also steer clear of lightweight or shriveled bulbs, because these may have lost too much moisture to recover well.

Large bulbs are likely to give the most impressive performance. The biggest tulip and daffodil bulbs, for example, produce larger flowers on taller, thicker stems. But if you're willing to give bulbs a year or two to build themselves up in your garden, you'll get fine results with smaller sizes of most kinds of bulbs—and their lower cost makes them a good buy.

PLANTING BULBS

To speed up planting, use a bulb planter (left) or excavate the entire planting area to the correct depth (right).

Like most plants, bulbs need good drainage. If your soil drains very poorly, it's best to plant on a slope or in raised beds. You can prepare an entire bed for bulbs alone, or intersperse bulbs among existing plants. To plant a bed, remove weeds and other vegetation. Spread 1 to 3 inches of an organic amendment over the soil and sprinkle on a complete fertilizer, following the label directions for amounts. Dig or till in these additions, rake the soil smooth, and you're ready to plant.

In most soils, bulbs should be planted about three times as deep as the bulb is wide. In hot climates or sandy soils, plant slightly deeper; in heavy soils, plant slightly shallower. Most bulbs can be set quite close together to provide a mass of blooms, but keep in mind that closely spaced bulbs will need dividing sooner than those given more room to grow. For spacing, see the individual descriptions starting on page 368.

To plant bulbs among other plants, use a trowel or bulb planter to dig a hole for each bulb, making the hole a couple of inches deeper than the recommended plant-

NATURALIZING BULBS

Some bulbs, corms, and tubers can be planted in meadows, fields, or sunny woodlands, where they will perform year after year as though they were wildflowers. By choosing bulbs that

adapt to naturalizing and that thrive in your climate and location, you can enjoy an annual display without much work. However, if bulbs aren't likely to receive enough water naturally, be prepared to supply it through irrigation.

Partly because burrowing rodents and deer avoid them, daffodils are among the most prolific naturalizers.

The traditional naturalizing method is to broadcast a handful of bulbs over the desired planting area, and then plant them where they fall. To achieve a more realistic effect, you may need to adjust the pattern slightly; the drift should be denser at one end or near the center, as if the bulbs began to grow in one spot, and then gradually spread to colonize outlying territory. After you have the pattern you want, use a trowel or bulb planter to set the bulbs at their preferred depths.

Following bloom, fertilize the bulbs and allow the foliage to remain until it withers. After number of years, overcrowding may cause a decrease in the number of flowers. When this happens it's time to dig, divide, and replant.

ing depth. Add a handful of compost, set in the bulb, and cover with soil.

After planting, water thoroughly to establish good contact between bulb and soil and to provide moisture to initiate root growth.

TIPS

- Buy bulbs early for best selection.
- Buy the largest-size bulbs available.
- Water thoroughly after planting.
- To extend flowering, mix early, midseason, and late-blooming varieties.

A Sampler of Bulbs

Ornamental onion (*Allium*)

Anemone (*Anemone blanda*)

Crocus

Ornamental onion (*Allium*) Bulb, zones 3–11, depending on species. Regular water during growth and bloom; full sun or partial shade. Bears roundish clusters of small flowers at ends of leafless stems that range in height from 6 inches to 5 feet tall. Many are delightfully fragrant. Bloom in spring or summer with flowers in white and shades of pink, rose, violet, red, blue, and yellow. In spring or fall, plant as deep as their height or width, whichever is greater. Space smaller ones 4–6 inches apart, larger ones 8–12 inches apart.

Belladonna lily (*Amaryllis belladonna*) Bulb, zones 8–11. Regular water while leaves grow in winter; dry during summer. Best in areas with warm, dry summers and wet winters. Straplike leaves grow from clump becoming about 1 foot tall, 2 feet wide. Leaves die back by early summer. About six weeks later, 2–3 foot flower stalks rise from bare earth, each topped by cluster

of 4–12 fragrant, trumpet-shaped pink flowers. Plant dormant bulbs after bloom, about 1 foot apart. All parts of this plant are poisonous if consumed.

Anemone (*Anemone blanda*) Tuber, zones 6–10. Regular water; partial shade. Sky blue flowers held above a low mat of soft, hairy leaves in spring. Plant in fall or spring, setting tubers 1–2 inches deep and 8–12 inches apart. Great ground cover under trees.

Tuberous begonia (*Begonia hybrida*) Tuber, zones 9–11 (or dig and store over winter). Regular water; light shade. Spectacular summer- to fall-blooming bulbs most often grown in pots. Available in every flower color except blue, including many multicolored types. Flower form also varies from single to double and from frilly to roselike. Plant form is upright to pendulous (ideal for hanging baskets), 12–18 inches tall. Plant in early spring.

Fancy-leaved caladium (*Caladium bicolor*) Tuber, zones 10–11, or dig and store over winter. Regular water during growth. Grown for large and colorful leaves, especially in southern U.S. and Hawaii. Many varieties; most are 2 feet high and wide. All need rich soil, high humidity, and warmth (rarely below 60°F). Outdoors, plant in spring, knobby side up so tops are level with soil surface. Keep moist and fertilized.

Crocus Corm, zones 3–11. Regular water during growth and bloom; full sun or partial shade. Most crocuses bloom in late winter or early spring, bearing tubular 1½- to 3-inch-long flowers in a rainbow of colors. Others, including saffron crocus (*C. sativus*) and *C. speciosus*, bloom in fall, with flowers rising from bare earth weeks or even days after planting. Plant corms of both spring- and fall-blooming types as soon as they are available in autumn, setting them 2–3 inches deep and 3–4 inches apart in light, porous soil.

Freesia

Snowdrop (*Galanthus nivalis*)

Dutch hyacinth (*Hyacinthus*)

Dahlia Tuberous root, all zones. Regular water during growth and bloom; full sun (partial shade where summers are hot). Blooming from summer through fall, dahlias are available in numerous colors and floral forms. Flowers range from 2–12 inches across; plant height varies from 1–7 feet or more (stake varieties that grow more than 4 feet tall). Plant after the last frost in spring, setting roots 4–6 inches deep. Space tall varieties 4–5 feet apart, shorter ones 1 to 1½ feet apart. Although roots can be left in the ground where winter temperatures remain above 20°F, gardeners in most areas prefer to dig them annually.

Freesia Corm, zones 8–11. Regular water during growth and bloom; full sun or partial shade. In spring, wiry 1- to 1½-foot stems bear spikes of tubular flowers in almost all shades but green. Plant in fall, 2 inches deep and 2 inches apart. Freesia naturalizes readily.

Snowdrop (*Galanthus nivalis*) Bulb, zones 3–9. Regular water during growth and bloom; full sun or partial shade. Among the first bulbs to bloom as winter draws to a close. Plants grow 6–8 inches tall, bearing one nodding bell-shaped white flower on each stalk. Best suited to cold-winter climates. Plant bulbs in fall, setting them 3–4 inches deep and 3 inches apart.

Gladiolus Corm, zones 6–11. Regular water during growth and bloom; full sun. These long-time favorites have sword-shaped leaves and flaring funnel-shaped flowers borne in slender spikes. Large summer-flowering garden kinds (grandiflora hybrids) grow 3–6 feet tall and come in a wide variety of colors. Plant corms in spring after soil has warmed; they'll bloom in 65–100 days. To enjoy an extended flowering season, plant corms at one- to two-week intervals over a period of four to six weeks. Set each corm about four times deeper than it is

thick; space 4–6 inches apart. In the zones listed, corms can overwinter in the ground, although many gardeners prefer to dig them up. In colder regions, they must be dug and stored in a frost-free location.

Dutch hyacinth (*Hyacinthus*) Bulb, zones 4–11. Regular water during growth and bloom. Dutch hyacinth is a spring bloomer with 1-foot-tall spikes densely packed with waxy, bell-like fragrant flowers in shades of blue, purple, red, pink, buff, and white. It grows best in cold-winter areas, where it lasts from year to year; in these zones, plant in September or October. In mild areas, bulbs will not persist and are best treated as annuals; plant from October to December. Set bulbs 4–5 inches deep, 4–5 inches apart.

Iris Rhizome, zones 3–11, depending on type. Full sun or light shade. Regular water during growing season. The most widely grown irises are bearded kinds that grow from

A Sampler of Bulbs

Bearded iris

Snowflake (*Leucojum aestivum*)

Hybrid lilies (*Lilium*)

rhizomes. Bearded irises come in a dazzling array of colors and color combinations; plant sizes also vary widely. Plant in July or August in cold-winter zones, in September or October where summers are hot. Space rhizomes 1–2 feet apart, setting them with their tops just beneath the soil surface and spreading out the roots.

African corn lily (*Ixia maculata*) Corm, zones 8–11. Regular water during growth; keep dry once leaves begin to fade. Leaves are narrow and grasslike. Spikes bearing 2-inch flowers come on wiry stems in late spring. Plant in fall, setting corms 4 inches deep, then mulch.

Snowflake (*Leucojum aestivum*) Bulb, zones 3–11. Regular water during growth and bloom; full sun to light shade. Small, nodding white flowers with green-tipped segments reach about 1½ feet tall in late winter to spring. Prefers shade in hot climates. Great for naturalizing

under trees. Plant in fall, 3–4 inches deep and 4 inches apart.

Hybrid lilies (*Lilium*) Bulb, zones 4–11. Keep soil moist; full sun or partial shade. Asiatic hybrid lilies bloom in early summer on strong, stems 1½ to 4½ feet tall. The 4- to 6-inch blossoms come in colors ranging from white through yellow and orange to pink and red. Oriental hybrids bloom later, in midsummer to early fall. Their 2- to 6-foot stems bear big (up to 9-inch), fragrant flowers with pink or white petals marked with center stripes and speckles. Plant as soon as possible after you get them. Space 1 foot apart. Cover smaller bulbs with 2–3 inches of soil, medium-size ones with 3–4 inches, and larger ones with 4–6 inches.

Grape hyacinth (*Muscari armeniacum*) Bulb, zones 3–11. Regular water during growth and bloom; full sun or light shade. Grape hyacinth's narrow, grassy leaves emerge in fall and live through

winter's cold and snow. Small, urn-shaped blue flowers with the scent of grape juice are carried in 8-inch spikes, blooming in spring. Plant bulbs in fall, setting them 2 inches deep and 3 inches apart.

Daffodil and narcissus (*Narcissus*) Bulb, zones 3–11. Regular water during growth and bloom; full sun to part shade. Easy to grow and generous with their spring flowers, daffodils are classified into 12 divisions, based in part on differences in flower form. Divisions include the familiar trumpet daffodils, large- and small-cupped types, and double forms. Besides yellow and white, colors include shades of orange, apricot, pink, and cream. Plant bulbs twice as deep as they are tall, spacing them about 6–8 inches apart.

Ranunculus (*Ranunculus asiaticus*) Tuber, zones 8–11. Regular water during growth and bloom; full sun. Peonylike blooms held above fresh fernlike foliage on 1½-foot stems in

Ranunculus (*Ranunculus asiaticus*) Harlequin flower (*Sparaxis tricolor*) Tulip (*Tulipa*)

early spring. Many shades of white, cream, yellow, orange, red and pink. Plant in fall, 2 inches deep and 6–8 inches apart. In cold-winter areas, plant in spring and grow as an annual, or dig and store in the fall.

Harlequin flower (*Sparaxis tricolor*) Corm, zones 9–10. Regular water during growth and bloom, dry after; full sun. Brilliant blooms above clumps of swordlike leaves over a long period in late spring; 12- to 18-inch-tall flower stems bear spikelike clusters of small, funnel-shaped blossoms. Each flower has a yellow center, surrounded by a dark color, and another color—red, pink, orange, or purple—on the rest of the petals. Plant corms 2 inches deep, 3–4 inches apart: in fall where corms are hardy in the ground, in early spring in colder regions. Dig and store the bulbs in fall in cold-winter climates.

Tiger flower (*Tigridia pavonia*) Bulb, zones 8–11, 1½–2½ feet. Regular

water; full sun, partial shade in hot summer areas. Flashy summer blooms are up to 6 inches across. The three outer segments of each triangular flower are red, pink, orange, yellow, or white; the cuplike center and three smaller inner segments are usually boldly blotched with contrasting hues. An individual flower lasts only one day, but because each stem carries a number of buds, bloom lasts for several weeks. Plant in spring after the weather warms. Set bulbs 2–4 inches deep, 4–8 inches apart. Dig and store in fall in cold climates.

Tulip (*Tulipa*) Bulb, zones 3–11. Regular water during growth and bloom; full sun to part shade. Hybrid tulips come in a multitude of colors, including bright shades, pastels, and even nearly black. Eleven categories are early- to late-blooming, 6 inches to 3 feet tall. Flowers very widely in form, too, from the classic egg-shaped blossoms to those that look like lilies or peonies. Bloom season

ranges from mid- to late spring, depending on variety. Most need an extended period of winter chill for best performance. In mild climates, refrigerate tulip bulbs for six weeks before planting (never near apples) and treat the plants as annuals. Otherwise, plant bulbs in fall, setting them three times as deep as they are wide, spaced 4–8 inches apart.

Calla lily (*Zantedeschia aethiopica*) Rhizome, zones 8–11, 2–4 feet. Moderate to ample water; full sun, light shade in hot-summer climates. Large, white to cream cornucopia-shaped flowers held beautifully above shiny rich green arrow-shaped leaves in spring and early summer. Excellent cut flower. Plant from fall through early spring; set rhizomes 4 inches deep, 1 foot apart. Needs moist soil year-round. Can become weedy. Semievergreen, does not dig and store well. Several other callas may also be available, including shorter-growing hybrids with cream, pink, orange, or lavender blooms.

Ornamental Grasses

UNMATCHED TEXTURE AND A REFINED, NATURAL LOOK

If you're looking for special effects in your garden, consider planting ornamental grasses. These versatile plants offer beauty and grace while demanding minimal care in return. Once used almost exclusively in prairie or native gardens, they are now finding their way into elegant and even formal landscapes.

Ornamental grasses bring new dimensions of texture, color, height, and graceful motion to the border, highlighting and enlivening groups of more traditional perennials. Varying in size from low tufts to giants rising to 8 feet or taller, the many choices can serve as edgings, mix with midsize perennials, and provide accents or focal points; most are also excellent for containers. Many have variegated or colored leaves as well as interesting

blooms, and the foliage and flowering stems often persist into autumn and winter.

Massed groups of clumping grasses can create the same color impact as landscape shrubs. The taller plants, such as zebra grass (*Miscanthus sinensis* 'Zebrinus'), can make effective hedges and privacy screens. In small gardens, use ornamental grasses as specimens or as accents in borders. In large gardens, fill wide borders with grasses that have airy textures and interesting colors. If you have a pond in your garden, try planting some moisture-loving grasses, such as

Showy and plumelike flower clusters of maiden grass lend an imposing presence to a summer border garden.

A Sampler of Herbs

BASIL **DILL** **MINT** **OREGANO** **PARSLEY**

Basil This fragrant annual needs warm weather to grow well. Plants typically reach 1½ to 2 feet tall. Besides varieties with large green leaves, you'll find purple basils and dwarf or small-leaved sorts.

Chives A hardy perennial in all zones, chives make a pretty addition to an ornamental garden. Each plant forms a clump of narrow onion-flavored leaves up to 2 feet high. Rosy purple flowers are also edible.

Dill The fresh or dried leaves and the seeds of this versatile annual herb are a popular seasoning for many foods—including, of course, dill pickles. The plants grow 3–4 feet high, sporting soft, feathery leaves and flat clusters of small, yellow flowers.

Mint These perennials (hardiness varies by type) spread rapidly by underground stems. Spearmint is the preferred kind for cooking; it has shiny, bright green leaves and reaches 1–2 feet tall. Peppermint, great for flavoring tea, grows to 2 feet or taller. Unlike most other herbs, mint thrives not only in sun but also in partial to full shade.

Oregano A perennial herb that grows well in all zones, oregano is popular in Italian, Greek, and Spanish cooking. Use its leaves fresh or dried. Many kinds are available; of these, Greek oregano is considered one of the most flavorful. Plants reach 2 feet tall and spread at a moderate rate by underground stems.

Parsley A biennial that's usually grown as an annual, curly-leaf parsley is an attractive edging for herb, vegetable, or flower gardens. In cooking, it's prized for garnishes. Flat-leaf parsley (also called Italian parsley) has a stronger flavor and is favored for seasoning many dishes. Both sorts grow 6–12 inches tall.

Rosemary A shrubby perennial with aromatic needlelike foliage, rosemary is available in numerous varieties, in heights ranging from 1½ to 6 feet. Most are hardy in zones 8–11, but 'Arp' has survived temperatures as low as −10°F. Rosemary is widely used as a ground cover or low hedge and needs little water. Set plants 2–3 feet apart.

Sage A perennial adapted to zones 5–11, but not picky about where it grows. Strong-flavored sage comes not only in the traditional soft gray-green variety, but also in decorative forms with yellow-and-green, purple, or tricolored (gray, white, and purplish pink) foliage. Plants form dense bushes to 3 feet tall.

Sweet marjoram Sweet marjoram is a perennial in zones 9–11; elsewhere, it is treated as an annual or grown in containers and moved indoors for winter. Plants reach 1–2 feet tall; the tiny gray-green leaves have a sweet floral scent and a milder flavor than oregano (to which sweet marjoram is closely related).

CHAPTER 12

Plant Maintenance and Care

Designing, building, and planting your landscape is only the first, although admittedly a busy, phase of landscaping. It's followed by caring for your new plants in such a way that they grow well and meet the potential that you chose them for. Careful watering, pruning, and fertilizing—especially during the first two or three years of a new landscape—make all the difference.

But perhaps you have a long-established landscape that needs only rejuvenation. In this chapter, you'll see how to give neglected plants the care and attention they need to shine.

IN THIS CHAPTER
WATERING • MULCHING
FERTILIZING • PRUNING
LAWN CARE • PEST SOLUTIONS

Watering and Composting
WHEN, HOW, AND HOW MUCH

Watering with a watering can or hand-held nozzle is just right for seed beds and seedlings but is usually inadequate for mature plants. They need enough water to really soak in and do the plants good.

How much water do plants need? How often should you water, and what's the best way to do it? How can you conserve water? This section addresses these and other important—and often perplexing—questions.

WATERING GUIDELINES

Plants, like animals, need water to live. A seed must absorb water before it can germinate. Roots can take up nutrients only when water is present in the soil; water transports nutrients throughout plants. And water is essential to photosynthesis.

But how much water your plants need and how frequently they need it depend on a number of interrelated factors, including soil texture, the plants themselves, their ages, and the weather.

Your soil's ability to absorb and retain water is closely related to its composition. Clay soils absorb water slowly and also drain slowly, retaining water longer than other soils. Sandy soils, in contrast, absorb water quickly and drain just as quickly. Loam soils absorb water fairly rapidly and drain well, but not too fast. You can work in organic amendments to help clay soils absorb water faster and drain better and to make sandy soils more moisture retentive. For more on soil texture and organic amendments, see pages 300 and 301.

After their roots are established, different sorts of plants have widely differing water needs. Plants native to semiarid and arid climates, called xerophytes, have evolved features that allow them to survive with little water and low relative humidity. They may have deep root systems, for example, or leaves that are small, hairy, or waxy.

The majority of familiar garden plants, however, are adapted to moist soil and high relative humidity. Called mesophytes, they usually have broad, thin leaves. Keep in mind that all young plants, including xerophytes, require more frequent watering than mature plants until their root systems become well established. And many annuals and vegetables require regular moisture throughout the growing season if they are to bloom well or produce a good crop.

Weather affects water needs, as well. When it's hot, dry, and windy, plants use water very rapidly, and young or shallow-rooted ones sometimes can't absorb water fast enough to keep foliage from wilting. Such plants need frequent watering to keep moisture around their roots at all times. During cool, damp weather, on the other hand, plants require much less water. Water needs are lower during winter, too, when the days are short and the sun is low on the horizon.

Because soil texture, plant type and

A soil sampling tube allows you to see and feel soil moisture several inches into the soil without making a large hole.

age, and weather are all variable, following a fixed watering schedule year-round (or even all summer) isn't the most efficient way to meet your plants' needs. Always test your soil for moisture and look at the plants before you water. To check the soil around new transplants and in vegetable and flower beds, dig down a few inches with your fingers or a trowel; if the top 1 to 2 inches are dry, you probably need to water. In a lawn or around established trees and shrubs, a soil-sampling tube (left) is useful. It allows you to test moisture at deeper levels without digging a hole that could disturb roots. Leaves can also can tell you when it's time to water: Most will look dull or roll in at the edges just before they wilt.

When you do water, aim to soak the plants' root zones. As a general guideline, the roots of lawn grasses grow about 1 foot deep; roots of small shrubs and other plants reach 1 to 2 feet deep. While the taproots of some trees and shrubs may grow more deeply into the soil, most roots concentrate in the top 2 to 3 feet. Watering below the root zone only wastes water.

To check how far water penetrates in your soil, water for a set amount of time (say, 30 minutes). Wait for 24 hours, and then use a soil-sampling tube or dig a hole to check for moisture. You'll soon learn to judge how long to water each plant to soak its root zone thoroughly.

WATERING METHODS

Methods for applying water to your landscape range from simple hand-held sprayers and hose-end sprinklers to more complex drip systems and underground rigid-pipe systems. The method(s) appropriate for you depend on how often you need to water a landscape of the size of yours and how much equipment you want to buy.

Sprinkling

Watering with a hand-held nozzle or fan may be enjoyable for you, but it takes too long to truly soak the soil.

HOSES

A hose can make the task of watering your garden easy or difficult. If you buy an inexpensive hose that's prone to kinking, you'll spend more time cursing than watering. But if you purchase a durable, kink-free type, it will last much longer and work more efficiently.

Unreinforced vinyl hoses are inexpensive and lightweight, but they're also the least durable and most prone to kinking. Reinforced vinyl hoses are less likely to kink and are lightweight, which is important if you have to move the hose around a lot. Rubber hoses, which have dull surfaces, are the heaviest and toughest types. They kink in hot weather but work well in cold weather. Reinforced rubber-vinyl hoses are flexible, kink resistant, moderately heavy, and durable.

Hoses are sold by length and have various inside diameters ($\frac{5}{8}$-inch, $\frac{3}{4}$-inch, and 1-inch hoses are common). Although the difference in hose diameter may seem slight, the water volume each carries varies greatly. If you have low water pressure or if you must run your hose uphill, you'll need all the pressure and flow you can get. Buy the largest diameter, shortest hose that's practical for your situation.

Hand-watering is, however, useful for new transplants, seedlings, and container plants, because you can apply the water gently and exactly where it's needed.

Hose-end sprinklers, which essentially produce artificial rainfall, offer the simplest way to apply water over a large surface. Many plants, particularly those that like a cool, humid atmosphere, thrive with this sort of overhead sprinkling. This method also rinses dust from foliage and discourages certain pests, especially spider mites. But sprinkling has some negative aspects, as well. First, it's wasteful. Wind can carry off some water before it even reaches the ground, and water that falls or runs off onto pavement is lost, too. In humid climates, sprinkling encourages some foliage diseases, such as black spot and rust, although you can minimize this risk by sprinkling early in the morning,

A portable sprinkler with an adjustable watering pattern lets you select the size of the area covered and, to some degree, the shape. Some include built-in timers.

information on installing a rigid pipe irrigation system, see pages 212 through 217.

To use water effectively, you need to know how fast water penetrates your soil and the delivery rate of your sprinklers. As the illustration below left shows, 1 inch of water (from sprinkling or rainfall) moistens about 12 inches in sandy soil, 7 inches in loam, and 4 to 5 inches in clay. Thus, if you want to water to a depth of 12 inches, you'll need to apply about 1 inch of water to sandy soil, 2½ to 3 inches to clay soil.

To determine delivery rate, place a number of equal-size containers (straight-sided coffee cups, for example) at regular intervals outward from the sprinkler, as shown below. Then turn on the water and note how long it takes to fill a container with an inch of water. This test will also show you the delivery pattern, because the containers will typically fill at different rates. To ensure that every area ultimately receives the same amount of water, you'll need to move the sprinklers so that the coverage overlaps.

so that leaves dry quickly as the day warms. Another potential drawback is that plants with weak stems and/or heavy flowers bend and can break under a heavy load of water.

Traditionally used for watering lawns, underground pipe systems with risers for sprinkler heads remain the best system for watering medium-sized to large lawns and low-growing ground covers. For more

Soaker hoses

These hoses, the forerunners of drip-irrigation systems, are still quite useful for slow, steady water delivery to plants in rows. They're long tubes made of perforated or porous plastic or rubber, with hose fittings at one or both ends. When you attach a soaker to a regular hose and turn on the water supply, water seeps or sprinkles from the soaker along its entire length. You also can water wide beds by snaking soakers back and forth around the plants; trees and shrubs can be watered with a soaker coiled in a circle around the plant. You'll probably need to leave soakers on longer than you would sprinklers; check water penetration with a trowel or soil-sampling tube.

How soil texture affects watering: Applied to sandy soil (left), 1 inch of water penetrates about 12 inches deep. In loam soil (center), the same amount of water reaches a depth of 7 inches. One inch of water penetrates only 4 inches in clay soil.

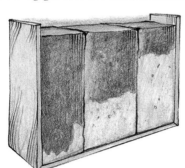

Check a sprinkler's delivery rate and pattern by placing equal-size containers at regular distances from the sprinkler.

Soaker hoses are either perforated plastic, or porous rubber, like this one. Attach it to a hose, and water seeps out along its entire length.

Flood watering

Flooding (soaking) is an effective way to supply enough water to the extensive, deep root systems of large shrubs and trees. Make a level basin for the plant by forming a ridge of soil several inches high around its drip line. You'll usually need to fill the basin more than once to ensure that water penetrates throughout the entire root zone. If the soil in the basin hasn't absorbed all the water within a few hours, make a channel in the ridge around it to let the excess drain away.

If you grow vegetables or flowers in rows, you can build adjoining basins for large plants, like squash, or make furrows between rows (see illustration at above right). To minimize damage to roots, construct the furrows when the plants are young, before their root systems have spread. Broad, shallow furrows are generally better than deep, narrow ones: The wider the furrow, the wider the root area you can soak, because water moves primarily downward rather than side to side. And a shallow furrow is safer for plants—nearby roots are less likely to be disturbed when you scoop out the furrow, and they're likewise less apt to be exposed if a strong flow of water goes through it.

Like drip, furrows work well for plants prone to leaf diseases. Use a bubbler attachment on a hose to break the water's flow.

Drip watering

For the greatest water savings, use drip irrigation for trees, shrubs, perennials, and vegetables. The opposite of flood watering, drip watering means applying water slowly, drip by drip. Drip sprinklers, called emitters, operate at low pressure, and they deliver a low volume of water compared to standard sprinklers. Because the water is applied slowly on or near the ground, there is no waste from runoff and little or no loss to evaporation. You position the emitters to deliver water just where the plants need it, and you control penetration by varying the time the system runs and/or varying the emitters' delivery capacity, rated in gallons per hour—gph. You can also regulate the volume of water delivered to each plant by varying the type and number of emitters you set up for each.

Besides water conservation, the chief advantage of drip systems is flexibility. You can tailor them to water individual plants by providing each with its own emitter(s), or you can distribute water over larger areas with microsprays. A standard layout may include hookups to two or more valves. Because the lines are on the ground (they're easily concealed with mulch) and are made of limber plastic, changing the system is simple: Just add or subtract lines and emitters, as needed.

Your drip system can be attached to a hose end or screwed into a hose bibb. Or, if you prefer, you can connect it permanently to your main water source. For more information on how to install a drip-irrigation system, see page 218.

MULCH SAVES WATER, REDUCES WEEDS

Like any other seeds, most weed seeds require sunlight, warmth, and moisture to germinate and grow. Mulches block light from the soil below, thus preventing the seedlings from becoming established. They also help keep soil moist and modulate its temperature. You can choose from organic or inorganic mulches.

Organic mulches gradually decompose, adding humus to the soil and giving it a loose, crumbly texture (thus mak-ing it easier to pull any weeds that do appear). Before laying down any organic mulch, clear existing weeds from the soil, because those that are already established can grow right through the mulch. Use a 2- to 4-inch-thick layer on paths and around plants, but take care not to cover the plants' crowns. Too much moisture near the crown will rot many plants.

Inorganic mulches include gravel and stones, black plastic, and landscape fabrics.

Gravel, river rock, and other kinds of stones make permanent mulches that can suppress weeds effectively—as long as you install them over weed-free soil to begin with. Many gardeners place landscape fabric under gravel.

LEFT: Use a drip emitter to deliver water at a precise rate and place.
RIGHT: Weed-free straw makes an excellent and attractive mulch.

CONSERVING WATER

Water is a limited resource everywhere. Alhough the eastern half of the United States typically receives enough (or sometimes too much) precipitation, droughts do occur, and parts of this area sometimes go for several years without enough water to meet the needs of the local population. Most low-elevation areas of the western United States have low rainfall rates and a long dry season—and although the overall western water supply remains virtually fixed, ever more people are putting demands on it. Thus, conserving water is (or should be) a concern everywhere. Here are a few tips for waterwise gardening.

USE WATER-CONSERVING PLANTS Some plants need a lot of water to survive; others perform better with less. You can find water-thrifty trees, shrubs, flowering plants, ground covers, and even some grasses for your garden. Some provide seasonal color, others year-round green. The key is to choose plants that are well adapted to the natural conditions of your region.

GROUP PLANTS WISELY Place thirsty ones together and drought-resistant plants elsewhere. Put plants that need regular watering on a separate irrigation system and schedule.

LIMIT TURF AREAS A lawn requires more irrigation than almost any other landscape feature. Limit its size to just what you need for your purposes and choose a grass or grass mix adapted to your climate (see pages 339). Consider replacing at least part of your lawn with hardscape materials or alternative plants.

IRRIGATE EFFICIENTLY Make sure your watering practices and devices use water as efficiently as possible.

IMPROVE THE SOIL Routinely cultivate your soil and incorporate organic matter. You'll improve the soil's ability to resist evaporation and retain moisture.

MULCH Place a layer of organic or mineral material over soil and around plants. Mulch greatly reduces moisture loss (because it reduces evaporation), reduces weeds, and slows erosion.

MAINTAIN YOUR GARDEN Tighten faucets so they don't drip. Water plants only when needed, not by the clock or calendar. Avoid runoff, which wastes water.

CONTROL WEEDS These garden intruders consume water needed by more desirable plants.

WATERING TREES

Water trees and shrubs by soaking soil up to and just beyond the drip line, the area below outermost branch tips. Feeder roots are normally concentrated here because rain usually collects here. As plants grow and roots extend beyond the canopy, irrigation must too.

Black plastic, available in rolls, is especially helpful in a vegetable garden. Besides effectively preventing weed growth, it warms the soil early in the season, speeding the growth of heat-loving plants like melons. Place the plastic over the soil, then cut slits in it where you want to plant seeds or transplants. Remove the plastic at the end of the growing season, because by this time it will usually have degraded too much to use again.

Mulch of black plastic conserves moisture and prevents weed growth.

LEFT: Spread landscape fabric or mulch over the planting area and secure corners and sides with heavy wire staples or soil.
RIGHT: Use a knife to cut openings; tuck flaps back around plant base.

Landscape fabrics, sold in nurseries and garden supply centers, are made of woven polypropylene, spun-bonded polyethylene, or a combination of other synthetic materials. Unlike plastic sheeting, they are porous and allow air and water to reach the soil. Density and porosity vary; denser fabrics are better for suppressing weeds.

Landscape fabrics are available in various widths and lengths. They're best used in permanent plantings around trees and shrubs. Install them around existing plants or cut slits in them to accommodate new ones.

Before you install the fabric, eliminate weeds. Unroll the fabric and estimate where to cut it. Overlap seams by at least 3 inches to avoid gaps through which weeds can grow. Anchor the outer edges of the fabric with plastic pegs, nails, or heavy wire staples.

After installation, cover the fabric with 2 to 3 inches of organic mulch, such as bark chips, or with a thinner layer of pea gravel. The mulch protects the fabric from ultraviolet degradation and improves its appearance.

COMPOSTING

This natural process converts raw organic materials into a valuable soil conditioner. Use it to improve a soil's texture, boost its nutrient content, and make it more water retentive. Besides benefiting the garden, composting lightens the load at the landfill: You recycle garden debris at home rather than consigning it to the dump.

A pile of leaves, branches, and other garden trimmings will eventually decompose with no intervention on your part. This type of composting is called slow or cold composting. With a little effort, however, you can speed up the process. If you create optimum conditions for the organisms responsible for decay (by giving them the mixture of air, water, and the carbon- and nitrogen-rich nutrients they need), the compost pile will heat up quickly and decompose in a few months. Such hot composting also destroys many (though not all) weeds and disease pathogens.

You can make compost in a freestanding pile, such as shown in the photo at top of page 394, or use some

HOW MUCH MULCH?

Bulk quantities of organic mulch are sold by the cubic yard. Determine how many square feet you want to cover (multiply the area's length by its width), then consult the chart to determine the approximate amount of mulch you need.

TO COVER THIS AREA	2 IN. DEEP	3 IN. DEEP	4 IN. DEEP
100 square ft.	$\frac{2}{3}$ cubic yard	1 cubic yard	1$\frac{1}{3}$ cubic yards
250	1$\frac{2}{3}$	2$\frac{1}{2}$	3$\frac{1}{3}$
500	3$\frac{1}{3}$	5	6$\frac{1}{3}$
1,000	6$\frac{2}{3}$	10	13$\frac{1}{3}$

sort of enclosure (see below). Regardless of which method you choose, though, the fundamentals of composting are the same.

Gather materials You'll need approximately equal amounts by volume of brown matter and green matter. Brown matter is high in carbon and includes dry leaves, hay, sawdust, straw, wood chips, and woody prunings. Green matter is high in nitrogen; it includes grass clippings, fruit and vegetable scraps, coffee grounds, tea bags, crushed eggshells, and manure from cows, horses, goats, poultry, and rabbits. The compost will heat up faster if you collect all the ingredients in advance and assemble the pile all at once. Don't use bones, cat or dog waste, dairy products, meat scraps, badly diseased or insect-infested plants, or pernicious weeds (such as bindweed, quackgrass, and oxalis) that might survive composting.

Chop materials Shredding or chopping large, rough materials into smaller pieces (ideally no larger than 1 to 2 inches) allows decay-producing organisms to reach more surfaces and thus speeds up the entire composting process. Shredder-chippers and lawn mowers are good tools to use for this purpose. You can also chop the materials with a machete on a large wooden block. Shredding dry leaves is a good idea, too; collect leaves in an open area and just run a lawn mower over them.

Build the pile Building the pile like a layer cake makes it easier to judge the ratio of brown to green materials. Start by spreading a 4- to 8-inch layer of brown material over an area at least 3 feet square; then add a layer of green material about 2 to 8 inches deep. Layers of grass

Composting proceeds somewhat faster and neater in a contained bin, but otherwise it's the same as in a freestanding compost pile like this one.

clippings should be only 2 inches deep; less-dense green materials can be layered more thickly. Add another layer of brown material and sprinkle the pile with water. Mix these first three layers with a spading fork.

Continue adding layers, watering, and mixing. To heat up efficiently, the pile should be about 3 feet tall, giving it a volume of 1 cubic yard.

Turn the pile In just a few days, the pile should have heated up dramatically. In time, it will decompose on its own, but you can hurry things along by turning the contents to introduce more oxygen—which is needed by the

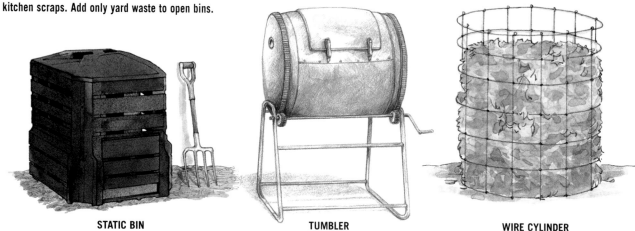

Compost bins with tops that close and keep pests out are suitable for kitchen scraps. Add only yard waste to open bins.

STATIC BIN   **TUMBLER**   **WIRE CYLINDER**

organisms responsible for decomposition. With a spading fork or pitchfork, restack the pile, redistributing it so that the materials originally on the outside are moved to the pile's center, where they'll be exposed to higher heat. If necessary, add water; the pile should be as moist as a wrung-out sponge. Turn the pile weekly, if possible, until it is no longer generating internal heat and most of the materials have decomposed.

Use the compost Finished compost is dark and crumbly, with a pleasant, earthy aroma. Mix it into your planting beds or use it as a mulch. If some of the material from the compost pile's exterior is still coarser than you prefer for either a soil amendment or mulch, simply incorporate it into your next compost pile. To obtain a finer-textured compost to use as potting soil for containers or for starting seeds, sift the finished compost through a screen with ½-inch mesh.

COMPOSTING SYSTEMS

You can make compost in a freestanding pile or in a homemade structure, or use a purchased manufactured composter.

Freestanding compost piles These piles should be at least 3 feet high and wide; at this size, their mass is great enough to generate the microbial activity needed for heating the materials. The upper size limit is about 5 feet high and wide; a pile larger than that may not receive enough air at its center. When you decide where to make the pile, allow space alongside for turning.

Wire cylinders or hoops For these, use welded wire, chicken wire, or snow fencing, supporting it with stakes if necessary. The cylinder or hoop should be about 4 feet in diameter and 3 to 4 feet tall. To turn the pile, lift the cylinder and move it to one side, and then fork the materials back into it.

Three-bin systems Bin systems are more complex than freestanding piles or those corralled with wire, but they also offer a more flexible way to make compost. One bin holds new green and brown material; the center one contains partly decomposed material; while a third bin holds finished or nearly finished compost. Turn the material in each bin weekly, moving decomposed material to the right. (The bin for nearly finished compost will be empty for a few weeks at the start.)

For a picture of a three-bin compost system and construction details, see page 268.

Manufactured composters These include various sorts of tumblers, which make it easier to turn materials and produce finished compost quickly. Most are turned with a crank, but some roll on the ground or are turned with foot treads. Such devices provide a tidy way to make compost, especially in small gardens.

Another manufactured composter is the static compost bin, in which the contents sit without turning (though occasional aerating with a spading fork is helpful). You add new materials at the top; the finished compost is removed through a door at the base. Though tidy, these units produce only fairly small amounts of compost—and they do so rather slowly.

COMPOSTING WITH WORMS

Worm composting, or vermicomposting, is an efficient way to compost fruit and vegetable scraps from the kitchen in a small amount of space. Many nurseries sell red wiggler worms and bins for housing them; you can also use a covered homemade wooden bin (about 2 feet square and 8 to 16 inches deep). Fill the bin with bedding made from shredded newspaper, then place it in a shaded, rain-protected location where it won't freeze or overheat from sun exposure. Feed the worms kitchen scraps; 2 pounds of worms will process about 7 pounds of fruit and vegetable scraps each week. After three to six months, you can begin harvesting the compost, which looks like dark, rich soil.

A Guide to Fertilizers

WHEN, HOW, AND HOW MUCH

Use a siphon attachment to pull concentrated liquid fertilizer from a bucket or container, dilute it into the water stream, and apply through the hose.

In order to thrive, plants need light, air, water, and a place for their roots to grow. They also need a continuous supply of nutrients, most of which come from the soil. When the natural supply of nutrients isn't adequate, gardeners add fertilizer to make up the difference.

The nutrients plants need for good health are typically divided into three groups: macronutrients, secondary nutrients, and micronutrients.

Fertilizer sections at garden centers may befuddle you. The shelves are piled with boxes and bottles, the floors covered with bags stacked high. Labels identify the package contents as rose food or vegetable food, lawn fertilizer or general-purpose fertilizer. You may also find bins filled with bonemeal, blood meal, or hoof-and-horn meal—all labeled "natural fertilizer." Choosing the right products to keep your plants healthy may be more than a bit confusing.

CHECKING OUT NUTRIENTS

Nitrogen (N), phosphorus (P), and potassium (K) are the primary plant nutrients. They are always listed on the labels of packaged fertilizers, usually in prominent type. The three numbers are also called the guaranteed analysis and the N-P-K ratio. For example, a fertilizer that's labeled 10-8-6 contains 10 percent nitrogen, 8 percent phosphorus, and 6 percent potassium. Any fertilizer that contains all three primary nutrients, such as 10-8-6, is called a complete fertilizer.

Of the three primary nutrients, nitrogen is generally in shortest supply, so it needs the most frequent replenishing. Fertilizers supply nitrogen in water-soluble (fast-release) or insoluble (slow-release) forms. Soluble nitrogen becomes available to plants quickly. Insoluble nitrogen must be broken down by soil microorganisms before plants can use it. Most fertilizers contain both forms of nitrogen, although labels don't always specify the percentages.

Plants also need smaller amounts of secondary nutrients—calcium, magnesium, and sulfur—and trace amounts of micronutrients, including iron, manganese, and zinc. These secondary and micronutrients are already present in most garden soils, so they're not always included in general-purpose fertilizers but are often sold as separate supplements.

Well-stocked garden centers offer all of the basic kinds of fertilizer: controlled release (foreground), soluble crystals (left center), and liquid (right center), as well as organic (rear).

NATURAL OR CHEMICAL?

You can buy fertilizers in either natural or chemical form. Plants can't distinguish nitrogen that came out of cow from nitrogen that came out of a factory. People, on the other hand, have their preferences, and for good reasons. For example, many natural fertilizers take good advantage of materials that would otherwise be waste products and disposal problems. Another good reason to choose one over the other is cost. On a pound-for-pound basis, manufactured fertilizers are usually much less expensive than natural ones. Applied properly, both kinds have their uses.

Natural fertilizers are derived mostly from animal waste and dead organisms. These include all kinds of animal manures, fish emulsion, and meals made from blood, bone, alfalfa, cottonseed, kelp, and soybeans.

Most natural fertilizers contain lower levels of nutrients than chemical products do. Because they tend to release nutrients over a longer period of time, they're less likely to burn plants (although some fresh manures can do so). However, because they depend on soil organisms to make the nutrients available, they don't contribute much to plant needs when the soil is cold and the key organisms are less active. Natural fertilizers also improve the texture of the soil and increase the amount of beneficial microorganisms. For best results, apply natural fertilizers in late fall or early spring.

Chemical fertilizers are mass-produced by industrial means. They usually have higher levels of nutrients and a larger percentage of soluble nitrogen than do natural fertilizers. The fast release of soluble nitrogen is often a plus in chilly weather, when cool-season crops and spring-flowering shrubs and trees can use a boost. To avoid burning plants, apply chemical fertilizers to soil that's moist, and then water thoroughly after application.

Excess fertilizer washes off lawns into storm drains ultimately collecting in nearby waterways.

FERTILIZERS CAN POLLUTE, TOO

While many gardeners are aware that improper use of pesticides can harm the environment, they may not realize that fertilizers pose some of the same risks. Plants can absorb only a certain amount of nitrogen at one time; when you fertilize with synthetic nitrogen fertilizers, excess nitrates remain in the ground to be washed away by rain or watering. They drain into rivers, lakes, and bays, either directly (through runoff) or indirectly (by penetrating the groundwater—deep beneath the soil). They increase algal growth in the water, disrupting the ecosystem.

To make sure you don't unintentionally contaminate water sources, determine how much nitrogen is actually needed to keep plants and lawns healthy. Start out by using a low-nitrogen fertilizer, and then gradually increase the percentage of nitrogen until you see satisfactory growth. You might consider switching to natural fertilizers. With few exceptions, natural fertilizers typically have low percentages of nitrogen, and their nitrogen is released slowly, more closely matching the plants' needs and leaving little excess to be washed away.

LIQUID OR SOLID?

You can buy natural and chemical fertilizers in liquid or solid form.

Liquid fertilizers, including fish emulsion and water-soluble crystals, get nutrients to the roots immediately. But because the nutrients usually last only a couple of weeks in soil, liquid fertilizers need to be applied more often. Liquids are useful for feeding plants in containers and hanging baskets.

Solid fertilizers are usually sold as granules or pellets. They can be broadcast or spread over lawns and ground covers or dug or forked into soil around the root zones of trees, shrubs, and perennials.

Other solids include controlled-release fertilizers. These are sold as spikes or beadlike granules that

Use a hand-cranked spreader to scatter fertilizer granules and a cultivator to work them into soil.

release nutrients over a period of time, assuming certain temperature and moisture conditions. Because they release nitrogen slowly and steadily, most of it is used by the plant, and very little is washed away by rain or irrigation.

WHEN TO FERTILIZE

To get your plants off to a good start, fertilize when the growth cycle of plants begins. Many gardeners use a general-purpose fertilizer at this time (an evenly balanced formulation or one slightly higher in nitrogen); others

FERTILIZER SELECTION GUIDE

The chart below describes several common natural and chemical fertilizers. The N-P-K ratios listed are typical, but they vary widely among manufacturers. In general, fertilizers formulated for lawns and other plants grown for their leaves have higher nitrogen levels; fertilizers that maximize flowering and fruiting have higher phosphorus. When you shop, you'll also see specialty fertilizers formulated for specific plants, such as roses, fruits, vegetables, and (of course) lawns. While these fertilizers are not necessarily unique, the directions on the label are specific to the featured plants, so they're more useful for those plants than are the general directions on a general-purpose fertilizer.

NATURAL

FERTILIZER TYPE	Blood meal	Cottonseed meal	Fish emulsion	Fish pellets
N-P-K RATIO	13-0-0	6-2-1	5-1-1	8-5-1
BENEFITS, USES	Good source of nitrogen in both soluble and insoluble forms. Scratch it into the soil around plants. Store away from cats and dogs.	Acidifies soil as it fertilizes, making it useful where soils are commonly alkaline and for plants, such as azaleas, that require acidity.	Acts fairly quickly and gently. Excellent for container plants and leafy vegetables. Fishy odor can attract cats and raccoons.	Blend the pellets into the soil of vegetable beds at planting time. Fish odor can attract animals.

CHEMICAL

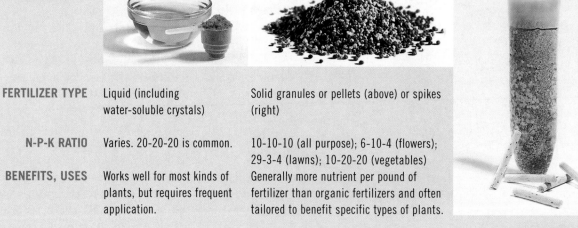

FERTILIZER TYPE	Liquid (including water-soluble crystals)	Solid granules or pellets (above) or spikes (right)
N-P-K RATIO	Varies. 20-20-20 is common.	10-10-10 (all purpose); 6-10-4 (flowers); 29-3-4 (lawns); 10-20-20 (vegetables)
BENEFITS, USES	Works well for most kinds of plants, but requires frequent application.	Generally more nutrient per pound of fertilizer than organic fertilizers and often tailored to benefit specific types of plants.

Use a spading fork to work a dry granular fertilizer deep into a new garden bed where nutrients will do the most good. Water afterward.

Apply dry fertilizers over the root area and use a cultivator or water it into soil. Be careful to not damage surface roots.

add only nitrogen. How often you fertilize later in the year depends on the plant. Heavy feeders benefit from regular applications of general-purpose fertilizers and extra nitrogen throughout the growing season. Others—often those that evolved in nutrient-poor environments—may need only one annual feeding with a general-purpose fertilizer, or they may flourish with no feeding at all.

Applying fertilizer accurately to a lawn requires a drop spreader.

APPLYING FERTILIZER

Use a spading fork to work a dry granular fertilizer into a new garden bed. This technique puts phosphorus and potassium at a level where they can best be absorbed by plant roots. Water thoroughly after incorporating the fertilizer.

Around plants with roots close to the surface, gently scratch the soil with a cultivator. Apply a dry granular fertilizer and water thoroughly. Because roots may extend several feet beyond the drip line, be sure to spread fertilizer out wide enough to reach all the roots.

Liquid fertilizers can be applied with a watering can. You can also use an injector device to run the fertilizer through your watering system. A simple siphon attachment (page 396) draws a measured amount of fertilizer into a hose from concentrate.

TIPS

- Wait two to three weeks after planting to apply liquid fertilizers.
- Controlled-release fertilizers are more convenient and less polluting than others.
- Organic fertilizers improve soil structure as they release nutrients.

Pruning
KEEP PLANTS HEALTHY AND GOOD-LOOKING

Most trees, shrubs, and vines need pruning from time to time. Make most pruning cuts just above a bud, as shown here.

In a well-planned, well-pruned garden, you're rarely aware of pruning. Trees and shrubs grow in perfect proportion to each other, complementing your house and other structures rather than overwhelming them. In fact, most people notice pruning only when it's done badly.

This section discusses how and when branches grow—information that will help you understand how and when to prune. You'll also review the four basic pruning cuts and learn when each should be used.

WHY PRUNE?

If you choose the right plant for the right location and give it plenty of room to expand, you probably won't need to prune too often. You may have to cut back a few stems or branches now and then as the plant matures, but pruning won't be a major task.

Sometimes, however, circumstances make pruning a necessity. A tree's branches may block your view as you back out of your driveway, creating a safety hazard, or you may move into a house with a garden so woefully neglected that it has turned into a jungle. These and several other key reasons to prune are listed here.

To maintain safety Remove low-growing branches if they impede passing vehicles or obscure oncoming traffic from view. You may also need to take out split or broken branches before they have the chance to come crashing down on a person, car, or building. It's wise, too, to prune out low-hanging, whip-like branches (especially those with thorns) that may strike passersby.

To alter or rejuvenate growth Neglected, overgrown shrubs can sometimes be turned into small multitrunked trees if you remove their lower limbs; this may be a better approach than digging out the shrub and planting another in its place.

To direct growth Pruning influences the direction in which a plant grows: Each time you make a cut, you stop growth in one direction and encourage it in another. This principle is important to keep in mind when you train young trees to develop a strong branching structure.

To remove undesirable growth Prune out unwanted growth periodically. Cut out wayward branches, take out thin growth that's too dense, and remove suckers (stems growing up from the roots) and water sprouts (upright shoots growing from the trunk and branches).

To promote plant health Trees and shrubs stay healthier if you remove branches that are diseased, dead, pest-ridden, or rubbing together.

Three Ds of Pruning

Begin any pruning job by getting rid of the three Ds—dead, damaged, and dysfunctional growth. Here, a broken limb, hanging branches, crossing branches, and water sprouts are shown to be removed.

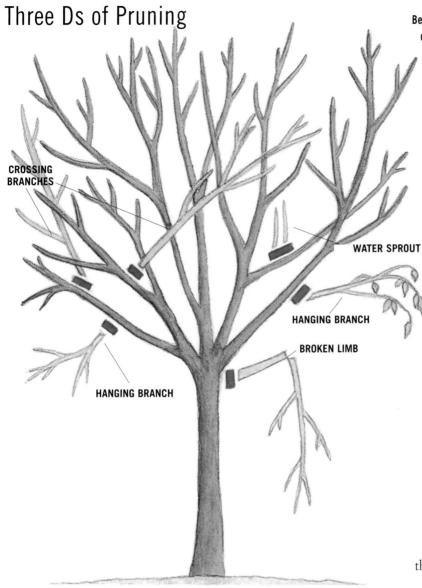

CROSSING BRANCHES

WATER SPROUT

HANGING BRANCH

BROKEN LIMB

HANGING BRANCH

WHEN TO PRUNE

Learning when to prune a particular plant is every bit as important as knowing how to do the actual job. The timing is easier to understand if you know a little about plant metabolism. Most plants produce new leaves and stem growth from spring through midsummer. Photosynthesis proceeds most intensively during this time, producing food (in the form of sugars) for the plant.

As full summer heat sets in, the sugars are gradually transferred to the plant's woody parts and its roots, where they're stored during the winter dormant period. When spring arrives, the stored sugars are used to start new growth. Pruning is timed to harmonize with this cycle; it is typically done either late in dormancy or during summer. For some plants, a combination of both late-dormancy and summer pruning often yields the best results.

Note that these guidelines are most pertinent to climates with four distinct seasons and definite winter chill. In warmer-winter areas, timing will vary depending on the particular plant's native climate. If you have any doubts about the best time to prune a particular plant, ask your Lowe's nursery personnel or your cooperative extension office for advice.

Pruning in late dormancy Many plants, especially deciduous trees and shrubs, are best pruned in late winter or early spring, just before they break dormancy. Heavy frosts have abated, so the plants are less likely to suffer cold damage at the point where you make your cuts. Sugars are still stored in larger branches, trunks, and roots, so little food will be lost to pruning. Deciduous plants are still bare, so you can easily spot broken and awkwardly growing branches and decide

To create particular shapes You can prune a line of closely planted trees or shrubs as a unit to create a hedge. If you're a hobbyist who practices topiary, you can prune trees and shrubs into fanciful shapes.

To produce more flowers or fruits Flowering plants and some fruit trees are pruned to increase the yield of blossoms and fruit and to improve their quality. You'll need, for example, to remove spent flowers from roses throughout their bloom time. For some fruit trees, you'll make many small, precise cuts each dormant season. Although this sort of pruning sometimes ranks as a tedious chore, remember that your efforts will pay off in lavish bloom and generous crops of fruit at harvest time.

Pruning a shade tree

In winter, an overgrown hawthorn tree is dense and twiggy.

Early spring after pruning, the crown of the tree is more open and airy.

The following summer, the pruned tree is much more attractive.

how to direct growth. And because growth will soon start, your pruning cuts will stimulate new growth in the direction you want.

For flowering trees and shrubs, you'll need to know whether the flowers are produced on old or new growth. If early spring flowers come on last year's wood—as in the case of forsythia, flowering quince (*Chaenomeles*), and flowering trees, such as peach and plum (*Prunus*)—you'll lose many flowers by pruning before plants break dormancy. It's best to wait until flowering has finished before pruning. But plants such as cinquefoil (*Potentilla*), that bear flowers on leafy new growth formed in spring can safely be pruned while dormant.

Pruning in summer A second time to prune is in late summer, when sugars needed for the next year's growth are moving into large limbs, trunks, and roots and will not be seriously depleted by pruning. Some gardeners like to thin plants in summer, because it's easier to see how much thinning is really needed when

branches are still thickly foliaged. And because growth is slower at this time of year, pruning is less likely to stimulate new growth—an advantage when you're thinning. In cold-winter regions, don't do summer pruning later than one month before the first frost; if you do, an early frost may damage the plant at the point of the cuts.

Pruning evergreens

Although evergreen trees and shrubs don't drop their leaves, they approach a near-dormant state during the winter months. The group includes broadleaf evergreens—such as boxwood (*Buxus*) and camellia—and conifers, among them spruce (*Picea*) and pine.

Broad-leaved evergreens are usually best pruned in late dormancy or in summer, as outlined above. For flowering broad-leaved evergreens, however, timing is a bit more precise; you'll need to prune with an eye toward preserving flower buds. Prune after bloom for evergreens flowering on last season's growth; prune before spring

SCISSORS-CUT SHEARS

ANVIL CUT SHEARS

Shorten new spring growth to control the size and shape of whorl-branching conifers, such as this pine.

growth begins for those that bloom on new growth.

Most conifers are pruned only in their first two or three years in order to direct their basic shape; from then on, they're best left alone. Some of the most badly botched pruning you'll see is on conifers that have been pruned too severely, usually to keep them confined to a too-small location—although a few conifers, including arborvitae (*Platycladus* and *Thuja*), yew (*Taxus*), and hemlock (*Tsuga*), lend themselves to shearing into hedges. When you do need to prune a conifer, the timing will depend on whether the plant is a whorl-branching or random-branching type.

In whorl-branching conifers, the branches radiate out from the trunk in whorls. Members of this group include fir (*Abies*), spruce (*Picea*), and pine (*Pinus*). These trees produce all their new growth in spring; buds appear at the tips of new shoots as well as along their length and at their bases. On pines, the new shoots are called candles, because that's what they look like until the needles open out.

Prune whorl-branched conifers in early spring. To induce branching, you can pinch or cut anywhere along the new growth, being sure to do so before the shoots harden. When the tree is still relatively small, you can nip back the pliant new growth of the leader (the central upward-growing stem) and all side branches to make a denser, bushier plant. If you cut into an older stem, however—even at a point where it bears foliage—no new growth will sprout from below the cut.

Unlike whorl-branching sorts, random-branching conifers have branches that grow randomly along the

REMOVING A BRANCH

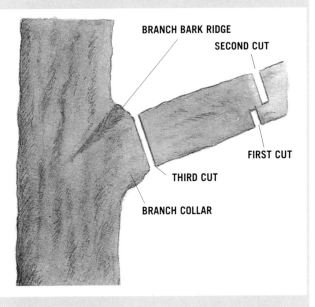

When removing heavy branches, avoid ripping the bark by shortening the branch to a stub before cutting it off at the branch collar. Use a sharp pruning saw and make these three cuts as described below:

1. About a foot from the branch base, make a cut from the underside approximately a third of the way through.
2. About an inch farther out on the branch, cut through the top until the branch rips off. The branch should split cleanly between the two cuts.
3. Make the final cut by placing the saw beside the branch bark ridge and cutting downward just outside of the branch collar. (If the branch angle is very narrow, cut upward from the bottom to avoid cutting into the branch collar.)

trunk. These plants don't limit their new growth to spring, but grow in spurts throughout the growing season. Trees of this type include cedar (*Cedrus*), cypress (*Cupressus*), dawn redwood (*Metasequoia*), redwood (*Sequoia*), giant sequoia (*Sequoiadendron*), bald cypress (*Taxodium*), and hemlock (*Tsuga*). Prune these as you would deciduous and broad-leaved evergreen trees. New growth will sprout from below the pruning cuts as long as the remaining branch bears some foliage; in general, no new growth will develop from bare branches, but hemlock is an exception. It's best to prune random-branching conifers right before new growth begins in spring.

Growth Buds on a Branch

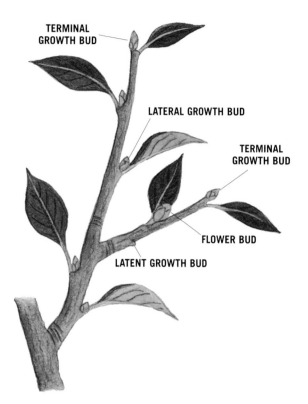

TERMINAL GROWTH BUD

LATERAL GROWTH BUD

TERMINAL GROWTH BUD

FLOWER BUD

LATENT GROWTH BUD

UNDERSTANDING GROWTH BUDS

Pruning makes sense when you understand the role and locations of growth buds. Select the bud you want to keep and cut just beyond it. The resulting growth will vary depending on the bud. If your pruning is to have the effect you want, you'll need to learn to recognize three different kinds of growth buds.

A terminal bud grows at the tip of a shoot and causes the shoot to grow longer. These buds produce hormones that move downward along the shoot, inhibiting the growth of other buds on that shoot.

Lateral buds grow along the sides of a shoot and give rise to the sideways

Cutting Above the Bud

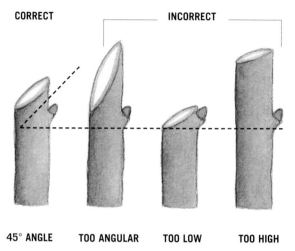

CORRECT   INCORRECT

45° ANGLE   TOO ANGULAR   TOO LOW   TOO HIGH

growth that makes a plant bushy. These buds stay dormant until the shoot has grown long enough to diminish the influence of the hormones produced by the terminal bud or until the terminal bud is pruned off—then they begin their growth. If you remove lateral buds, you'll redirect growth to the terminal bud; the shoot will lengthen dramatically and tend to grow upward.

Latent buds lie dormant beneath the bark. If a branch breaks or is cut off just above a latent bud, the bud may develop a new shoot to replace the wood that has been removed. If you need to repair a damaged plant, look for a latent bud and cut above it.

PRUNING CUTS

There are four basic pruning cuts, each aimed at producing a different effect. For cuts that involve cutting above a growth bud, make your cut as shown at left above. Angle it at about 45°, with the lowest point of the cut opposite the bud and even with it; the highest point about ¼ inch above the bud.

BOW SAW

LOPPERS

HEDGE SHEARS

Pinching is one of the easiest "cuts" to make without cutting: You simply pinch off a terminal bud with your thumb and forefinger. This stops the stem from elongating and encourages bushy growth. It is typically done on annual and perennial flowers and on some vegetables. Also use it to direct growth of small-leaved shrubs and give the plant an even shape.

HEADING

Heading means cutting farther back on the shoot than you would for pinching. In most cases, the lateral bud has already grown a leaf, and you cut right above the leaf. Usually done with hand-held pruners, heading stimulates the buds just below the cut, encouraging dense growth.

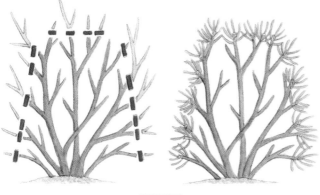

SHEARING

Shearing, customarily used to create a hedge or a bush with spherical or square form, is a form of heading that makes no attempt to cut back to a bud. However, because plants chosen for this treatment typically have many lateral buds close together, you'll usually end up cutting near a bud. Shearing stimulates many buds to produce new growth, so you'll be repeating the job regularly after you start. Because this method cuts right through leaves, it's best done on small-leaved plants, where damage is less noticeable. Use hand-held or electric hedge shears for this kind of pruning.

THINNING

Thinning reduces the bulk of a plant with minimal regrowth: Each cut removes an entire stem or branch, either back to its point of origin on the main stem or to the point where it joins another branch. Because you remove a number of lateral buds along with the stem or branch, you're less likely to wind up with clusters of unwanted shoots than you are when making heading cuts. (A common mistake of inexperienced gardeners is to make a heading cut when a thinning cut is needed.) Use hand-held pruners, loppers, or a pruning saw to make thinning cuts, depending on the thickness of the branch being cut.

ELECTRIC HEDGE SHEARS

TIPS

- Use scissors-cut hand shears for precise cuts on branches up to $1/2$ inch thick.
- Use long-handled loopers for the extra leverage needed to cut branches up to $1^3/4$ inches.
- Use bow saws to cut large limbs quickly.

A smaller lawn means big savings in water use and mowing time, especially if you choose a drought-tolerant, low-maintenance grass, such as this buffalo grass lawn in San Antonio, Texas.

Lawn Care

WATERING, MOWING, AND FERTILIZING

The key to a great lawn—one that is dense, evenly green, and has few pests or weeds—is not doing just one thing right; it's doing a combination of things right. A great lawn results from a balanced program of proper watering, fertilizing, mowing, and aerating. And that's assuming you've planted a type of grass that's well adapted to your area (for more about choosing the right grass, see pages 338 to 345). But assuming you've got a reasonably healthy lawn to start with, here's how to keep it beautiful.

WATERING

Although lawns do need lots of water, many gardeners are too generous, often providing twice the amount the lawn really needs. Overwatering does more than just waste water. It leaches fertilizer and natural soil nutrients from the root zone and creates perpetually wet conditions that can encourage disease. And a heavily watered lawn grows faster and requires more mowing.

In general, warm-season grasses require less moisture than cool-season types; the tall fescues are among the least needy of the cool-season ones. On average, however, most grasses need 1 to 2 inches of water per week, whether from rainfall, irrigation, or both. To encourage roots to grow deep, water infrequently, adding the 1 to 2 inches all at one go. If you simply sprinkle on a little water each day, the roots will stay near the surface. If there is then a prolonged dry spell or if you forget to water, the root system won't be able to draw enough water from deeper in the soil to survive.

After watering, wait until the top inch or two of soil has dried before watering again. To check, probe the soil with a thick piece of wire or a long screwdriver. It will move easily through moist soil but stop when it reaches firmer, dry soil. You can also use a soil-sampling tube (see page 389). An even faster way to determine whether a lawn needs watering is simply to walk across it. If your

dead patches and water well. If the grass doesn't come back on its own, reseed or resod.

Chinch bugs are ¼-inch-long, gray black insects that suck juices from grass blades. They cause brownish yellow patches in lawns, primarily in St. Augustine and zoysia grasses (and sometimes in bluegrass and creeping bent grass), especially in hot or drought-stressed conditions. To diagnose, sink an empty can (open at both ends) into the ground at the edge of a patch. Fill the can with water. If chinch bugs are present, they'll float to the surface. To minimize spread, keep the area well watered. Chemical controls include insecticidal soap, pyrethroids, and sevin.

Sod webworms aren't worms at all, but small, hairless gray caterpillars—the larvae of tiny buff-colored moths that, if present, can be seen flying close to the lawn's surface in the evening. Sod webworms feed on grass blades. Symptoms are small dead patches of lawn that appear in spring and enlarge during summer. To diagnose, drench an area of lawn near the dead spots with a solution of 1 tablespoon liquid dishwashing detergent diluted in 1 gallon of water. The larvae will come to the surface. If you find more than 15 larvae in a square yard, treat the lawn. For chemical control, use *Bacillus thuringiensis*, insecticidal soap, neem, pyrethroids, or sevin. If you don't want to use chemicals, you may be able to reduce the pest population by improving lawn care. Don't overwater or overfertilize; dethatch and aerate (page 412) regularly.

White grubs is a catchall name for the soil-dwelling larvae of various kinds of beetles, including June bugs (named for the month when they are usually noticed), rose chafers, and Japanese beetles. The larvae of all these beetles feed on lawn roots. They're typically white with brown heads; when exposed, they curl up in a C-shape. Signs of their presence include distinct, irregularly shaped brown patches in the lawn; damage is usually most severe in late summer. Because the roots have been eaten, the dead patches pull up easily. Remove a patch and dig into the soil; if you find more than one grub per square foot, treat the soil. Correct identification of the grubs will help you choose the best means of treatment; for help in identifying them, take a few to a Lowe's, or a cooperative extension office. Nematodes control many kinds of grubs. Chemical controls include halofenizide and imidacloprid.

Fairy rings are small to large circular patches of dark

green grass surrounding areas of dead or light-colored grass; mushrooms may or may not be present at the perimeter of the green area. The rings result from a fungal disease common in lawns growing in soil high in organic matter. To control the problem, aerate the soil, apply a nitrogen fertilizer formulated for lawn care, and keep the lawn wet for three to five days.

Rust is a fungal disease. Among lawns, it affects primarily bluegrass and ryegrass. Grass blades turn yellowish to reddish brown throughout, small reddish pustules form in groups on older blades and stems, and the

Dandelion   Crabgrass

Bermuda grass   Yellow oxalis

blades eventually die. The best solution for rust is to apply a nitrogen fertilizer formulated for lawn care, water regularly, and mow more frequently.

Weeds infesting the rest of your garden will also attempt to establish themselves in the lawn. A healthy lawn isn't at high risk. Its grass stems grow thickly together, making it difficult for weed seeds to reach soil, germinate, and take root. But if the lawn is in poor condition and patchy soil is exposed, weed infestation is likely.

Some warm-season grasses—bermuda and zoysia, in particular—can themselves be weeds if accidentally introduced into a lawn of a different grass type. The controls noted for bermuda grass noted on page 423 are also effective against zoysia. Other lawn weeds include common mallow, crabgrass, dandelion, oxalis, plantain, quack grass, and spotted spurge.

① **Check your lawn** for thatch, accumulated dead stems, roots, and other debris that impedes the penetration of water. A small amount of thatch, less than ½ inch, is normal.

② **Dethatching machine** slices through mat of old turf so new seeds can reach soil. Dethatching also promotes air circulation and eliminates hiding places for pests.

Renovating a Lawn

Dethatching and aerating Controlling thatch is one of the most important—and most overlooked—parts of lawn care. Thatch is simply the layer of dead grass, roots, and debris that accumulates between the soil surface and the green grass blades above. Over time, it forms a thick mat, hindering water and air from reaching the soil and providing an environment that can encourage pests and diseases. Dethatching can help prevent these problems.

Almost every lawn needs dethatching about once a year or whenever the thatch reaches a thickness of about ½ inch. To check, just work your fingers into the grass and note the depth of the thatch layer. Dethatch cool-season grasses in fall, warm-season types in early spring.

If your lawn is small, you can dethatch it with a special dethatching rake. The sturdy, very sharp, crescent-shaped

DETHATCHING RAKE

tines slice into the thatch, and you then rake it up. For larger lawns, you may prefer to rent a dethatching machine. Similar in appearance to a large, heavy gas mower, it has knifelike blades that slice the turf vertically. Make several crisscrossing passes to cut and loosen the thatch, and then rake up and remove all debris.

Dethatching machines have several settings. For most grasses, adjust the blades to a high setting and 3 inches apart; for tougher grasses, such as bermuda and zoysia, set the blades lower and about an inch apart.

Aeration, a method of punching holes into the lawn to allow moisture, oxygen, and nutrients to penetrate the soil, also helps break up thatch. Its primary goal is to loosen compacted soil; it's often needed for lawns grown in clay soils and those subject to heavy foot traffic. You can do the job more than once a year, if necessary. If you aerate once annually, do it in fall for cool-season grasses, in spring for warm-season sorts.

You can aerate soil with a hand tool. Press the cutting end into the soil with your foot, and then lift it out along with a 2-inch, cylindrical plug of sod. Hand aeration is certainly good aerobic exercise, but it can be time consuming if you have a large lawn. For good-sized areas, a gas-powered aerator does the job faster; rent one from supply centers offering garden-machine rentals. (You may also see spike-soled sandals sold as aerating tools: You walk back and forth over the lawn wearing this footgear, and the spikes will supposedly

3 **Power aerators** remove cylindrical plugs of grass and soil, leaving small holes in the lawn where turf seeds can germinate. Aerating also improves air and water circulation.

4 **Rake up and remove soil** and debris brought to the surface by the dethatching and aerating process.

penetrate the soil. Unfortunately, the spikes are both too short and too thin to do an efficient job. Save your money.)

After the lawn has been aerated, clear away the plugs and spread a layer of organic matter, such as compost or soil conditioner, over the lawn. Water the organic matter in, and it will seep into the holes left by the plugs, improving the soil's texture.

LAWN RENOVATION

At some point, you may move into a home with a tired, worn lawn. Before you decide that you need to remove it and start over from scratch, see if it can be renovated.

As a first step, give the lawn good care. Check for diseases and pests, control any you find, and get rid of weeds. At the best time of year for your type of grass,

5 **Scatter seeds** of a top-quality lawn seed over the aerated and dethatched lawn. Follow up with fertilizer, a light mulch, and water.

dethatch and aerate, being sure you do a thorough job. You want to be certain that grass seed will be able to reach the soil to germinate. Rake up and remove all debris.

Buy a grass seed compatible with your climate and the use the lawn will receive (see pages 338 to 345). Apply both seed and a complete granular controlled-release fertilizer over the lawn. Top-dress the area with an organic amendment, such as compost or soil conditioner. It will seep into the holes made during aeration, improving the soil, and will also provide some protection for the germinating grass seeds.

Water the lawn lightly and evenly and continue to water often enough to keep it constantly moist until the seeds are fully sprouted and the new blades are about a third taller than their optimum height (this usually works out to 2 to 3 inches tall). You may need to water three, four, or more times a day if the weather is warm. After the new grass is tall enough, you can mow it, taking off only the top third. At this time, begin a regular watering program, but avoid walking on the lawn for another four to six weeks.

Pests are rare in this garden because the plants are appropriate to the climate, and because the diversity of plants encourages beneficial insects and birds, essential partners in pest control.

Managing Garden Pests

KNOWING WHEN—AND WHEN NOT—TO TAKE ACTION

The notion of pest control—where control implies eradication—has been superseded by the concept of pest management. The management concept acknowledges that many perceived "problems" are natural components of gardens, and the presence of pests doesn't necessarily spell trouble. In a diversified garden, most insect pests are kept in check by natural forces (such as predators and weather). If pests reach damaging levels, however, temporary intervention may be needed to restore a balance.

Because of this natural system of checks and balances in a garden, it makes sense to determine which form of intervention will return the situation to a normal balance with the least risk of destroying helpful (as well as harmless) organisms that maintain the equilibrium. Action choices range from doing nothing (giving nature a chance to correct the imbalance), to using restraints (washing plants, thereby repelling or physically destroying the damagers), to

implementing biological controls (improving the helpful side of nature's control system), or, as a last choice, using chemical controls.

THE INTEGRATED APPROACH (IPM)

More and more gardeners are turning to physical restraints and biological controls as a first line of defense against garden pests because they want natural gardens that are safer for children, pets, and wildlife. Yet garden experts acknowledge the need for at least occasional treatment with chemical controls. This approach—the preferred use of natural and mechanical controls, plus chemicals as a discretionary second choice—is called integrated pest management, or IPM for short. Increasingly, IPM is being used in parks, city landscapes, and greenhouses.

The following points explain how to implement IPM in your own garden. Most are just good common sense, but it helps to see how basic gardening practices influence pest problems.

Select well-adapted plants Choose plants that are adapted to your area and that are resistant to your region's pest and disease problems. Plants stressed by inhospitable climate or from lack of water or nutrients are more vulnerable to damaging organisms than are their healthy, well-cared-for counterparts.

Adjust planting time If by planting early you can avoid a pest, do so. For instance, a common pest of beans, spider mites, are most troublesome when the weather turns hot. By planting beans early, as soon as soil warms, you can avoid them. Keep records of planting dates and temperatures so you can make adjustments from season to season.

Pick large pests like tomato hornworm by hand (or with a tool).

Try mechanical controls Handpicking, traps, barriers, floating row covers, or strong water sprays can reduce or thwart many pests, especially in the early stages of a potential problem. Cleanup of plant debris can remove the environment in which certain pests and diseases breed or overwinter.

Yellow sticky card attracts and traps tiny whiteflies.

Accept minor damage A totally pest-free garden is neither possible nor desirable. Allow natural control methods to play the major role in maintaining a healthy balance between pests, beneficial insects, and the many harmless insects and creatures that are normal in gardens.

Use less-toxic alternatives Release or encourage beneficial insects; use soaps, horticultural oils, botanical insecticides (such as natural pyrethrins and neem), and one of several packaged forms of *Bacillus thuringiensis*. Realize that beneficial insects may take a while to reduce the pests they prey upon and that you may have to use nonchemical controls at more frequent intervals than you would chemical controls. And although many natural insecticides have a relatively low impact on the environment, they can be harmful to humans if used carelessly. Follow instructions exactly.

SYNTHETIC INSECTICIDES

Here are the most common insecticides, listed by active ingredient, with the most common trade names in parentheses. Broad-spectrum insecticides kill a wide variety of insects. Use them only as a last resort as their victims usually include many nonpest insects. Systemic insecticides are absorbed by plants, rendering all parts toxic for days or weeks.

ACEPHATE (ORTHENE) A synthetic poison (one absorbed by the plant and incorporated into its tissues), this broad-spectrum product is used against aphids, beetles, caterpillars, grasshoppers, leaf miners, mealybugs, thrips, root weevils, whiteflies, other pests. Don't use on edible crops. Toxic to honeybees and birds.

CARBARYL (SEVIN) Broad-spectrum contact insecticide. Controls most chewing insects but is not effective against many sucking types. In fact, it often increases problems with the latter by destroying natural predators. Registered for use on edible crops. Highly toxic to honeybees, fish, and earthworms.

IMIDACLOPRID (MERIT) Systemic. Controls a variety of pests in lawns and ornamentals. Particularly effective against hard-to-control pests like scale and borers. Toxic to fish.

MALATHION Broad-spectrum contact insecticide that controls aphids, beetles, caterpillars, mealybugs, scales, thrips, whiteflies, other pests. Registered for use on edible crops. Toxic to honeybees, birds, and fish.

PYRETHROIDS Synthetic versions of plant-based pyrethrins, pyrethroids are increasingly being used in pesticides and are effective against many household and garden pests. Active ingredients include permethrin, cyfluthrin, esfenvalerate, and others. Less hazardous to humans, birds, and mammals than many other pesticides; toxic to honeybees and fish.

Use chemicals prudently on those rare occasions you need one. Before you buy a chemical control and apply

Ladybugs earn their good name by consuming common pests.

it, be sure you have correctly identified the problem. Use a pesticide only to solve a problem if both the pest and the plant it is preying on are listed on the pesticide's label. If you are at all uncertain, ask a Lowe's nursery associate or your nearest cooperative extension office.

COMMON INSECT PESTS

The following insects are familiar garden troublemakers through most of North America.

Aphids are tiny green, yellow, black, or pink insects—soft and sometimes winged. They cluster thickly on new growth; heavy infestations will stunt new growth. In trees, the secretions of the sticky "honeydew" they produce will drip on everything beneath the branches.

Controls Hose them off or spray with insecticidal soap, imidacloprid, neem, pyrethrum products, malathion, or acephate.

Beetles are hard-shelled insects that chew holes in leaves and flowers; in larval phase, they're ground-dwelling grubs that often feed on lawns. Japanese beetles are a major summer foliage pest in the eastern United States.

Controls Hand pick, use pheromone traps, or spray with imidacloprid, neem, pyrethrum products, carbaryl, or malathion.

Borers are burrowing insects that cause limbs and branches to die. Telltale signs may be small holes in a tree or shrub branch accompanied by bits of sawdust nearby. Those borers that tunnel beneath bark may show no entry holes but may leave bits of sawdust in bark crevices. Young softwood trees and plants stressed from improper care are particularly vulnerable. For prevention, wrap trunks of newly planted specimens with special protective wrap. Adult moths lay eggs on bark, so the best time to intervene is when larvae are newly hatched and before they enter the wood. Reduce plant stress by providing better care, such as more water.

Controls Drench soil with imidacloprid.

Caterpillars and worms include many multilegged, crawling larvae of moths and butterflies. They range from the relatively innocuous inchworm to the voracious, highly destructive gypsy moth caterpillar.

Controls Handpick or spray with *Bacillus thuringiensis*, neem, carbaryl, or acephate.

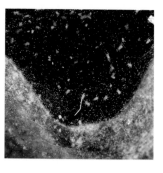

Mites are tiny spider relatives found on leaf undersides (webbing is often present); leaf surface is pale and stippled. Foliage eventually dries out and turns brown.

Controls Wash mites from foliage with a strong blast of water. Use native predatory mites. Spray with insecticidal soap, summer oil, neem oil, or sulfur.

Scale insects begin life as tiny crawlers, but their adult stage attaches to stems and leaves, covering their bodies with protective, waxy shells. Typically they congregate in colonies.

Controls Adult scale can be rubbed off by hand (for light infestations) or sprayed with a dormant oil (for deciduous plants in winter only). For the juvenile, crawler stage, spray with summer oil, carbaryl, malathion, imidacloprid, or acephate.

Snails and slugs are night-feeding pests. Snails have shells, slugs don't. They feast on leaves, stems, and flowers, leaving telltale trails of silvery slime.

Controls Handpick and destroy. Containers filled with beer and set at ground level attract the pests, which then fall in and drown. Use barriers: Surround plants or beds with rings of diatomaceous earth or enclose containers and raised beds with copper strips. Use baits containing nontoxic iron phosphate. Apply metaldehyde bait (but keep it away from children, pets, and birds).

Whiteflies are tiny white pests that fly up in a cloud when disturbed; they suck plant juices from leaf undersides. Damaged foliage is sometimes stippled and may eventually curl and turn brown. **Controls** Hose off plants frequently with water jets; spray directly with insecticidal soap. Or try neem, pyrethrum products, and horticultural oil. Stronger insecticides kill beneficials, often increasing problems.

COMMON BENEFICIAL INSECTS

Some of the creatures described here are naturally present in gardens; others, as noted, can be introduced to reduce various pest populations. Spiders and centipedes are also important predators, as are toads, frogs, and birds.

Ground beetles range from $\frac{1}{2}$ to 1 inch long; most are shiny black, though some are also marked with bright colors. The smaller species eat other insects, caterpillars, cutworms, and soil-dwelling maggots and grubs. Some larger species eat slugs and snails and their eggs.

Lacewings An adult lacewing is an inch-long, flying insect with lacy, netted wings and long antennae. The immature or larval form looks something like a $\frac{1}{2}$-inch-long alligator; it has visible legs and is equipped with pincers at the mouth end. Lacewing larvae devour aphids, leafhoppers, mealybugs, mites, psyllids, thrips, whiteflies, and other insects; adults of most species feed only on nectar, pollen, and honeydew from garden plants. Larvae are commercially available.

Ladybugs are familiar garden helpers and their larvae (which look like $\frac{1}{4}$-inch-long six-legged alligators with orange and black spots or stripes) feed on aphids, mealybugs, and the eggs of many insects. Mail-order and

garden centers sell lady beetles, but once released they often fly away rather than staying in your garden. Freeing them at night or keeping them contained for the first few days may encourage them to remain.

Parasitic nematodes include several species of microscopic worms. Also known as beneficial or predatory nematodes, they're effective against several hundred kinds of insects, including cucumber beetles, cutworms, flea beetles, grubs, root weevils, and sod webworms. They attack the larvae, releasing a toxic bacterium that kills the host. Can be purchased. Effectiveness depends on proper soil conditions and release techniques.

Soldier beetles are narrow, $\frac{3}{4}$-inch-long, typically red or orange insects with leathery-looking black, gray, or brown wing covers. Adults eat aphids and other soft-bodied insects; the tiny soil-dwelling larvae attack smaller insects. Adults also feed on pollen and nectar.

Syrphid flies, also known as flower or hover flies, are important naturally occurring beneficials. Adults have bodies banded with yellow; they look a bit like bees but have only one set of wings. While adults feed only on nectar and pollen, the larvae (tapered green or gray maggots with small fangs) consume dozens of aphids each day.

Tachinid fly adults are gray and, bristled, look something like houseflies. They feed only on nectar, but their tiny, spined, green larvae parasitize pests such as armyworms, cutworms, stinkbugs, and smaller beetle larvae. Many species, each attacking specific insects.

ANIMAL PESTS

A number of animals, including gophers, moles, squirrels, field mice, and deer can damage gardens and plants.

You may be able to keep tunneling moles, gophers, and ground squirrels out of gardens and beds by surrounding them with underground fencing 3 to 4 feet deep. But that's not very practical. You can also use barriers for raised beds, or plant bulbs and landscape plants in wire baskets. As a last resort, try traps or poison baits, following the manufacturer's instructions.

Deer are thriving throughout North America, and a pair like this can decimate a garden in one evening.

The best way to keep aboveground animals out of your garden is to build a strong fence. Deer fencing should be at least 7 feet high. Fencing to keep out rabbits should be a few feet high but also extend 6 inches below ground. To keep mice and other animals from feeding on bark, wrap trunks with protective materials. For more information on keeping animals out of your garden, consult your local cooperative extension office.

DISEASES

A healthy plant, like a healthy human being, is better able to resist the microorganisms that cause disease. Focus on keeping your plants strong and vigorous, and you'll have already taken an important step toward preventing problems. Sometimes, though, diseases will appear despite your best efforts. But if you're familiar with their symptoms and the controls that can be used against them, you'll have a better chance of stopping them before they can get established.

Fungi, bacteria, and viruses are the pathogens most often responsible for plant diseases. Unlike green plants, these organisms are incapable of manufacturing their own food and must instead take it from a host plant. Fungi can live in the soil, but the bacteria and viruses that cause plant problems can't survive outside their host.

Fungi multiply by tiny reproductive bodies called spores (their equivalent of seeds), which they produce in great quantity. Spores of some fungi enter plants through the roots; others land on leaves, where they attach and complete their life cycle. A single fungus-infected leaf may release 100 million spores, which drift through the garden and onto new hosts with even the slightest breath of air.

Bacteria need water and warmth to multiply, so the diseases they cause tend to be more prevalent in warm, wet climates. These single-celled organisms are easily transmitted by rain, splashing irrigation water, and gardeners working among plants. They enter plants through a wound or natural opening.

Viruses are even smaller than bacteria; they can reproduce only within the actual cells of the host organism. Some viruses are transmitted by insects, such as aphids, leafhoppers, and thrips; others are carried by infected seeds and pollen. Viruses also enter plants through wounds and cuts.

DISEASE PREVENTION

You can't always prevent a disease from attacking a prized plant. The bacterial infection fireblight, for example, can enter blossoms readily if there is rain just at the time of bloom; you'd have to control the weather to stop it. A mosaic-virus-infected bare-root rose won't exhibit symptoms until it leafs out.

Luckily, good gardening practices will fend off many diseases. To keep plant problems under control, take the following steps.

Keep plants healthy by giving them the water, light, and fertilizer they need to flourish.

Buy disease-resistant plants You'll find tomatoes that are resistant to verticillium wilt and flowering pear trees less likely to succumb to fireblight, for example. Vegetable seed packets are labeled to indicate the particular plant's disease resistance; plant tags on fruit trees or ornamental trees and shrubs sometimes also include this information. Your cooperative extension office can often provide information on plants resistant to diseases that may cause problems in your area.

Transplant carefully to minimize root damage. When broken, roots are susceptible to certain soilborne diseases.

Avoid injuring plants when you work in the garden. An

Continued on page 420

PRODUCTS FOR DISEASE PREVENTION AND CONTROL

A number of products are aimed at disease prevention or control. These include preventives, products that prevent diseases from occurring but can't control them after they become established; eradicants, which help control diseases after they have appeared (many simply protect new growth); and systemics, materials that are taken up by plant roots and act as preventives, eradicants, or both. Controls described here are the most useful and commonly available ones. Other less widely sold products are mentioned in the descriptions of specific plant diseases. The products below are listed by the accepted common name of the active ingredient; that is, the actual chemical that prevents or controls the disease or diseases listed on the package label. Some widely used trade names, if they differ from the common name, are noted in parentheses. Before you buy, read the label to make sure you're getting the active ingredient you want. Always dispose of pesticides in a safe manner.

NATURAL FUNGICIDES AND BACTERICIDES

Natural fungicides and bactericides are products whose active ingredients originate in a plant, animal, or mineral, or whose action results from a biological process (as in a product containing live bacteria that combat harmful fungi). "Natural," however, does not mean "harmless:" Some of these products can harm people or plants if not used properly. When using any product, read label directions carefully and follow them exactly. The package will clearly state the plants and diseases for which the control product is registered for use, and it is illegal to use it on a plant or to control a disease not so listed.

BAKING SODA, SODIUM BICARBONATE
You can buy baking soda sprays, but it's easy to make your own by mixing 2 teaspoons each of baking soda and fine-grade horticultural oil with 1 gallon of water. This solution helps to control powdery mildew on roses. Commercial versions contain a sticky ingredient to help keep the spray on the plant.
COPPER COMPOUNDS (BORDEAUX MIXTURE)
General-purpose fungicides and bactericides used to prevent fireblight, peach leaf curl, shot hole, brown rot, and other foliar diseases. Toxic to fish.
COPPER SOAP FUNGICIDE
Broad-spectrum fungicide used to control many plant diseases, including rust, black spot, and powdery mildew.
LIME SULFUR, CALCIUM POLYSULFIDE
Used as a spray in winter (when plants are dormant) to prevent various leaf spots and peach leaf curl. Very caustic; wear goggles and plastic gloves when applying.
NEEM OIL (ROSE DEFENSE AND OTHERS)
Used to prevent and control black spot, powdery mildew, and some other foliar diseases. (Also used as an insecticide and miticide.) Toxic to fish.
POTASSIUM BICARBONATE (REMEDY, OTHERS)
Used to control powdery mildew. May not be registered in all states.
SULFUR (SULFUR DUST, OTHERS)
Controls powdery mildew, rust, and other diseases. Do not use in conjunction with horticultural oil sprays or when the outdoor temperature is above 85°F.

SYNTHETIC FUNGICIDES

Synthetic fungicides are manufactured compounds that don't normally occur in nature. Here are the ones most useful for home gardeners.
CHLOROTHALONIL (DACONIL, OTHERS)
Broad-spectrum liquid fungicide used to prevent powdery mildew, leaf spots, gray mold, scab, and a variety of lawn and other diseases. Toxic to fish.
MYCLOBUTANIL (IMMUNOX)
Liquid systemic for prevention and eradication of many common diseases of lawns, roses, and fruit trees.
TRIADIMEFON (FUNGI-FIGHTER; FORMERLY BAYLETON)
Wettable powder; systemic used for the prevention or eradication of powdery mildew, rust, and some lawn diseases. Toxic to fish.
TRIFORINE (FUNGINEX)
Liquid systemic for prevention and eradication of powdery mildew, rust, black spot, and a variety of other diseases. You must wear goggles and a face mask during application. Keep animals out of treated areas.

Continued from page 418

open wound on a plant stem or tree trunk readily admits bacteria and fungi.

Avoid wet-weather garden work You may unwittingly spread waterborne pathogens as you move about from one spot to the next.

Install a drip-irrigation system (see pages 218 and 219) or use soaker hoses to minimize the splashing water that can spread waterborne diseases.

Raking is more than a fall ritual that keeps the garden neat. It also removes diseased leaves so they can't infect new growth next spring.

Remove diseased plants If certain plants are constantly afflicted by disease, eliminate them from the garden and replace them with less trouble-prone choices. This solution is simpler than attempting to control the disease, and it removes sources of further infection.

Dispose of infected plants and plant parts right away. Throw them out with the trash; don't compost them. Some pathogens may be killed by the heat generated during decomposition, but it's better not to take the chance.

Keep the garden clean Do a thorough fall cleanup each year. Remove weeds, because pathogens may overwinter on them. In mild-winter areas, strip off any diseased leaves remaining on plants; rake up and discard all diseased leaves on the ground. You may also want to rake up other garden debris; although it can serve as a good mulch (if undiseased), it also shelters ground-dwelling pests.

COMMON DISEASES

Anthracnose is a fungus that attacks new shoots and leaves in spring, causing them to turn brown and die; in older leaves it causes large, irregular brown patches and premature leaf drop. Spores are spread by rainfall and sprinkling, so the disease is severe in wet springs but disappears in warm, dry weather. It overwinters in cankers on twigs it has killed, only to reinfect new growth in spring. To prevent, cut out all dead twigs and branches.
Controls Spray with lime sulfur during the dormant season. Use chlorothalonil in spring (check with your cooperative extension service for timing in your area).

Black spot is a fungal disease that thrives in high-humidity areas with ample summer rain. It attacks roses exclusively. Young leaves show black, irregular circles, sometimes surrounded with a yellow halo, that then drop from the plant. Heavy infestation can defoliate a plant, thus preventing it from building up nutrient reserves.
In cold-weather regions, badly infected plants can become so depleted that they may not survive the winter.
Controls Prevent the disease by planting resistant rose varieties. Remove and destroy all diseased foliage in fall. Some gardeners have had good luck controlling black spot with weekly applications of a baking soda and summer oil spray; to make the solution, mix 2 teaspoons baking soda and 2 teaspoons summer oil with a gallon of water. Others report success with soap sprays

or sulfur. Chemical controls include chlorothalonil, myclobutanil, and triforine. Repeat applications of spray will be needed as long as the weather conditions favor the development of the fungus.

Powdery mildew shows up as a powdery white to gray coating on leaves, stems, and flower buds. It attacks a wide variety of plants, including beans, clematis, dahlia, grape, hydrangea, rose, strawberry, tomato, and zinnia, as well as apple, maple, oak, peach, and sycamore trees. Heavy infestations debilitate and disfigure plants. Favored by moist air, poor air circulation, and shade but needs dry leaves to become established.

Controls To prevent powdery mildew, plant resistant varieties and routinely spray plants with jets of water to wash off fungus spores. Increase sunlight to plants by avoiding overcrowding. In the fall, discard infected flowers, fruits, and plants. Sulfur may help; on roses and other flowering plants, try a baking soda and summer oil spray (see the preceding entry on black spot). Some gardeners report success with antitranspirant sprays sold to protect tender plants from cold. Such sprays keep the surface temperature of treated leaves somewhat higher than that of the surrounding air; apparently they also prevent mildew spores from attaching to foliage. Chemical controls include triforine and myclobutanil.

Root rots are caused by fungi and are mostly active in warm, wet, or poorly drained soils. Young leaves turn yellow and wilt; plants may be stunted or may wilt and die, even in moist soil. Trees and shrubs may die a branch at a time.
Controls Plant resistant varieties. Keep soils moist but do not overwater. Improve drainage. No chemical management. Consult local cooperative extension service for additional information.

Rust is a fungus of many different types, and each type is specific to a certain plant. Yellow, orange, red, or brown pustules appear on leaf undersides; the powdery spores are spread by wind and water.
Controls Buy resistant varieties. Because rust spreads fastest in wet conditions (leaves must be wet for at least 4 to 5 hours for spores to germinate), you can minimize spread by curtailing overhead watering. Remove and discard most affected leaves; dispose of infected leaves that drop to the ground and clean up all debris in fall. Sulfur and summer oil may help (do not apply them simultaneously; the combination is toxic to plants). Chemical controls include chlorothalonil, myclobutanil, triadimefon, and triforine (especially on roses).

Sooty mold is caused by a number of different fungi. This disease can afflict any plant. It shows up as a powdery dark brown or black coating on leaves, hence the name. The responsible fungi live on a plant's natural secretions and on the honeydew excreted by aphids, mealybugs, and scale. While fairly harmless on its own, sooty mold may weaken a plant if combined with extensive insect damage.
Controls Reduce the population of honeydew-excreting insects. Rinse small, ornamental plants by hand; hose down larger infected areas (such as trees or expanses of ground covers). There is no chemical control.

CONTROLLING WEEDS

Weeds are wild plants (and some invasive cultivated plants, like bamboo, English ivy, and honeysuckle) that compete with your garden plants for water, nutrients, and space. They're inevitable, but you can manage them. Prevention through mulches, landscape fabrics, and blanketlike ground covers is the first line of defense. Hand-weeding before weeds set seed is also critical. If you're vigilant for a few years, you'll be rewarded with a sharp decline in your garden's weed population.

Because they develop extensive root systems, perennial

Two common weeds often require repeated treatments to eliminate; they are yellow nutsedge (left) and bindweed (right).

weeds are more difficult to manage after they've grown past the seedling stage—to get rid of the plant, you have to dig out the roots. Hasten their demise by repeatedly cutting back the tops, which stresses the plants, but it may take several seasons to eradicate the weeds. Annual weed seeds can be windborne or delivered by birds, arrive in nursery containers, or be present in certain mulches (so use only mulches that are weed-free).

Herbicides are powerful chemicals that can damage desirable plants and contaminate water and soil. Before buying one, always read the label to ensure you have the correct product for the weeds in your garden.

Herbicides are classified according to what stage of weed growth they affect, as well as by how they damage weeds.

Pre-emergence herbicides work by inhibiting the growth of germinating weed seeds and very young seedlings; they do not affect established plants. To be effective, they must be applied before the seeds sprout. Before applying these chemicals in ornamental gardens, remove any existing weeds. Some pre-emergence products are formulated to kill germinating weeds in lawns; these may be sold in combination with fertilizers, which increase the vigor of the lawn and improve its ability to compete against weeds. (Such dual-purpose products should not be treated solely as fertilizers and reapplied whenever the lawn needs feeding—for that purpose, use a regular lawn fertilizer.) Some pre-emergence products must be watered into the soil, while others are incorporated into it. Some may also harm seeds you sow later in the season. Check the label to learn how long the product remains active in the soil.

Postemergence herbicides act on growing weeds rather than on seeds. They damage plants in different ways. Those that are translocated must be absorbed by the

Simple hand cultivators remain the best all-round weed control.

plant through its leaves or stems; they then kill it by interfering with its metabolism. Contact herbicides kill only the plant parts on which they are sprayed; regrowth can still occur from roots or unsprayed buds.

When using any herbicide, read the label directions carefully and follow them exactly. The package will clearly state the weeds that the product controls and the other plants, if any, around which it can be safely used; it is illegal to apply it to any plant not designated as a target. Always dispose of pesticides in a safe manner.

The following products are listed alphabetically by the accepted common name of the active ingredient— the actual chemical that controls the weed or weeds

listed on the package label. Some widely used trade names, if they differ from the common name, are noted in parentheses. Before you buy, read the label to make sure you're getting the active ingredient you want.

Synthetic herbicides are manufactured compounds that don't normally occur in nature. Natural herbicides are products whose active ingredients originate in a plant or mineral.

One-gallon pressure sprayer is commonly used to apply herbicides.

NATURAL HERBICIDES
Common natural herbicides include the following:

CORN GLUTEN MEAL (SUPPRESSA, OTHERS) Pre-emergence. Used to control some germinating weed seeds in lawns. This product is also a fertilizer, serving to thicken lawns and thus suppress weed growth (some research shows that this may be its primary contribution to weed control).

HERBICIDAL SOAP (SUPERFAST, OTHERS) Postemergence. Contact herbicide that degrades quickly. Kills top growth of young, actively growing weeds; works most effectively on annual weeds. Made from selected fatty acids (as are insecticidal soaps).

SYNTHETIC HERBICIDES
Common synthetic herbicides include the following:

FLUAZIFOP-BUTYL Postemergence. A translocated herbicide that controls actively growing grasses. Can be sprayed over many broad-leaved ornamentals without damaging them; check the label.

GLUFOSINATE-AMMONIUM (FINALE) Postemergence. Contact herbicide that damages or kills many kinds of weeds. Take care not to apply to desirable plants.

GLYPHOSATE (ROUNDUP) Postemergence. Translocated herbicide that kills or damages any plant it contacts. Effective on a broad range of troublesome weeds, but must be used with care to avoid contacting desirable plants.

ORYZALIN (SURFLAN) Pre-emergence. Used to control annual grasses and many broad-leaved weeds in warm-season turf grasses and in gardens.

PENDIMETHALIN (PROWL) Pre-emergence. Used to control many grasses and broad-leaved weeds in turf and in ornamental plantings. Toxic to fish.

SETHOXYDIM (GRASS-GETTER) Postemergence. Translocated herbicide that controls many grasses growing in ornamental plantings; check the label.

TRICLOPYR (BRUSH-B-GON, TURFLON ESTER) Postemergence. Translocated herbicide. Depending on formulation, used on cool-season turf to control broad-leaved weeds and Bermuda grass; also used to control hard-to-kill woody plants. Use with care to avoid damaging desirable plants.

TRIFLURALIN: Pre-emergence. Controls many grasses and broad-leaved weeds in turf and ornamental plantings. Toxic to fish.

Index

Page numbers in *italic* indicate photographs and illustrations.

A

Abelia grandiflora (glossy abelia), 320
Abies concolor (white fir), 314, *314*
accents, *162*
accessories and ornaments, 12–13, 290–291
Acer (maple), *17*
  circinatum (vine maple), 189
  griseum (paperbark maple), 197
  palmatum (Japanese maple), *15, 21, 30,* 179, 189, 310
  rubrum (red maple), 310
Achillea (yarrow), *65,* 181, 183, *332,* 348
acid soil, 303
Adiantum pedatum (maidenhair fern), 197
adobe, *91,* 102–103
Aegopodium podagraria (bishop's weed), 334
Aesculus carnea (red horsechestnut), 310
African corn lily, 370
African daisy, 50, 337, *337*
Agapanthus (lily-of-the-Nile), 203
Agastache rupestris (giant hyssop), 183
Agave spp., *21, 47, 64,* 192
Ageratum houstonianum (floss flower), 360, *360*
Agrostis stolonifera (creeping bent grass), 344, *344*
Ajuga reptans (carpet bugle), 334, *334*
Akebia quinata (fiveleaf akebia), 330
Albizia julibrissen (silk tree), 310
Alcea rosea (hollyhock), 181, 365, *365*
Alchemilla mollis (lady's mantle), *15, 57, 60, 97,* 348, *348*
alkaline soil, 303
Allamanda cathartica (common allamanda), 203
Allium (ornamental onion), 368, *368*
Alopecurus pratensis (foxtail grass), 374, *374*
Alpinia zerumbet (shell ginger), 203
alyssum, *60, 107,* 183, 361
Amaryllis belladonna (belladonna lily), 368
Amelanchier spp. (serviceberry), 183, 310
amethyst flower, 360
Anemone (anemone), 179, 368, *368*
angel's trumpet, *62*
annual flowers, 358–364. *See also specific annuals*
  planting, 358–359
  sampler of, 360–364
  using, 358
anthracnose, 420
Antirrhinum majus (snapdragon), 363, *363*
aphids, 416
apple, 184, 198, 312, *312*
Aquilegia (columbine), 189, 348, *348.376*
arborists, 171
arbors, *9, 10, 11, 12, 14, 15, 19, 22, 24, 35, 39, 44, 94, 97, 99, 147, 149*
  building instructions, 131, 254–255
  designing, 128–131, 166, *167*
arborvitae, 315
Arbutus menziesii (madrone), 189

architects and designers, 170–171
Archontophoenix cunninghamiana (king palm), *316,* 317, *317*
Arctostaphylos spp. (bearberry, manzanita), 183, 190, 191, 334, *334*
Arctotheca calendula (cape weed), 334
Arrhenatherum elatius bulbosum (bulbous oat grass), 374
Artemisia (wormwood), *155,* 348
artist's gardens, 52–53
Asclepias tuberosa (butterfly weed), 183, 348, *377*
ash, 311
Asian-style gardens, *21, 30–31, 122*
Asplenium bulbiferum (mother fern), 179
Aster
  amellus (Italian aster), 183
  frikartii, 199
  novae-angliae (New England aster), 348, *348*
Astilbe (false spiraea), 189, 348
Athyrium spp., *195,* 197
Aucuba japonica (Japanese aucuba), 320
autumn fern, 197
axis, *162*
azalea, *147,* 181, 189, 197, 326

B

baby's breath, 350
baby's tears, 337
bachelor's button, 363
backyard gym project, 270–271
bactericides, 419
Bahia grass, 345
Baileya multiradiata (desert marigold), 192
balance, landscape principle, 87
balled-and-burlap plants, selecting and planting, 307
bamboo
  gates and fences, *31, 122*
  golden, 203
  heavenly, 325
bamboo palm, 317
banana, flowering, 203
banana shrub, 201
barbecue grills, 280–281
barberry, *139,* 320, *320*
bare-root plants, selecting and planting, 307
basil, *49, 384,* 385
batter gauges, 231
bayberry, 324
beans, 184, 382, *382*
bearberry, 183, 190, 334, *334*
beard tongue, 352, *377*
bear's foot hellebore, 189, 197, 199
beebalm, 351, *351*
beetles, 416, 417
beets, 184, 383
Begonia, 195, 368
belladonna lily, 368
bellflower, 181, 349
bells-of-Ireland, 181
belvederes. *See* gazebos

Berberis thunbergii (Japanese barberry), 320, *320*
Bergenia, 348
berms and mounds, 209
Bermuda grass, 344, *411*
Beschorneria yuccoides, 191
Betula
  nigra (river birch), *33, 141,* 198, 310
  pendula (European white birch), 310
biennials, 358–359, 365
birch. *See Betula* (birch)
birds
  birdhouses, 294–295
  feeders and seed, 292–293
  landscaping for, 14–15, 58–59, 182–183
  providing water, 294
bishop's hat, 189, 197
bishop's weed, 334
black-eyed Susan, *346,* 352, *352, 377*
black-eyed Susan vine, 362, *362*
black spot, 420–421
blanket flower, *51, 65,* 183, 350, *350*
bleeding heart, 50, *57,* 189, 197, 349, *349*
blood meal, 398
bluebeard, 321
bluebells, *57*
blueberry, 184, 187
blue blossom, 191
blue fescue, 199, 335, *373, 374–375*
blue flax, *377*
blue gramma grass, 344
bluegrass, 345, *345*
blue lyme grass, 375
blue oat grass, 375, *375*
blue star creeper, *373*
bolts, 79
borers, 416
borrowed scenery, *163*
Boston ivy, *328,* 331
Bougainvillea, 191, 330, *330*
Bouteloua gracilis (blue gramma grass), 344
boxwood, *138,* 179, 320
brick, 96–99
  cutting, 233
  edges for paths and patios, 92–93
  laying in sand, 233
  patios, 91, 232
  patterns, *99*
  sizes, 98–99
  steps, *111,* 239
  types of, 96–97
  walls, *124,* 127, *127, 137*
Briza media (quaking grass), 374
broccoli, 383
Browallia (amethyst flower), 360
bubble diagrams, 157
Buchloe dactyloides (buffalo grass), 344, *344*
Buddleia spp. (butterfly bush), 181, 192, 194, 320, *320*
buffalo grass, 344, *344*
bugs, 414–417
building codes, 151, 206
building permits, 151, 206
bulbous oat grass, 374

bulbs, 181, 366–371. *See also specific bulbs*
burning bush, 323, *323*
Butia capitata (pindo palm), 203
butterflies, 59, *59,* 182–183
butterfly bush, 181, 192, 194, 320, *320*
butterfly weed, 183, 348, *377*
Buxus microphylla (Japanese boxwood), 320

C

cabbage, 383, *383*
cabbage palm, 203, 317
cactus, *58,* 192
Caesalpinia mexicana (Mexican bird of paradise), 192
Caladium, 50, *63,* 368
Calamagrostis acutiflora (feather reed grass), *373, 374*
Calendula officinalis (calendula), 363, *363*
California fuchsia, 191
California lilac, 321, *321*
California poppy, *55, 65,* 363, *376*
calla lily, 371
Callistemon citrinus (lemon bottlebrush), 320, *320*
Calluna vulgaris (heather), 320, 334, *334*
Camellia spp., 179, 320
Campanula (bellflower), 181
   carpatica (Carpathian bellflower), 349
   medium (Canterbury bells), 365, *365*
Campsis tagliabuana (trumpet creeper), 330
candytuft, 364
Canna, 63, 203
Canterbury bells, 365, *365*
cape weed, 334
Carex spp. (sedge), 189, 374, *374*
Cariss grandiflora (Natal plum), 321
Carmel creeper, 334
Carolina jessamine, 330, *330*
Carpathian bellflower, 349
carpet bugle, 334, *334*
carrots, 184, 383
Caryopteris clandonensis (bluebeard), 321
catch basins, 211, *211*
caterpillars, 416
Catharanthus roseus (Madagascar periwinkle), 360, *360*
catmint, *45, 60, 106,* 351
cattail, 183
Ceanothus spp., 191, 321, *321,* 334
cedar, *31,* 190, 314, *314*
Cedrus spp. (cedar), *31,* 190, 314, *314*
Celosia argentea (celosia), 360
cement, 207, 223
Centaurea cyanus (bachelor's button), 363
centipede grass, 344
Ceratostigma plumbaginoides (dwarf plumbago), 334
Cercidium spp. (palo verde), 192
Cercis canadensis (eastern redbud), *310,* 310
Chaenomeles (flowering quince), 321, *321*
chairs, selecting outdoor, 274–277
Chamaecyparis obtusa (hinoki cypress), 194

Chamaedorea spp. (bamboo palm), 317
Chamaemelum nobile (chamomile), 334
Chamaerops humilis (European fan palm), *316,* 317
chamomile, 334
chaparral plants, 379
Chasmanthium latifolium (sea oats), 374
chaste tree, 181
Chelone obliqua (turtlehead), 183
cherry, flowering, 181, 187, 189, 313
Chihuahuan sage, 192
children. *See* family-centered landscaping
chinch bugs, 411
Chinese fan palm, 317
Chinese fringe flower, 324
Chinese holly, 323–324
Chinese jasmine, 331, *331*
Chinese pistache, 312–313
Chinese wisteria, *142,* 331
Chitalpa tashkentensis (chitalpa), 311
chives, 385
Christmas rose, 199
Chrysanthemum
   coccineum (painted daisy), 349, *349*
   paludosum (miniature marguerite), 363
   parthenium (feverfew), 181
cinquefoil, 326, *326,* 337
Cistus (rockrose), 321
Citrus, 314
Clematis spp., *143,* 330, *330*
climate and plant selection, 298–299. *See also* microclimates
coffeeberry, 191
Colchicum speciosum, 199
coleus, 50, 195, 203, *288*
Colorado blue spruce, 315, *315*
columbine, 189, 348, *348,* 376
comfort, designing for, 10–11
compost and composting, 393–395
compost bins, 268–269, *394,* 395
computer-aided design, 171
concrete block walls, 124, *125,* 126, *126,* 127, *127,* 228–229, 231
concrete, cast
   edges for paths and patios, 92, 93
   finishes, *103, 223, 227, 227*
   foundations/footings, 124, 226
   mixing, 222–223
   paths, 102–103
   patios, *91,* 222, 224–225
   pouring a slab, 224–225
   safety, 207
   steps, 239
   surface treatments, 102, *103*
   tools, 225
concrete pavers, *91,* 100–101, 100–101, 232–233
coneflower, *16, 51, 58, 155,* 181, 187, *346,* 350, *350*
conifers. *See* evergreens
Consolida ambigua (larkspur), *155,* 181, 363
container gardening, *12,* 50–51, 194–195
container nursery plants, selecting and planting, 306

contractors, hiring, 170–171, 206
contracts, 207
cook's garden, 48–49
coral bells, 195, 197, 199, 350
Cordyline australis (dracaena), 191
coreopsis, *14, 46*
   annual, 360
   perennial, 181, 199, *349, 349*
corkscrew willow, 181
corn, 184, 382
Cornus (dogwood)
   florida (flowering dogwood), 181, 311, *311*
   kousa, 181
   stolonifera (redtwig dogwood), 183, 321, *321*
Cortaderia selloana (yellow pampas grass), 374
Cosmos, 16, 32, 181, 360, *360*
Cotinus coggygria (smoke tree), 321
Cotoneaster spp. (cotoneaster), 322, *322,* 335, *335*
cottage gardens, 44–45, *98*
cottonseed meal, 398
courtyard gardens, 40–41, *42, 50*
crabapple, 198, 312, *312*
crabgrass, *411*
cranberry bush, 199
cranesbill, *155,* 179, 336, 350
crape myrtle, *117, 138, 140,* 312, *312*
Crataegus (hawthorn), *58,* 311, *311*
creeping bent grass, 344, *344*
creeping zinnia, 362
creosote bush, 192
Crinum asiaticum (grand crinum), 201
crocosmia, 181
Crocus spp. (crocus), 199, 368, *368*
cucumbers, 382
Cuphea hyssopifolia (Mexican heather), 203
Cupressocyparis leylandii (Leyland cypress), 314
Cupressus arizonica (Arizona cypress), 314
cutting garden plan, 180–181
Cycas revoluta (sago palm), 203
Cynodon dactylon (bermuda grass), 344, *411*
cypress, 314

D

daffodils and narcissus, 181, 199, 370
Dahlia, 181, 369
dame's rocket, 183
dandelion, *411*
Daphne spp., 197, 201, 322
date palm, 203, 317
daylily, 201, 350, *350*
deadheading, 347
dead nettle, 336, *336*
decks, *31, 71*
   building instructions for basic, 234–235
   cleaning, 236, *237*
   construction basics, 74–75
   designs, 72–73
   finishing and preserving, 79, 236, *237*
   hardware, 78–79
   lighting, 80, *81*

Index

lumber choices, 76–77
railings, *80, 81, 81*
steps, 110–111
vs. patios, 70
decorative details, 12–13, 290–291
deer grass, *289*
Delosperma (ice plant), 335, *335*
Delphinium elatum, 349
deodar cedar, 190, 314, *314*
desert garden, 192–193
desert ironwood, 192
desert marigold, 192
design. *See* landscape design
dethatching and aerating lawns, 412–413
Deutzia gracilis, 322, 322
Dianthus spp., *45,* 50, 181, 349, 365
Dicentra spp. (bleeding heart), 50, *57,* 189, 197, 349, *349*
Digitalis purpurea (foxglove), *47,* 181, 365, *365*
dill, 385
dining outdoors
barbecue grills, 280–281
dining spaces, *10, 11, 22, 38, 70, 71, 82, 83, 84,* 88–89, *129, 130,* 222
outdoor kitchens, *88, 89,* 282–283
diseases, prevention and control, 418–421
dividing perennials, 347, *347*
Dodonaea viscosa (hop bush), 322
dogwood. *See Cornus* (dogwood)
Douglas fir, *57,* 189
Dracaena marginata, 203
drainage, 210–211, 302
drip irrigation systems, 212–214, 217, 218–219, 391
Dryopteris spp. (woodfern), 195, 197
dry wells, 211, *211*
Duchesnea indica (Indian mock strawberry), 335
dust masks, 207
Dutch hyacinth, 369, *369*
dymondia, *53*

E

Echinacea (coneflower), *16, 51, 58, 155,* 181, 187, *346,* 350, *350*
edges for paths and patios, 92–93
edible landscape plan, 184–185
Elaeagnus
angustifolia (Russian olive), 311
pungens (silverberry), 322
Eleutherococcus sieboldianus (five-leaf aralia), 183
English ivy, 336, *336*
English laurel, 326
Enkianthus, 189
entryways, *19, 24–25, 29, 55, 83,* 102
Epimedium spp. (bishop's hat), 189, 197, 335, *335*
Eremochloa ophiuroides (centipede grass), 344
Erica (heath), 322, *322*
Eriogonum crocatum (saffron buckwheat), 191
Eriophyllum nevinii, 191
Erodium reichardii (cranesbill), 179

Escallonia exoniensis (escallonia), 322
Eschscholzia californica (California poppy), *55, 65, 363, 376*
Eucalyptus, 314
Euonymus
alata (burning bush), 323, *323*
fortunei (wintercreeper), 335
japonicus (evergreen euonymus), 322–323
Eupatorium rugosum, 197
Euphorbia, 189
European fan palm, *316, 317*
evapotranspiration (ET), 407
evergreen huckleberry, 191
evergreens. *See also specific evergreens*
dwarf conifers, *12, 60, 61*
pruning, 402–403
sampler of, 314–315

F

fairy rings, 411
false spiraea, 189
family-centered landscaping
building a backyard gym, 270–271
designing for family activities, 34–35
family garden plan, 186–187
play areas, 112–113
fan palm, *63, 316,* 317
feather grass, *373, 375, 375*
feather reed grass, *373,* 374
fences, 118–121, 166
in Asian-style gardens, *30, 31*
basic board, building instructions, 240–241
lattice, building instructions, 242
parts of, 120
picket, *9, 16, 44, 119, 121, 146*
regulations regarding, 120
setting posts, 241
split-rail, *27,* 119
styles, 121
wood and wire, building instructions, 243
ferns, *20, 62, 179,* 189, 195, 197
fertilizers and fertilizing, 396–399, *409,* 409–410
fescue. *See Festuca* (fescue)
Festuca (fescue)
arundinacea (tall fescue), *338,* 344, *344*
glauca (blue fescue), 199, 335, *373,* 374–375
rubra (fine fescue), 344–345
feverfew, 181
Ficus spp. (fig), *63, 179,* 203, 330
fig, *63, 179,* 203, 330
fir. *See Abies*
fireplaces, *9, 83, 85, 88, 89,* 222
fire safety, 65–67
firethorn, 326, *326*
fish emulsion and pellets, 398
five-leaf aralia, 183
flagstones, *19, 95,* 106–107, 227, 229, 248–249
flannel bush, 191, 379, *379*
flax, *21, 377*
floors, outdoor, 168–169

floss flower, 360, *360*
flowering quince, 321, *321*
flowering tobacco, 361
focal points, *163*
footings and foundations, 124, 226
forget-me-not, 364, *364*
formal gardens, 28–29
Forsythia spp., 181, 323, *323*
fountain grass, 187, 195, *373, 375*
four o'clock, 201
foxglove, *47,* 181, 365, *365*
foxtail grass, 374, *374*
Fragaria (strawberry), 187
fragrant garden, 200–201
framing connectors, 78, 78–79
Fraxinus pennsylvanica (green ash), 311
Freesia, 369, *369*
Fremontodendron (flannel bush), 191, 379, *379*
fungicides, 419
furniture, selecting outdoor, 80, 274–277

G

Gaillardia (blanket flower), *51, 65,* 183, 350, *350*
Galanthus nivalis (snowdrop), *57,* 369, *369*
Galium odoratum (sweet woodruff), 189, 335
Galphimia glauca (shower of gold), 203
Gardenia spp. (gardenia), 201, 323, *323*
gates, *9, 12, 31, 39, 41, 44,* 122–123, 244–247
Gaultheria procumbens (wintergreen), 197
gayfeather, 183, 351
Gazania rigens leucolaena (trailing gazania), 335–336
gazebos (summerhouses, belvederes), *71,* 104, *108,* 128–131, 132–133
Gelsemium sempervirens (Carolina jessamine), 330, *330*
Geranium (cranesbill), *155,* 336, 350
geranium (*Pelargonium*), *43, 107,* 181, 187, 195, 201
germander, 191
germander sage, 191
Geum (prairie smoke), 181, *379*
ginger lily, 201
Ginkgo biloba (ginkgo), 311, *311*
gladiolus, 181, 369, *369*
Gleditsia tricanthos inermis (honeylocust), 183, 311
globe amaranth, 360
globe mallow, 193
gloriosa daisy, *51,* 181
goldband Japanese sedge, 374, *374*
goldenrain tree, 311–312
golden trumpet tree, 203, 313
Gomphrena (globe amaranth), 360
grading, 208–209
grape hyacinth, 370
grapes, *147,* 181, 184
grapevine, ornamental, 195
grasses, ornamental, *17, 21, 51, 64,* 372–373, *379. See also specific grasses*
grasses, turf. *See* lawns
gravel paths, *27, 32, 94, 105,* 249

ground covers
    planting and maintenance, 332–333
    roses, 356
    sampler, 334–337
grubs, lawn, 411
gum, 314
Gymnocladus dioca (Kentucky coffee tree), 197
Gypsophila paniculata (baby's breath), 350

H

Halesia monticola (mountain silverbell), 181
Hamamelis intermedia (witch hazel), 198, 323
Hardenbergia violacea, 330, *331*
hardware, deck, *78*, 78–79
harlequin flower, 371, *371*
hawthorn, *58*, 311, *311*, 326
heath, 322, *322*
heather, 203, 334, *334*
Hedera helix (English ivy), *328*, 336, *336*
hedges, *39*
    defining spaces, 166, *167*
    formal, *28, 29*
    for privacy, 137–139
    rose, *139*, 356
    shearing, 405
Hedychium coronarium (common ginger lily), 201
Helianthemum, 332
Helianthus annuus (sunflower), 183, 185, 360
Helichrysum bracteatum (strawflower), 361
Heliconia psittacorum (parrot heliconia), 203
Helictotrichon sempervirens (blue oat grass), 375, *375*
heliopsis, *46*, 181
heliotrope, 181
Helleborus spp. (hellebore), 191, 197, 199, 350
Hemerocallis (daylily), 201, 350, *350*
hen-and-chickens, *60*
herbicides, 422–423
herbs, 48–49, 184, 190–191, 384–385
Hesperis matronalis (dame's rocket), 183
Heteromeles arbutifolia (toyon), 191
Heuchera spp. (coral bells), 195, 197, 199, 350
Hibiscus rosa-sinensis, 203, 323
hillsides. *See* slopes
hinoki cypress, 194
Holdeman, Eric and Mary, 174–175
holly, *25, 138*, 198, 314, 323–324
hollyhock, 181, 365, *365*
honeylocust, 183, 311
honeysuckle. *See Lonicera* (honeysuckle)
hop bush, 322
horsechestnut, 310
horsetail, *63*
horticulturists, 171
hoses, 389, 390
Hosta spp. (plantain lily), 50, *57, 97*, 351, *351*
    in landscape plans, 181, 187, 189, 195, 197, 201
Howea fosteriana, 195
Hyacinthus (Dutch hyacinth), 369, *369*
Hydrangea
    macrophylla (big leaf, garden hydrangea), 179, 323

quercifolia (oakleaf hydrangea), *97*, 197, 198, 323, *323*
    serrata, 194
hydrozones, 213
Hypericum calycinum (St. Johnswort), 197, 336
hyssop, 183

I

Iberis umbellata (globe candytuft), 364
iceland poppy, 364
ice plant, 335, *335*
Ilex spp., *25, 138*
    cornuta (Chinese holly), 323–324
    meserveae (evergreen holly), 198, 324
    opaca (American holly), 314
    verticillata (winterberry), 198, 324, *324*
    vomitoria (yaupon), 179, 324
Impatiens, *20*, 179, 187, 195, 203, *288*, 361, *361*
Imperata cylindrica (Japanese blood grass), 199, 375, *375*
Indian grass, 199
Indian mock strawberry, 335
insecticides, 415
insects
    beneficial, 417
    pests, 416–417
integrated pest management (IPM), 414–415
Ipomoea tricolor (morning glory), *45*, 361
Iris, *56*, 181, 187, 369–370, *370*
    cristata (crested iris), 197
    douglasiana hybrid, *376*
    Dutch, *65*, 181
    pallida (Dalmatian iris), 197
    sibirica (Siberian iris), 189
    tectorum (Japanese roof iris), 197
irrigation systems, planning and installation
    drip, 217, 218–219, 391
    misters, 219
    planning, 212–214
    sprinkler, 215–217, 407–408
    timers, 213, 215
ivy, *43, 328, 331*, 336, *336*
Ixia maculata (African corn lily), 370

J

Japanese anemone, 179
Japanese anise, *138*
Japanese aucuba, 320
Japanese blood grass, 199, 375, *375*
Japanese boxwood, 179, 320
Japanese holly, *25*
Japanese maple, *15, 21, 30*, 179, 189, 310, *310*
Japanese painted fern, 195, 197
Japanese pieris, 325, *325*
Japanese spurge, 179, 189, 199, 337, *337*
jasmine, 179, 331, *331*
Jasminum polyanthemum (jasmine), 179, 331, *331*
Joe Pye weed, 346
joints, wood furniture, 277
juniper, 324, *324*, 336

Juniperus spp. (juniper), 324, *324*, 336
Justica spicigera (Mexican honeysuckle), 192

K

kalanchoe, *53*
Kalmia latifolia (mountain laurel), 197
Kentucky bluegrass, 345, *345*
Kentucky coffee tree, 197
kids. *See* family-centered landscaping
king palm, *316*, 317, *317*
kitchens, outdoor, *88, 89*, 282–283
Koelreuteria paniculata (goldenrain tree), 311–312
kohlrabi, *49*

L

lacewings, 417
ladybugs, *415*, 417
lady fern, 195
lady palm, 317
lady's mantle, *15, 57, 60, 97*, 348, *348*
Lagerstroemia indica (crape myrtle), *117, 138, 140*, 312, *312*
lamb's ears, 189, 194, 353
Lamium maculatum (dead nettle), 336, *336*
landscape design, 144–175
    basic decisions, 146–149
    computer software, 171
    creating rooms, 38–39, 166–169
    do-it-yourself, 174–175
    drawing the plan, 150, 156–159
    hiring professionals, 170–171, 206, 207
    principles, 85–87, 160–163
    site analysis, 150–155
    staking out the design, 172–173
    terms, 162–163
    tricks, 164–165
landscape fabrics, 393
landscape plans, 176–203
    Alabama fragrance garden, 200–201
    Arizona desert landscape, 192–193
    California hillside garden, 190–191
    Florida tropical garden, 202–203
    Illinois all-season garden, 198–199
    Missouri edible landscape, 184–185
    Northeast rooftop garden, 194–195
    Pennsylvania shade garden, 196–197
    South Carolina side yard, 178–179
    Tennessee family garden, 186–187
    Virginia cutting garden, 180–181
    Washington native plant garden, 188–189
    Wisconsin wildlife garden, 182–183
landscape professionals, hiring, 170–171, 206, 207
Lantana montevidensis, 336
larkspur, *155*, 181, 363
Larrea tridentata (creosote bush), 192
latches, *246, 247, 247*
Lathyrus odorata (sweet pea), 364, *364*
lattice fence, 242
lattice panels, 259, *259*
lattice porch skirt, building instructions,

Index

258–259

Lavandula (lavender), *14, 21,* 189, 191, 194, 351

lavender, *14, 21,* 189, 191, 194, 351

lavender cotton, *106,* 191

lawnmowers, 408–409

lawns, 338–345, 406–413
    designing lawn areas, 168, *169,* 338
    dethatching and aerating, 412–413
    fertilizing, *409,* 409–410
    mowing and trimming, 408–409
    plugs and sprigs, 343
    problems, 410–412
    regional grass selections, 339, *339*
    seeding, 340–342
    sod, 341, 342
    turf grass sampler, 344–345
    watering, 406–408

leather leaf sedge, 374

legal considerations, 151, 206

lemon bottlebrush, 320, *320*

Lenten rose, 191, 197, 199

lettuce, 383

Leucojum aestivum (snowflake), 370, *370*

Leucophyllum spp., 192

Leucothoe walteri, 197

Leymus arenarius (blue lyme grass), 375

Liatris spicata (gayfeather), 183, 351

licorice plant, *274*

lighting fixtures and techniques, 80, *81,* 284–287

Ligustrum japonicum (wax leaf privet), 324, *324*

lilac, 181, 189, 327, *327*

Lilium (hybrid lilies), *118,* 199, 370, *370*

lily-of-the-Nile, 203

lilyturf, *33,* 336–337, *337*

linden, 313, *313*

Linum perenne (blue flax), *377*

Liquidambar styraciflua (sweet gum), *17,* 312

Liriodendron tulipifera (tulip tree), 197, 312

Liriope (lilyturf), *33,* 336–337, *337*

Livistona chinensis (Chinese fan palm), 317

Lobelia erinus, 364

Lobularia maritima (sweet alyssum), 183, 361

Lolium perenne (perennial ryegrass), 345

London plane tree, 313

Lonicera spp. (honeysuckle), 331, *331*
    heckrottii (Goldflame honeysuckle), 181, 331
    japonica (Japanese honeysuckle), 183, 331
    periclymenum (woodbine honeysuckle), 201
    sempervirens (trumpet honeysuckle), 181, 187, 195, 331, *331*

Loropetalum chinense (Chinese fringe flower), 324

lot sizes and shapes, 156–159

love-in-a-mist, *55*

lumber, types and grades, 76–77

Lunaria annua (money plant), 365

lungwort, 352

Lupinus albifrons collinus (silver lupine), 191

M

Madagascar dragon tree, 203

Madagascar periwinkle, 360, *360*

madrone, 189

Magnolia
    grandiflora (Southern magnolia), 201, *314,* 314–315
    soulangiana (saucer magnolia), 190, 312

Mahonia aquifolium (Oregon grape), 189, 197, 324

maiden grass, *8, 372,* 375

maidenhair fern, 197

maintenance, minimizing, 32–33

Malus, 184, 198, 312, *312*

Malva moschata (musk mallow), 183

manzanita, 190

maple. See *Acer* (maple)

marguerite, 363

marigold, *49,* 187, 362, *362*

marjoram, *384,* 385

Matthiola incana (stock), 364, *364*

meadow rue, 189

Mediterranean fan palm, *63,* 317

Mediterranean-style gardens, *21, 40, 65*

melons, 184, 382, *382*

Mertensia (Virginia bluebell), 197, 351

Mexican bird of paradise, 192

Mexican heather, 203

Mexican honeysuckle, 192

Mexican poppy *(Argemone), 54*

Michelia figo (banana shrub), 201

microclimates, 152–153, 299

Mimulus hybrids (monkey flower), 361, *361*

mint, 385

Mirabilis jalapa (four o'clock), 201

Miscanthus sinensis (maiden grass, silver grass), *8,* 194, *372,* 375

mites, 416

mock orange, 181, *319,* 325, *325*

Molina caerulea (moor grass), 375

Moluccella laevis (bells-of-Ireland), 181

Monarda didyma (beebalm), 351, *351*

mondo grass, 203

money plant, 365

monkey flower, 361, *361*

morning glory, *45,* 361

Morus alba 'Pendula' (weeping mulberry), 187

moss rose, 187, 362

mother fern, 179

mounds and berms, 209

mountain ash, European, 183

mountain laurel, *137,* 197

mountain silverbell, 181

mowers, 408–409

mowing strips, *33, 338*

Mucsari armeniacum (grape hyacinth), 370

Muhlenbergia capillaris (muhly grass), *373*

mulberry, *140,* 187

mulches and mulching, 391–393

Musa coccinea (flowering banana), 203

musk mallow, 183

Myosotis sylvatica (forget-me-not), 364, *364*

Myrica spp. (myrtle), 324

myrtle, *57,* 324

N

nail sizes, 78, *78*

Nandina domestica (heavenly bamboo), 325

Narcissus (daffodil, narcissus), 181, 199, 370

nasturtium, 195, 364

Natal plum, 321

native plants, 378–379. *See also* wildflower gardens
    in landscape plans, 188–189, 190–191, 192–193

naturalizing bulbs, 367

nature in the landscape, 14–15. *See also* wildlife

nematodes, parasitic, 417

Nemesia, 364

Nepeta (catmint), *45, 60, 106,* 351

Nerium oleander (oleander), 325

New England aster, 348, *348*

New Zealand flax, *21*

Nicotiana alata (flowering tobacco), *274,* 361

nursery stock, selecting and planting, 305–307

Nymphaea (water lily), 195

Nyssa sylvatica (tupelo), 312, *312*

O

oak, 187, 197, 313, *313,* 315. Also see *Quercus*

oakleaf hydrangea, *46, 97,* 197, 198, 323, *323*

oat grass, 374, 375, *375*

oleander, 325

Olneya tesota (desert ironwood), 192

Ophiopogon, 203, 337, *337*

Opuntia ficus-indica (prickly pear), 192

oregano, 385

Oregon grape, 189, 197, 324

organic matter, adding to soil, 300–301

ornamental onion, 368, *368*

ornaments and accessories, 12–13, 290–291

Osmanthus fragrans (sweet olive), 325

Osteospermum (African daisy), *50,* 337, *337*

Oxalis (sorrel), 189, *411*

Oxydendrum arboreum (sorrel tree), 181

P

Pachysandra terminalis (Japanese spurge), 179, 189, 199, 337, *337*

Pachystachys lutea (yellow shrimp plant), 203

Paeonia (peony), 181, 351, *351*

painted daisy, 349, *349*

painted tongue, 362

paints and painting, *42, 52, 53,* 276, 278–279

palms, *63,* 195, 203, 316–317

palo verde, *54,* 192

pampas grass, 374

pansy, 364

Papaver
    nudicaule (iceland poppy), 364
    orientale (oriental poppy), 189, 352

paperbark maple, 197

Parney cotoneaster, 322

parsley, 385

Parthenocissus tricuspidata (Boston ivy), 331

Paspalum spp., 345

paths, *53,* 94–109, *148*

brick, *25, 70, 95,* 96–99
cast concrete, 102–103
concrete pavers, 100–101
cottage garden, *45, 45*
cut stone, *250*
designing, 94–95, *162, 164, 165*
edges for, 92–93
flagstone, *19, 95,* 106–107, 248–249, *248–249*
gravel, *27, 32, 94,* 105, *249*
lighting, *284, 285,* 286, *286*
stepping-stones, 251
stone, 106–107
wood, 108–109
wood chips and bark, 105–106
patios, 70–73, 81–93
brick, *86, 87,* 232–233
cast concrete, *91, 222,* 224–225
concrete pavers, 232–233
design, 72–73, 82–87
dining areas, 88–89
edges, 92–93
landscaping principles, 85–87
paving options, 90–91
small, *43*
steps, 110–111
stone, *71, 86, 91*
vs. decks, 70
pavers. *See* concrete pavers
paving choices, 90–91
peace lily, 203
pear, flowering, 313
peas, *383, 383*
Pelargonium (geranium), *43, 107,* 181, 187, 195, 201
penetrating resins, 276
Pennisetum (fountain grass), 187, 195, *373, 375*
Penstemon spp., *54, 55, 60, 65,* 191, *289,* 352, *377*
peony, 181, 351, *351*
peppers, 185, 382
perennial flowers, 346–353. *See also specific perennials*
planting and caring for, 346–347
sampler of, 348–353
perennial ryegrass, 345, *345*
periwinkle, 337, 360, *360*
Perovskia atriplicifolia (Russian sage), *32, 346, 352, 352*
Persian shield, 50, 203
pests, 414–423
animals, 266, 418
diseases, 418–421
insecticides, 415
insects, 416–417
weeds, 421–423
Petunia hybrida (petunia), 50, *107,* 187, 195, 361, *361*
Philadelphus
coronarius (sweet mock orange), 181
virginalis (mock orange), *319,* 325, *325*
Phlox, 16, 46, 187, *332*
drummondii, 361
paniculata, 183, 352, *352*
Phoenix spp. (date palm), 203, 317, *317*

Photinia spp. (photinia), *137,* 325
Phyllostachys aurea (golden bamboo), 203
Picea spp. (spruce), 194, 315, *315*
pickerel weed, 195
Pieris japonica (Japanese pieris), 325, *325*
pilasters, 119
pindo palm, 203
pine. *See Pinus* (pine)
Pine Hill flannel bush, 191
pinks, 50, 181, 349
Pinus (pine), *141*
densiflora (Tanyosho pine), 198
mugo mugo (mugho pine), 325, *325*
resinosa (red pine), 183
strobus (white pine), 187, 315, *315*
thunbergii (Japanese black pine), 198, 315, *315*
wallichiana (Himalayan pine), 181
Pistacia chinensis (Chinese pistache), 312–313
Pittosporum tobira (tobira), 325
plans. *See* landscape design; landscape plans
plantain lily. *See Hosta*
Plantanus acerifolia (London plane tree), 313
planting
annuals, 358–359
grass seed, plugs and sod, 340–343
ground covers, 322–333
perennials, 306, 336
roses, 354–355, *355*
trees and shubs, 305–307
planting beds, 304–305
plant-lover's gardens, 46–47
plastic edges for paths and patios, 93
plastic mulch, 393
play areas, 112–113
plumbago, dwarf, 334
plum, flowering, 189
Poa pratensis (Kentucky bluegrass), 345, *345*
Podocarpus spp., 141, 203, 326
Polygonatum (Solomon's seal), 189
Polygonum aubertii (silver lace vine), 331
polyurethane, 276
Pontederia cordata (pickerel weed), 195
poppy, *55, 60, 64*
California, *55*
Iceland, 364
Mexican, *54*
Oriental, 189, 352
Shirley, *376*
porch skirt, building instructions, 258–259
Portulaca grandiflora (moss rose), 187, 362
posts, setting, 240, 241
potato vine, *35*
Potentilla (cinquefoil), 326, *326,* 337
powdery mildew, 421
prairie plants, 379
prairie smoke, *379*
pre-cast piers, 235
prickly pear, 192
pride of Madeira, *65*
primrose, *57,* 352
Primula (primrose), *57,* 352
privacy, 8–9, 116–117
using shrubs, 136–139
using structures (*See* arbors; fences;

gazebos; trellises; walls)
using trees, *116,* 140–141
using vines, 142–143
privet, wax leaf, 324, *324*
property analysis, 150–156
property deeds, 151, 206
proportion, landscape principle, 86–87
pruning
basic cuts, 404–405
branch removal, 403
evergreens, 402–403
ground covers, 333
growth buds and, 404–405
perennials, 347, *347*
roses, 355, *355*
shrubs, 319, *319*
trees, 67, *67,* 400–405
vines, 329
why and when, 400–402
Prunus, 313
blireiana (flowering plum), 189
cerasifera (purpleleaf plum), 313
laurocerasus (English laurel), 326
sargentii (Sargent cherry), 187
serrulata (Japanese flowering cherry), 189
subhirtella 'Autumnalis' (Autumn Higan cherry), 181
Pseudotsuga (Douglas fir), 57, 189
Pulmonaria (lungwort), 352
purpleleaf plum, 313
pussy willow, 181
pygmy date palm, 317
Pyracantha (firethorn), 326, *326*
Pyrus calleryana (flowering pear), 313

Q

quaking grass, 374
queen palm, 317
Quercus spp., 313, *313*
alba (white oak), 197, 313
rubra (red oak), 187
virginiana (Southern live oak), 315
quince, flowering, 321, *321*

R

railroad ties and timbers
edges for paths and patios, 92
steps, *223,* 238–239
raised beds, *49,* 256
building instructions, 266–267
screening out gophers and ground squirrels, 266
Ranunculus asiaticus, 370–371, *371*
raspberries, 181, 184
redbud, Eastern, 310, *310*
red maple, 310, *310*
redwood, coast, 190, 315
regional landscape plans. *See* landscape plans
rental yards, 207
retaining walls, 125, *125, 155,* 174, 209, *231*
Rhamnus californica (coffeeberry), 191
Rhaphiolepis indica (Indian hawthorn), 326
Rhapis spp. (lady palm), 317

Index

Rhododendron spp., *30, 147,* 181, 187, 189, 197, 199, 326, *326*
rock gardens, 60–61
rockrose, 321
rooftop garden plan, 194–195
rooms, creating outdoor, 38–39, 166–169
root rots, 421
rose
    'Abraham Darby', *357*
    'Ballerina', *45, 356*
    climbing, *9, 24, 143,* 181, 356, 357
    'Dortmund', *143*
    'Double Delight', *356*
    gardens, 26–27
    'Graham Thomas', *357*
    hedges, *139,* 356
    'Heritage', *357*
    Lady banks' rose, 191
    'Margo Koster', *356*
    'Nearly Wild', 50
    'New Dawn', *44*
    'Phyllis Bide', *24*
    planting and caring for, 354–355
    rugosa, 187
    sampler, 356–357
    'Sun Flare', 201
    'Sun Goddess', *45*
    'The Fairy', *27*
    'Zéphirine Drouhin', *27*
rosemary, *49,* 191, 326–327, *384, 385*
ruby grass, *21*
Rudbeckia hirta (black-eyed Susan, gloriosa daisy), 181, *346,* 352, *352, 377*
Ruellia peninsularis (Baja ruellia), 192
Russian olive, 311
Russian sage, *32, 346,* 352, *352*
rust, 411, 421

S

Sabal palmetto (cabbage palm), 203, 317
safety, 206–207
    reducing wildfire danger, 66–67
    using wood preservatives, 237
saffron buckwheat, 191
sage. *See Salvia* (sage)
sago palm, 203
saguaro, 192
Salix spp. (willow), 181
Salpiglossis sinuata (painted tongue), 362
Salvia (sage), *46, 49,* 181, *193, 332, 353, 358*
    argentea (silver sage), 365
    autumn sage, *58*
    chamaedryoides (germander sage), 191
    clevelandii (California blue sage), 191
    farinacea (mealycup sage), 50, 195
    officinalis (common, culinary), *384,* 385
    splendens (scarlet), 362, *362*
sandbox and slide project, 270–271
Santa Barbara daisy, *106*
Santolina neapolitana (lavender cotton), *106,* 191
Sanvitalia procumbens (creeping zinnia), 362

saskatoon, 183
Scabiosa, 45, 199
Scaevola, 195
scale insects, 416
scarecrows, *34, 48*
scarlet bugler, 191
Scotch heather, 320
screws, deck, 78
sealers, wood, 79, 276
sea oats, 374
seashore paspalum, 345
seasons, 16–17
    all-season landscape plan, 198–199
    changing sun and shade patterns, 152–153
sedge, 189, 374, *374*
Sedum (stonecrop), *46, 61, 64,* 353
    'Autumn Joy', *33, 346,* 353
    'Matrona', 183
    telephium, 187, 199
seedlings, selecting and planting, 305
Senegal date palm, 317
Sequoia sempervirens (coast redwood), 190, 315
service areas, 18–19
serviceberry, 310
shade gardens, *20,* 50, 56–57, 196–197
sheds. *See* storage
shell ginger, 203
shower of gold, 203
shrimp plant, 203
shrubs, 318–327. *See also specific shrubs*
    maintaining, 319
    for privacy, 136–139
    pruning, 405
    sampler, 320–327
side yards and gardens, *175,* 178–179
silk tree, 310
silverberry, 322
silver date palm, 203
silvergrass, 194
silver lace vine, 331
site preparation
    analysis, 150–155
    drainage, 210–211
    grading, 208–209
slopes, 154–155, 191, 209, 241
slugs and snails, 416–417
small gardens, 42–43. *See also* courtyard gardens; side yards and gardens
smoke tree, 321
snails and slugs, 416–417
snapdragon, 363, *363*
snowdrop, *57,* 369, *369*
snowflake, 370, *370*
soaker hoses, 390, *391*
sod, 341, 342
sod webworms, 411
soil, 300–303
soldier beetles, 417
Soleirolia soleirolii (baby's tears), 337
Solenostemon scutellarioides (coleus), 195, 203, *288*
Solomon's seal, 189
sooty mold, 421

Sorbus aucuparia (European mountain ash), 183
Sorghastrum nutans (Indian grass), 199
sorrel, 189
sorrel tree, 181
Southern live oak, 315
Sparaxis tricolor (harlequin flower), 371, *371*
Spathyiphyllum (peace lily), 203
speedwell, *46,* 181, 353, *353*
Sphaeralcea ambigua (globe mallow), 193
spiderwort, *155,* 353, *353*
spinach, 383
spinulose wood fern, 195
Spiraea spp., 181, 327, *327*
sprinklers, hose-end, 389–390, 407, *407*
sprinkler systems, 212–217, 407–408
    head styles, 215, *215*
    installing, 216–217
    planning, 212–214
    timers, 213, 215
    valves, *214,* 215
spruce, 194, 315, *315*
spurge, Japanese, 179, 189, 199, 337, *337*
squash, 185, 382
Stachys byzantina (lamb's ears), 189, 194, 353
stains, wood, 79, 276
star jasmine, 331
St. Augustine grass, 345, *345*
Stenotaphrum secundatum (St. Augustine grass), 345, *345*
Stepping-stones, 250–251
steps, 110–111, *223,* 238–239, 286
Stipa spp. (feather grass), *373, 375, 375*
St. Johnswort, 197, 336
stock, 364, *364*
stone
    cutting, 248, *248*
    edgings, 93
    paths, 106–107, 248–251
    patio surface, *91*
    steps, *110*
    walls, 124, *125, 127,* 229, 230–231
stonecrop. *See Sedum* (stonecrop)
storage, 18, *18, 19*
strawberry, 184, 187, 335
strawflower, 361
Strobilanthes dyerianus (Persian shield), 50, 203
structure, creating, 166–167
stucco, *14, 117,* 279, *279*
style, developing personal, 12–13
submersible pumps, 264–265
summerhouses. *See* gazebos
sun angles and exposure, 87, *152,* 153
sundrops, 55
sunflower, 183, 185, 360
sunflower, false, 181
sweet alyssum, 183, 361
sweet box, 189, 327
sweet gum, 312
sweet olive, 325
sweet pea, 364, *364*
sweet potato vine, *63*
sweet William, 365

sweet woodruff, 189, 335
Swiss chard, 383, *383*
Syagrus romanzoffianum (queen palm), 317
symmetry, *163*
Syringa vulgaris (common lilac), 181, 189, 327, *327*
syrphid flies, 417

T

Tabebuia chrysotricha (golden trumpet tree), 203, 313
tachinid flies, 417
Tagetes (marigold), *49*, 187, 362, *362*
Taxus spp. (yew), 315
terraces, *38*, *154*, *155*
Teucrium fruticans (bush germander), 191
Texas ranger, 192
textures, *162*
Thalictrum (meadow rue), 189
Thuja occidentalis (Eastern arborvitae), 315
Thunbergia alata (black-eyed Susan vine), 362, *362*
thyme, *65*, *384*, 385
tiger flower, 371
Tigridia pavonia (tiger flower), 371
Tilia cordata (little-leaf linden), 313, *313*
timbers, landscape. *See* railroad ties and timbers
tobira, 325
tomatoes, 185, 382, *382*
toyon, 191
Trachelospermum jasminoides (star jasmine), 331
Trachycarpus fortunei (windmill palm), 317
Tradescantia (spiderwort), *155*, 353, *353*
tree fern, *62*
trees. *See also specific trees*
    deciduous shade sampler, 310–313
    evergreen sampler, 314–315
    landscaping with, 308–309
    planting, 306–307
    for privacy, 140–141
    pruning, 67, *67*, 400–405
    shapes, 141
    staking and training, 309
    watering, 392
trellises
    building instructions, 256–257
    uses and designs, 134–135, *143*, 166, *167*, *234*
trompe l'oeil gates, *42*, *52*
Tropaeolum majus (nasturtium), 195, 364
tropical gardens, 62–63, 202–203
trumpet creeper, 330
Tulipa (tulip), *21*, 181, 199, 371, *371*
tulip tree, 197, 312
tupelo, 312, *312*
turtlehead, 183
Typha minima (dwarf cattail), 183

U

unity, landscape principle, 85

USDA Plant Hardiness Zone Map, 298–299
utilities, locating, 151, 210

V

Vaccinium
    corymbosum (blueberry), 184, 187
    ovatum (evergreen huckleberry), 191
variances, 206
variety, landscape principle, 85–86
vegetables
    cook's garden of vegetable and herbs, 48–49, *146*
    garden plan, 184–185
    planting and caring for, 380–381
    sampler of, 382–383
Verbena spp., 193, 363, *377*
Veronica (speedwell), *46*, 181, 353, *353*
Viburnum spp., 327, *327*
    in landscape plans, 180, 183, 197, 199, 201
Vinca minor (periwinkle), 337
vine maple, 189
vines
    for privacy, 142–143
    sampler, 330–331
    training and pruning, 329
    types of, 328–329
Viola (violet, pansy), 353, *353*, 364
violet, 353, *353*
Virginia bluebells, 197, 351
Vitex (chaste tree), 181
Vitis vinifera 'Purpurea' (ornamental grapevine), 195

W

walls, 124–127
    brick, *124*, *127*, *127*, *137*
    building instructions, 228–231
    concrete block, 124, *125*, 126, *126*, 127, *127*, 228–229, 231
    foundations for, 124, 226
    functions of, *38*, *39*, 166
    modular block, 231
    painted, *42*, *52*, *53*, *279*
    retaining, 125, *125*, *155*, 174, 209, *231*
    stone, *29*, *155*, *174*, 230–231
    stone veneer, 127, 229
    stucco, *14*, *117*, *279*, *279*
water conservation, 391, 392. *See also* mulches and mulching
water-conserving plants, 64–65
water gardening, 36–37, 262–265, 288–289
    fountains and basins, *26*, *28*, *31*, *37*, *40*, *41*, *50*, *81*, 264–265, 288–289
    installing a rigid pond liner, 262–263
    pebble fountain project, 265
    pond in a pot, project, 264
    ponds and pools, *15*, *20*, *31*, *36*, *41*, *43*, *62*, *101*, 182–183, 262–263, 288–289
    streams, *108*, *110*
    wall fountain project, 265
watering, 388–391, 406–408. *See also* irrigation systems

water lily, 195, 289
water sealers, 79
wax leaf privet, 324, *324*
weed control, 411–412, 421–423
weigela, 181
white fir, 314, *314*
whiteflies, 417
white snakeroot, 197
wildflower gardens, 54–55, *57*, 376–379. *See also* native plants
wildlife, 14–15, 58–59, 182–183, 292–295
windmill palm, 317, *317*
window box, building instructions, 260–261
winterberry, 198, 324, *324*
wintercreeper, 335
wintergreen, 197
Wisteria spp., *10*, *142*, 331
witch hazel, 198, 323
wood
    alternatives, 77
    fences, 240–243
    finishing and preserving, 79, 236–237, 275–276, 279
    lumber types and grades, 76–77
    paths, 108–109
    steps, *111*, 239
wood chips, *35*, 104–105
woodland gardens, 56–57, *57*, *105*, 196–197, 378–379
worm composting, 395
wormwood, *155*, 348

X

Xylosma congestum, 327

Y

yarrow, *65*, 181, 183, 332, 348
yaupon, 179, 324
yew, *47*, 315
yew pine, 203, 326
yucca, *65*

Z

Zantedeschia aethiopica (calla lily), 371
Zauschneria californica (California fuchsia), 191
Zinnia elegans (zinnia), *17*, 181, 358, 363, *363*
zone maps
    lawn grasses, *339*
    USDA hardiness, 298–299
zoning ordinances, 151, 206
Zoysia matrella (zoysia), 345